TURNING YOUR
HUMAN RESOURCES
DEPARTMENT
INTO A
PROFIT CENTER

Preface

This is a unique book on human resources management. Most such books focus on how to provide good *service*. In sharp contrast, this book zeros in on how to provide good service to an organization *and measurably improve corporate profitability*.

This book will prove valuable to at least three types of managers: (1) human resources managers and professionals, (2) executives who oversee the human resources function, and (3) other types of managers who wish to know how to turn their most valuable assets—people—into profits.

Two interesting incidents arose while writing this book. The first one involved a woman who called me after having attended one of my seminars on human resources profit center techniques. She happily recounted how she had used techniques presented in the seminar (and discussed in this book) to *measurably* improve her employer's profits by $1.1 million. She did this in only six months.

She told me that she had been hired as a personnel manager. The main expectation placed upon her was that of providing the usual human resources services. Her employer never asked her to do anything to enhance its profits.

Now, however, as a result of her profit improvement accomplishments, she has received a promotion and now participates in all top management meetings. She also earns a good deal more money. She is a profit center manager, not a cost center manager.

Shortly after hearing from this successful woman, I called an official of a Fortune 100 company. This company is renowned for certain of its human resources programs. Many articles have been published on these services. So, I assumed that this company would provide lots of examples of how its human resources management techniques had measurably enhanced profitability.

To my astonishment, the official told me, "We don't bother to measure the cost benefits of what our human resources function does. We just figure that it works, so why bother measuring it in dollars and cents?"

I was astonished that this company had never examined its human resources programs in terms of their impact on corporate profits. After all, this company was so large, had so much money, and employed so many respected human resources professionals. Surely, it possessed the funds and the brainpower to perform such cost-benefit studies.

So, I asked, "How about the work of *[name of company's highly qualified human resources manager]*? Hasn't he measured how his activities improve your company's profits?"

The company official hemmed and hawed. "Oh, well, ah, let's see. I guess you haven't heard. *[Name of highly qualified human resources manager]* is no longer with our company."

"What happened?" I asked, although I anticipated the inevitable response. "He worked for you for so long, why would he ever leave?"

The official replied, "Well, I can't go into details. But, he was let go because we weren't sure his work *really* helped the company."

In other words, this company "de-employed" that human resources manager because he did not prove that he had upgraded the bottom line. In effect, he had operated from a human resources cost center perspective.

Such tales are widespread in the human resources community. Every month brings news of many fine human resources managers losing their jobs, or staying in stagnant positions, because they do not show how they *measurably improve company profits*.

This book aims to change this situation for the better. It features an easy-to-use, six-part *Planning Model* to guide all profit center endeavors. Chapter 3 also contains a handy *Planning Schedule* for pinpointing how to make the human resources profit center a reality. This book also provides you with dozens of human resources-oriented solutions to specific business problems. These solutions are accompanied by case examples that show you how to put the human resources profit center into action.

The next step is yours to take. As Will Rogers observed, "If you're on the right track, you'll get run over if all you do is just sit there." I fervently hope you take action to become like the woman who improved her company's profits by over $1 million in only half a year. She is now reaping the rewards of being a human resources profit center manager. I also believe that you do not want to meet the fate of the highly qualified human resources cost center manager whom I have just described.

This book provides the tools, techniques, and practical guidance you need to start and manage a human resources profit center. The rest is up to you.

Grab the opportunity to enjoy the rewards that you produce for yourself and your company.

MICHAEL W. MERCER
Chicago, Illinois

TURNING YOUR HUMAN RESOURCES DEPARTMENT INTO A PROFIT CENTER

MICHAEL W. MERCER

amacom

AMERICAN MANAGEMENT ASSOCIATION

Library of Congress Cataloging-in-Publication Data

Mercer, Michael W., 1950–
    Turning your human resources department
into a profit center.

    Includes index.
    1. Personnel management.   2. Labor costs.
3. Profit.   I. Title.
HF5549.M349   1989   658.3   88-48024
ISBN 0-8144-5841-6

Printing number

10   9   8

To
Maryann Victoria,
my precious one

Acknowledgments

Many people offered information and advice during the creation of this book. Their input helped make this book a reality.

These people included George Arteaga of Wang Laboratories, Gerry Belko of F. S. B. Associates, Dee Birschel of International Foundation of Employee Benefits, Peter L. Bisulca of P. L. Bisulca Associates, Rita Black of International Business Machines, William Byham, Ph.D., of Development Dimensions International, Jim Coblin of Nucor Corporation, Merlin Davidson of Bethlehem Steel Corporation, Kenneth P. De Meuse of Intergraph Corporation, Bonnie Donovan of American Productivity & Quality Center, Gene Johannes of National Association of Suggestion Systems, William S. Jose II, Ph.D., of Control Data Corporation, Joseph Kipp of Bethlehem Steel Corporation, Andrew Littlefair of Mesa Limited Partnership, Susan Lokker of Chips & Technologies, Robert M. MacQueen of Rexnord, Inc., Sandra McNamara of First National Bank of Chicago, Vincent J. McNamara of VJ Associates, Jack J. Phillips of Secor Bank, James Poet of Combined Insurance Company of America, Marcy Rappaport of Johnson & Johnson, Sandra Secord of Unisys, Edward R. Stasica of Stasica & Associates, Jane Stein of Health Insurance Association of America, Joseph E. Troiani, M.A., M.H.A., C.A.C., of Comprehensive Care Corporation, and Pamela A. Wilder of G. D. Searle.

Also, I felt quite fortunate to work with three magnificent AMACOM editors: Adrienne Hickey, Michael Sivilli, and Eva Weiss. Their helpful suggestions and enthusiasm for this book always made me feel wonderful. I also feel grateful to Phyllis White of the American Management Association for asking me to speak at the Annual AMA Human Resources Conference and encouraging me to write this book.

Finally, I thank my family for showing me the importance of looking at both the human and financial sides of all business endeavors.

Contents

HOW TO START THE PROFIT CENTER / 246

PUBLICITY TO FUEL THE EXCITEMENT / 247

INCENTIVE PAY FOR HUMAN RESOURCES MANAGERS / 247

PROFILE OF A SUCCESSFUL HUMAN RESOURCES PROFIT CENTER / 247

CONCLUDING REMARKS AND A SHOT IN THE ARM / 249

TURNING YOUR
HUMAN RESOURCES
DEPARTMENT
INTO A
PROFIT CENTER

PART I
How to Start a Human Resources Profit Center

Chapter 1
Why Human Resources Departments *Must* Become Profit Centers

WHAT IS MOST IMPORTANT TO ANY BUSINESS

Every human resources manager must fully grasp and wholeheartedly accept the most essential fact of business life: The purpose of business is to make money.

The purpose of business is not to be nice. It is not to do good things. The purpose is not to make people feel good. All those outcomes are certainly praiseworthy, but they are not what makes the business world turn round.

Money is what makes the business world turn round. Perhaps you think that sounds somewhat hard-nosed or maybe even coldly calculating. But such reactions will never change the way people operate in the business world.

Human resources managers need to make a choice. They can continue to provide service that is valued to a degree. Or, human resources managers can fully enter the real business arena of their organizations by becoming part of the profit-generating team that runs the show.

After all, companies *must* focus on generating money, profits, and profit improvement. That is how all organizations exist—including the most altruistic, humanistic, people-oriented organizations. In fact, even so-called nonprofit organizations must produce a profit, because unless nonprofit organizations create profits, they do not have the funds necessary to continue operating.

All these realizations underline the importance of the bottom line, both figuratively and financially. That is what really counts. And anyone who fails to contribute to the bottom line quickly proves expendable to an organization. This is not meant to discount the innumerable good deeds and hard work that many people, including probably the vast majority of human resources professionals, perform in every enterprise. It just points out the extreme importance of human resources managers getting in the middle of the real, honest to goodness, nitty-gritty purpose of their companies, namely, playing *crucial roles* in generating improved corporate profitability.

Think about it from a somewhat different perspective. Take a look at any company's annual report. What does the annual report focus on? Profit. Money, financial statements, past profitability and projected profitability, sales, dividends, and sometimes even the price of the company's stock stack up as the typical annual report's main highlights. Just open the front cover and what do you see? Usually the first page features a letter from the company's chairman or president about the company's financial improvements (or rationales for financial downturns), marketing highlights, products, and future directions.

Notice that annual reports spend very little, if any, space on the sorts of activities that occupy most human resources managers' time. If human resources endeavors are lucky enough to receive a small amount of space, they usually appear in a rather unobtrusive place, probably for two reasons. First, the company does not want stockholders (who overwhelmingly desire to make a profit on the company's stock) to see that their money is being spent on activities that do not definitely increase profits. Second, most programs carried out by the human resources department simply are not viewed as an integral part of the real business of the corporation. They are nice, but potentially unnecessary, so the annual report omits most human resources endeavors.

It also would prove useful for human resources managers to look at the types of stories covered by major business periodicals, such as *The Wall Street Journal, FORTUNE,* and *Business Week*. The vast majority of their articles about companies focus on the corporations' finance, marketing, sales, manufacturing, research and development, or other non-human-resources functions. Why do major business publications generally ignore human resources endeavors in favor of reporting on other activities? The answer is simple: The focus of business is money, but usually human resources managers act as cheerleaders on the sidelines applauding the "real businesspeople," rather than as key players in the business field.

Fortunately, these typical scenarios readily can change for the better. Human resources managers no longer need to play second fiddle to their counterparts in other functions, such as sales, marketing, finance, manufacturing, operations, and research and development. The human resources management team definitely can make a big difference where it really counts—in its companies' profitability. This book shows how. It reveals ready-to-use techniques to turn the human resources cost center into a profit center.

HOW HUMAN RESOURCES MANAGERS ALMOST ALWAYS MISS THE MARK: THE ART OF DOING GOOD WHILE DOING NOTHING OF REAL VALUE

Imagine that you are the chairman of the board or president of a company. You walk into your office one morning and decide to examine the productivity of your top executives.

First, you pull out the record of your vice-president of sales. You note, to your horror, that sales under his direction have decreased or stayed flat. You probably have ample reason to fire your vice-president of sales.

Then you look at the achievements of your vice-president of finance. As you review this person's performance, you gasp as you realize that this executive arranged for corporate financing needs at too high a rate and also failed to maximize the return on money in your company's bank accounts. You gaze out the window as you ponder when the vice-president of finance must go.

Next, you decide to see how your vice-president of manufacturing is doing. You feel rather uncomfortable as you notice that this person's reign in the manufacturing arena has resulted in your company's need to spend more money to produce fewer widgets. Such a drop in manufacturing efficiency is the exact opposite of what the vice-president of manufacturing is supposed to do.

Before deciding what to do with the career of the vice-president of manufacturing, you open up the folder containing the results achieved by your vice-president of marketing. This executive has managed to get the company to take a chance on manufacturing a few products that proved to be duds in the marketplace. This vice-president, you say to yourself, will not stay around here very much longer.

Finally, you turn your attention to reviewing the results of your vice-president of human resources. This member of your executive team has managed to spend practically every penny in the human resources department's budget and has done *nothing* purposely and specifically linked to increasing your enterprise's profitability. In other words, the vice-president of human resources has done exactly what that person has always done. He "just did his job."

But somewhere, deep down in your mind, you feel a nagging question. Why do your vice-presidents of sales, finance, manufacturing, and marketing all rise or fall based on how they affect corporate profitability, while your human resources executive keeps his or her job (and even gets regular raises) without measurably improving the bottom line?

The above-described scenario occurs every day, in one form or another, in organizations around the world. Practically every executive lives and breathes by the bottom line except those in the human resources department and a few other staff or non-line functions. Somehow, companies have lulled themselves into accepting the unfounded fact that human resources managers cannot play key roles in generating greater corporate profits. Nothing can be further from the truth.

However, few human resources managers focus on corporate profit improvement, probably because most may not *know how* to affect profitability. Typically, human resources managers are not even *expected* to play any role in enabling their companies to make even one penny more. So, they act out their roles on the sidelines of the corporate drama.

For instance, many human resources managers pay special attention to their social service role. The vice-president of one medical supply company was asked to describe his proudest achievement during the past year. This seasoned veteran with over 20 years in human resources management happily recounted how his proudest accomplishment was the Bach's Lunch he orchestrated at his company on the birthday of composer Johann Sebastian Bach! When his company's financial fortunes began to tumble, this human resources executive was forced to "leave for personal reasons," which is a common euphemism for forcing someone to resign or being fired. And why not? After all, if any executive's crowning glory is a social event, then that manager certainly is off base when it comes to the company's reason for existence, namely, to make money. Unfortunately, all too many human resources professionals pride themselves on their agility at carving a cake, rather than on their role in carving out a profitable market niche.

Many human resources managers also spend a lot of their time carrying out high-class clerical duties. For example, many aspects of typical compensation or benefits work are more administrative than managerial. That is, quite a few components of such human resources endeavors can be explained in a straightforward manner so that a clerk, secretary, or administrative assistant could handle them. Nevertheless, many human resources managers spend their time sifting through administrative duties instead of creating and implementing profit improvement solutions to business problems.

At this point, it may be argued that someone must oversee administrative details, handle grievances, and counsel employees. That certainly is true. However, the fact remains that corporations always will place more value on someone who pulls in money than on someone who carries out "nice but not necessarily necessary" activities.

That is, business-oriented employees are more valued than service-oriented employees. This is not meant to degrade the contributions of human resources staff members who carry out non-profit-generating service endeavors. It merely acknowledges a fact that has been known for decades: Companies live and die by the bottom line. Anyone who adds to the bottom line is important. Anyone who does not invariably deserves, and receives, less status, recognition, prestige, power, and salary.

SURVIVAL VS. THRIVING: WHY THE HUMAN RESOURCES DEPARTMENT MUST BEGIN TO IMPROVE THE BOTTOM LINE, RATHER THAN JUST PROVIDING SERVICE

Since the human resources department almost invariably provides service, it generally exists outside the core of a company's business. That state of affairs accounts for the events that occur when a company feels a profit pinch: The human resources staff suddenly becomes readily expendable.

The business press frequently reports how one company or another has cut its human resources staff when it needed to trim overhead or corporate flab. Most human resources managers constantly feel the pressure that comes with being on a company's payroll without ever *proving* their worth in the company's actual bread-and-butter business. They do not thrive. For this reason, they never ensure for themselves secure positions or career progression.

Fortunately, this insecurity and fear of job loss can become a thing of the past *if* human resources managers will begin to turn their departments into profit generators for their companies. Actually, human resources managers possess no other viable alternative if they really want to get ahead. Here are five areas to consider in order to understand why they should have a vested interest in creating profit centers to benefit their companies and their careers.

1. *Business = Money.* As discussed in the beginning of this chapter, the spotlight in business is on improving the organization's financial picture. Human resources managers need to *play the game*. Anything less than being involved in the money-making or profit-improving side of an organization is like being a well-meaning spectator who roots for the team that does the *real* work out on the field.

Many companies spend 50 percent or more of their money on the people they employ. That is a huge chunk of gross revenues. Human resources professionals are in a perfect position to make this huge investment even more profitable.

2. *Who gets paid a lot and who gets paid less?* Companies tend to pay money

producers more than highly qualified employees who are not money producers, which is why it is not uncommon for a salesperson to earn more than a company president. After all, if a salesperson generates a lot of sales, why should the salesperson be paid any way other than handsomely? The results of salespersons' work make the company successful or unsuccessful, so they deserve compensation for their importance.

How are human resources managers compensated? Generally, human resources managers earn less than their counterparts in other departments who enhance corporate profitability. There is no reason for an organization to pay anyone a particularly large amount unless that person *measurably* improves the company's profitability. Human resources managers who wish to earn more money but do not want to change careers to do so, need to turn their human resources cost centers into profit centers. Then, they will warrant the sort of wages they desire.

3. *Who receives the highest level of respect?* In our society, employees that make money for their companies receive a lot of respect. People who mainly spend their budget without making money for the company receive lesser status. Respect is highly valued by many. And it can be earned by human resources managers who take the appropriate steps to become valuable to their organiations.

4. *Who gets laid off during financial downturns, mergers, and reorganizations?* When push comes to shove, almost every company keeps its employees who add to its bottom line. Everyone else proves all too readily unnecessary. During most money-saving changes, staff positions such as human resources and public relations quickly are eliminated.

In sharp contrast, employees who directly contribute to a company's prosperity rarely need to fret about whether someone will hand them a pink slip. They do not live with the dread that they will be told that their previously useful services simply are not required anymore.

5. *Whose career is most valued? Who is most sought after?* These questions address difficult career decisions. Every ambitious person in any business career wants to be wanted in the form of being sought after by in-house corporate executives, or in terms of who gets the most calls from executive recruiters who try to lure them away to bigger and better-paying positions. Both forms of being wanted can make or break a management career. Unfortunately, most human resources managers have not yet achieved the level of being sought after that they could because the most sought-after executives are those who can show that they favorably and measurably affect the bottom line. By learning how to do so, as explained in this book, human resources managers can enhance their career opportunities with corporate executives and headhunters.

IMPROVING PROFITABILITY

Given the importance of turning the human resources cost center into a profit center, the question now arises: What can human resources managers measure to show that they improved corporate profits? In general, human resources professionals can help improve profitability by figuring out ways to:

1. Increase profits
2. Decrease costs

3. Make employees more efficient
4. Improve productivity

The measurements of profits, costs, efficiency and productivity intertwine to some degree. For example, a decrease in costs results in greater profits. Or, improved productivity, such as enhanced efficiency, should result in increased profit. Nevertheless, it is necessary to keep all four of these measures in mind when using human resources techniques to improve company financial success. They provide the language of business when it comes to corporate profit improvement.

Let's look at these measures as they may relate to traditional human resources endeavors in compensation, benefits, training, recruiting, and equal employment opportunity. (These areas are selected examples only. The measures apply to a much broader range of human resources activities, as later chapters show.)

Compensation

Executives are more likely to favor a compensation manager who devised an incentive pay system that resulted in measurable profit improvement than a compensation manager who conducted a wage survey that merely aimed to keep the normal salary structure competitive. Why? Because the incentive pay plan will *reward employees for what they produce, not just for showing up*. That motivates employees to increase profits, which meets with tremendous enthusiasm from top management.

Benefits

Some benefits actually pay people for not working. For example, companies constantly face a problem of their own creation: Employees use their so-called sick days as de facto vacation days. Because of this problem, it is not uncommon for many employees to call in "sick" 5 or 10 days a year when actually all they are doing is sunning themselves on a beach or taking an extended weekend. From the company's perspective the result is (1) lower productivity, since the employee is not on the job, (2) payment of a day's wages to someone who is not even working, and (3) possible overtime pay to someone to substitute for the "sick" employee.

This all-too-typical situation leaves human resources professionals in an important position to effect change for the better. It is easy to see how a human resources professional who devises an absentee reduction program that *measurably* works will be more valuable to a company than an equally bright human resources professional who merely offers some new benefits ideas that will not noticeably improve productivity or decrease costs.

Training

Everyone seems to love the *idea* of training employees. However, few people bother to measure if training results in greater efficiency or job effectiveness. For example, it is one thing to train 50 salespeople; it is quite another to train 50 salespeople and then show that following the training, they sold more. The increased sales is dollars-and-cents proof that the training was effective. Merely recounting the *fact* that people were trained does not *show* that the training was worth more than the time and money invested in it.

Recruiting

Many human resources managers like to keep track of the cost per hire. That is a calculation of how much cost and time it took to hire a new employee. Looking at the cost per hire is fine, however, it easily could miss the boat. *The* make-it-or-break-it question is not how long it took to hire someone, or even how much the recruiting process cost, but whether a superb employee was hired. It is easy to hire average or below-average employees. It takes some focused work to make sure that the employees hired are above-average to excellent.

For instance, one human resources manager may brag about how inexpensively he hired some new employees. That provides no indication of the quality of those employees. In contrast, another human resources manager rightfully may brag about how he contracted with an industrial psychologist to develop a valid and reliable employment test to weed out job applicants who are similar to the company's average to below-average employees. Furthermore, the test accurately pinpoints which candidates possess job-related abilities that are similar to those of the company's above-average to excellent employees.

Using this employment test, the cost per hire, even though increased, readily would be of secondary importance to the fact that the test enables the company to choose the *best,* most productive job candidates. Let's say it costs more to hire someone using a validated and reliable employment test than it might cost without the test. This extra cost per hire might come from taking into account the cost for an industrial psychologist to develop and validate the test or perhaps the longer search necessary to find candidates who pass the test.

Regardless of the reason, in all likelihood any above-average to excellent employee hired using the test is bound to be worth much more to a company than any average to below-average employee. A human resources manager who recruits using accurate, validated employment tests probably could measure the improved productivity of the employees hired using the validated employment test over employees hired using traditional, but unvalidated, methods. So, top management probably would look quite favorably on the human resources manager who uses an on-target employment test that results in hiring highly productive employees.

On the other hand, executives may yawn and say "So what!" to themselves when a human resources manager talks in terms of cost per hire. The true measure of any recruiting program is the productivity of new employees, not just how much money or time it took to hire them.

Equal Employment Opportunity

Equal Employment Opportunity (EEO) complaints can cost a company a lot of money, time, and productivity. For this reason, it behooves any human resources manager to do whatever is needed to (1) reduce the number of complaints and (2) make sure that whatever complaints arise are not well founded enough to cost the company a penny in lost judgments or out-of-court settlements. For this reason, the profit-center-oriented human resources manager may wish to look at the number and types of EEO complaints that the company has received in the last year or two. Then, he or she can tackle the problem and *show* that he or she took actions that reduced the *number and cost* of EEO complaints filed against the company. Such a human resources manager would prove highly valuable to the company, since this manager contributed to the financial well-being of the organization.

On the other hand, another human resources manager may produce a letter-perfect Affirmative Action Plan (AAP). While such an AAP would be useful in a number of ways, it would not in itself *measurably* reduce the cost of EEO complaints against the company. Therefore, the manager probably would not receive the status, praise, and recognition that the profit-center-oriented EEO manager deserved and probably received.

HOW TO PROFITABLY USE THIS BOOK
FOR YOUR COMPANY—AND YOUR CAREER

This book presents a total package to human resources managers. It details a ready-to-use, pragmatic system for turning the human resources department into a corporate profit generator. As human resources managers accomplish this goal, they automatically propel their careers because they become important members of the business team.

Using the methods explained in this book, you can overturn the commonly held belief that much of human resources management may be *nice but not totally necessary* to the ultimate financial health of a company. Now it *is* possible for human resources managers in every organization to move to the forefront of producing *measurable business and financial improvements* for their organizations.

Within these covers is a wealth of ideas, information, and case examples to benefit companies. To put this book to profitable use, you will need to do the following:

1. *Use the Planning Model to turn human resources into a corporate profit generator.* The Planning Model is described in Chapter 2, and is used throughout the book to show how to operate a human resources profit center.

2. *Organize profit center endeavors using the Planning Schedule.* Chapter 3 discusses the Planning Schedule and explains how to use it.

3. *Implement the numerous human-resources-oriented solutions to business problems.* Many examples of human resources techniques that result in improved profitability are provided in this book. Put some of these into action.

4. *Follow pointers for encouraging organizationwide enthusiasm, commitment, and involvement.* Pointers for accomplishing this crucial feat are provided in Chapter 12.

By following this Profit Center system, the individual human resources manager can reap tremendous personal benefits, such as:

☐ Earning the status, recognition, and prestige that a business-oriented human resources manager deserves
☐ Earning higher bonuses, or even a percentage of the profit improvement created
☐ Being much more widely sought out by top executives and executive search firms who always have their eyes open for managers with profit improvement talent

Opportunities abound for the human resources manager who knows how to increase a company's bottom line. Keep in mind that the profit center system this book conveys certainly is not the typical status quo of human resources management. It is a progressive, forward-thinking approach that is needed and valued by companies desiring growth. It also is a highly practical system that human resources managers can use to their advantage. Human resources managers now must decide whether they want to remain part of the old way of mainly providing "service" of unmeasured value. Or, they can step into the new era of profit-oriented human resources management.

The choice is yours to make.

Chapter 2
The Six-Part Planning Model to Guide
the Human Resources Profit Center

WHY A PROFIT-FOCUSED HUMAN RESOURCES
MANAGEMENT MODEL IS NEEDED

Out of all major corporate functions, only the human resources function still clings to the notion that it can use action models that do not *directly* zero in on enhancing the corporate bottom line. Take, for instance, the examples provided by other typical departments within a company. What would any businessperson think of a strategic planning department that omitted profit improvements from the plans it develops? How would a company board of directors view a sales department that avoided mentioning how it proposed to increase sales? The same sorts of questions *should* be asked of *all* major departments in any company. All of them—marketing research, operations, manufacturing, inventory/logistics, finance—constantly need to demonstrate how they will aid the company's profitability.

Curiously, however, human resources departments act as if they were somehow exempt from needing to create and use planning models for their endeavors that turn business problems into profit improving, cost decreasing, efficiency enhancing, or productivity improving opportunities. The time is ripe for the human resources department to enter into the same business concerns shared by all other major departments. To do so, profit-oriented models, such as the one described in this chapter, will play a key role in making an ordinary human resources department into an extraordinary one.

HOW MOST HUMAN RESOURCES MODELS PROVE
LESS THAN DIRECTLY PROFIT-ORIENTED

Most human resources action models merely play tag-along with the plans created by other departments. For instance, the personnel and management succession plans flow out of an organization's annual and long-range business plans that are created by other departments. The training plan drafted by the human resources department stems from the technical and mangerial needs expressed by non-human-resources departments. Even the recruiting, compensation, and benefits plans come out of the needs generated by other departments' requirements to attract and retain talent.

None of these traditional human resources planning models show a proactive stance on the part of the human resources staff. All of them come into existence as useful adjuncts *after* another corporate department creates a profit-oriented plan that needs human resources input. These planning models do not noticeably directly improve the bottom line. For years, executives have called for human resources to become more proactive and involved in the guts of business operations. Until now, few, if any, planning models have emerged to do just that.

BREAKING HUMAN RESOURCES TRADITIONS: MAKING A PROFIT-ORIENTED PLANNING MODEL

A pragmatic planning model for human resources management is one that helps the human resources staff "take the ball and run with it" in terms of improving business profitability. It puts human resources managers into the driver's seat, rather than just having them push the car that other departments are driving.

The planning model *must* display three characteristics. It must be:

1. *Proactive*. The model must be one in which human resources managers pinpoint specific. *business* problems and then devise and implement human resources-oriented solutions to these problems.

2. *Profit-improvement focused*. To really play an important role in any business, the planning model needs to show how the plan can and will improve the bottom line.

3. *Succinct*. Keep It Short and Simple, or K.I.S.S. A model that is brief and easy to graphically display gets more attention and mileage than a model that proves lengthy and hard to grasp on paper.

THE SIX-PART PLANNING MODEL FOR TURNING HUMAN RESOURCES INTO A CORPORATE PROFIT GENERATOR

The *Planning Model* shown in Figure 2-1 fulfills the key requirements of a useful model for a human resources profit center. It proves proactive, definitely profit improvement-focused, and it is a fine example of a K.I.S.S. model, since it is so short and simple to follow.

This model proves fairly easy to use. Here is an explanation of each of the six parts of the model.

1. *Business problem*. First, a business problem needs to be clearly stated. It could be a problem with productivity, turnover, managerial effectiveness, sales, or a myriad of other business problems that every business must successfully handle in order to enhance profitability.

2. *Cost of business problem*. Here is where basic cost accounting comes into play. It is not enough merely to specify a business problem that needs to be handled. That would

Figure 2-1. Planning model for turning human resources into a corporate profit generator.

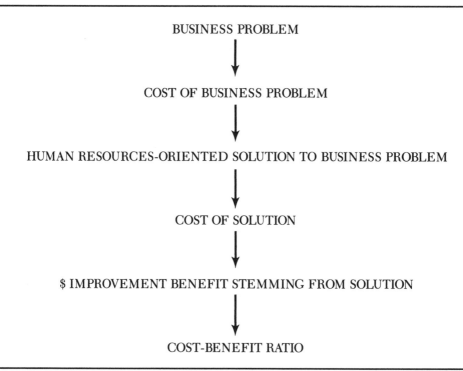

BUSINESS PROBLEM

↓

COST OF BUSINESS PROBLEM

↓

HUMAN RESOURCES-ORIENTED SOLUTION TO BUSINESS PROBLEM

↓

COST OF SOLUTION

↓

$ IMPROVEMENT BENEFIT STEMMING FROM SOLUTION

↓

COST-BENEFIT RATIO

be a passive and not profit-oriented approach. Instead, the human resources profit center *must* determine how much the problem costs. Only by having such cost figures can a human resources manager *measure* the cost-beneficial effectiveness of solutions to the business problem being tackled.

3. *Solution to business problem.* Now the human resources manager gets to show his or her ingenuity. The question arises: What specific human resources-oriented solutions could overcome the business problem? For instance, if productivity is the business problem, then some solutions might be better selection methods, quality circles or other productivity improvement programs, incentive pay systems, an attitude survey, employee assistance programs, suggestion boxes, teambuilding, or many other human resources-oriented solutions. Figure 3-1 clearly lists many possible solutions to a wide array of business problems. The chapters following Chapter 3 explain how to implement and measure each potential solution.

4. *Cost of solution.* Cost accounting again comes into use here to determine the dollars that need to be spent to implement the solution. This step also provides an important check in that almost all of the time the solution should cost less than the problem.

5. *Improvement benefit stemming from solution.* This part of the planning model enumerates the dollar improvement value resulting from the human resources-oriented solution. To create a worthwhile, cost-beneficial solution, the dollar improvement stem-

ming from the solution should be more than the cost of the problem and the cost of the solution. If it is not, then the solution was not worthwhile from a cost-benefit standpoint.

6. *Cost-benefit ratio.* This final step provides the crucial bottom line measure of how successful the solution proved. The cost-benefit ratio is similar to a return on investment figure. It tells how much money was earned compared to how much money was spent on the solution. (Actually, this should be referred to as the benefit-cost ratio, since the ratio is calculated by weighing the benefit stemming from the solution [part 5 of the Planning Model] compared to the cost of the solution [part 4 of the Planning Model]). For example, if a $100,000 improvement resulted from a $10,000 solution, then the cost-benefit ratio was 10:1. That is, for every one dollar spent on the solution, the organization reaped $10 in benefits. Such a cost-benefit ratio surely would be a great return on investment in any business venture.

HOW TO APPLY BASIC COST ACCOUNTING TO HUMAN RESOURCES MANAGEMENT

It is relatively simple to use basic cost accounting for the human resources profit center. This book provides dozens of case examples showing the use of simple cost accounting procedures. However, for many people, cost accounting seems complex and mysterious and perhaps difficult to grasp. Indeed, many companies find it hard to recruit enough good cost accountants. Yet, for the purposes of the human resources profit center, cost accounting is both necessary and easy to do, since it is very logical and straightforward.

How does one begin costing out a business problem, solution, or improvement benefit? Simply:

1. Jot down each possible expense or benefit
2. Calculate the dollars associated with each expense or benefit

A list of typical expenses or benefits that can be costed out are listed in Figure 2-2.

When costing out a problem, solution, or improvement benefit, be sure to take as many costs and benefits as possible into account. Obviously some are easier to measure than others. Nevertheless, human resources managers must take it upon themselves to calculate all the possible monies involved in any human resources solutions to business problems. That way everyone possesses a *measure* of how effective the human resources endeavors have been.

It should be noted that it is best to err on the side of doing conservative cost accounting. That is, do not try to stretch the extent of the profit improvement of a human resources solution. Instead, use conservative figures so that even the most cynical executive will feel compelled to admit that the human resources department's solutions indeed did improve corporate profitability.

HOW TO USE THE PLANNING MODEL ALL THE TIME

The human resources profit center needs to use the Planning Model in a number of its key endeavors, including:

☐ Analyzing and solving business problems from a profit-oriented, not just service-oriented, point of view

Figure 2-2. Typical expenses or benefits that can be calculated.

Productivity
Salaries and Benefits
Training
Recruitment
Turnover
Legal Fees
Sales
Testing
Consulting Fees
Surveys
Meetings
Interviewing
Waste
Returns
Absenteeism
Tardiness
Efficiency
Insurance
Workers' Compensation
Lay-Offs
Contracts

- ☐ Delivering presentations on profit center effectiveness
- ☐ Writing reports on human resources solutions for business problems
- ☐ Generating publicity about successes
- ☐ Training and reorienting human resources staff to the profit center way of carrying out their responsibilities

EXCELLING AT PRODUCING FINANCIAL RESULTS, NOT JUST PAPERWORK

The Planning Model is elegant in its simplicity. Keep it that way. Do not create a paperwork bureaucracy to carry out the human resources profit center. It is important to say this, because many human resources professionals feel that the more paperwork they create for other people to complete, the more valuable they make themselves look. However, that is not true. Moreover, this all-too-common proclivity evokes hostile snickers among non-human-resources staff.

In some organizations, the human resources department is mockingly referred to as the paperwork department, because human resources staffs often make people fill out lots of forms. There are the obvious ones, such as job applications, benefits forms, and tax withholding forms. Then, there are forms that need to be completed periodically, such as annual performance appraisal forms and interviewing forms.

In addition to these forms, human resources departments sometimes like to create even more paperwork. For example, one large chemical company's human resources department reacted to a top management complaint that the company's managers did not plan their work enough or develop their employees. So, the human resources department concocted a performance management system.

However, the implementation invented by the human resources department proved ponderous. Managers were forced to attend a three-day training session. The training taught managers how to use loads of forms the human resources department devised for the performance management system. After the training, each manager was required to meet with his or her employees to fill out lots of forms, many of them quite lengthy. These forms included documents to keep track of objective setting, quarterly follow-up forms, quarterly employee development plans and reports, annual performance appraisal forms, forecast of management potential forms, and more. There even was a form managers needed to fill out to order more copies of all of these forms!

As if that was not enough to occupy a good portion of any manager's potential work time, the human resources department created a full roster of seminars. Many of these seminars *required* attendance by employees in certain jobs or at certain levels of the organization.

It must be noted that the performance management system started off with a good goal. However, what began as a well-meaning service degenerated in practice into paperwork piled on top of paperwork.

Avoid any similar mistakes while creating the human resources profit center. It must act lean and mean. Getting *measurable results* is valued. Producing paperwork for anyone else to deal with is a bothersome nuisance. So, K.I.S.S. in everything the human resources profit center does.

Chapter 3
How the Human Resources Department
Can Turn Business Problems
into Profitable Opportunities

HOW TO START IMPROVING CORPORATE PROFITS

The first step in any profit improvement system is to *plan*. Little in life is accomplished without planning. The same holds just as true in business. The best ideas start with an inspiration then proceed to planning and, eventually, implementation. This chapter focuses on how to plan the activities of the human resources profit center. It includes the Planning Schedule for turning human resources into a corporate profit generator. The Planning Schedule plays an integral and on-going role in the human resources profit center.

But before discussing the Planning Schedule, it is necessary to delineate exactly what makes a good planning or goal-setting system. The goal-setting approach *must* include the following three major requirements. It must:

1. Be *measurable*
2. Include *deadline dates* by which each goal must be accomplished
3. Incorporate the *collaboration* needed to make sure the goals are reached

Properly used, the Planning Schedule presented in the next section incorporates all three of these goal-setting requirements. By doing so, the Planning Schedule also is intricately linked to key management areas, including the following:

• *Management by objectives*. Management by Objectives (MBO) in one form or another underlies almost all management planning methods. The Planning Schedule smoothly dovetails with all MBO-types of goal-setting methods.

• *Performance appraisal*. An important part of MBO is performance appraisal. Specifically, managers generally are appraised on how well they meet or exceed their goals. The

Planning Schedule provides a sound and objective basis for many performance evaluation components and discussions.

• *Training the human resources staff to use the profit center method*. An important aspect of every manager's job is to train his or her staff. Since the profit center method of managing human resources is foreign to most human resources professionals, they must receive training in how to think, plan, and operate using this method. A clearly laid out and easy-to-follow planning tool, such as the Planning Schedule, does a lot to help fulfill this need.

• *Interdepartmental collaboration*. Managers in any one department do not exist in a vacuum; instead, they work both with their employees and with managers from other departments. For this reason, a practical planning tool pinpoints specific business problems in *any* department. It then helps everyone involved advance step-by-step through the procedures needed to turn business problems into profit-enhancing opportunities. The Planning Schedule aids such interdepartmental collaboration.

PLANNING SCHEDULE FOR TURNING THE HUMAN RESOURCES DEPARTMENT INTO A CORPORATE PROFIT GENERATOR

The Planning Schedule, as shown in Figure 3-1, includes all six parts of the Planning Model (see Figure 2-1), along with the addition of three key components required for planning well. These three new components are:

1. A listing of *business problems* that occur in most organizations.
2. *Solutions* to each business problem. Explanations and examples of how to implement each solution are contained in subsequent chapters.
3. Space in which to write the *deadline date* by which a human resources manager plans to complete implementing a solution.

When using the Planning Schedule, a human resources manager first must determine what business problems listed in the schedule need to be overcome in his or her organization. Then, the best solution(s) can be chosen. It is important that a *specific deadline* be inserted so that there is a time frame for implementing any chosen solution. Also, when using the Planning Schedule, managers must cost out the expense attributed to the business problem. Then, the manager must specify the cost of the solution. After the solution is in place, the manager needs to calculate the dollars-and-cents improvement benefit, as well as the cost-benefit ratio.

ACTION-ORIENTED METHODS FOR PUTTING THE PLANNING SCHEDULE TO PROFITABLE USE

The Planning Schedule is only as pragmatic as its users make it. How can it be put to profitable use?

The answer lies in human resources professionals conducting action-oriented organizational research as part of putting the Planning Schedule into action. Many people consider research to be difficult to do and time-consuming. In fact, the action-oriented organizational research methods described here prove fairly simple, very logical, and exceedingly helpful for human resources professionals to carry out.

Figure 3-1. Planning Schedule for turning human resources into a corporate profit generator.

Business Problem	Cost of Business Problem	Solutions to Business Problems (Circle one or more)	Deadline for Implementing Solution	Cost of Solution	$ Improvement Benefit	Cost-Benefit Ratio
Productivity		• Piecework pay • Employee contests • Management bonus • Suggestion system • Interns and trainees • Gainsharing • Prorated merit salary increases following leaves of absence • Wellness program • Employee assistance program • Attitude survey • Teambuilding • Quality circles • Employment tests • Psychological assessments of management candidates • Assessment center • Intensive prehiring reference checks • Technical skills training				

Turnover, absenteeism, and
tardiness

- Piecework pay
- Prorated merit salary
  increases following
  leaves of absence
- Capped short-term
  disability benefits
- Reducing unemployment
  insurance costs
- Employer-supported child
  care
- Well pay and personal time
  banks
- Wellness program
- Employee assistance
  program
- Accident reduction
  program
- Attitude survey
- Exit interviews
- Realistic job previews
- Improving management
  succession
- In-house outplacement
  services
- Employment tests
- Psychological assessments
  of management
  candidates
- Assessment center

(continued)

(Figure 3-1 continued)

Business Problem	Cost of Business Problem	Solutions to Business Problems (Circle one or more)	Deadline for Implementing Solution	Cost of Solution	$ Improvement Benefit	Cost-Benefit Ratio
Work-group effectiveness		• Piecework pay • Employee contests • Gainsharing • Accident reduction program • Attitude survey • Teambuilding • Quality circles • Technical skills training • Performance management training				
Interdepartmental collaboration		• Gainsharing • Teambuilding				
Insurance costs		• Wellness Program • Employee assistance program • Accident reduction program • Intensive prehiring reference checks				
Sales force performance		• Commissions for —Salespeople				

	—Customer service representatives • Employee contests • Employment tests • Psychological assessments of management candidates • Assessment center • Training nonsales support staff to sell
Manager and executive effectiveness	• Management bonus • Exit interviews • Teambuilding • Improving management succession • Employment tests • Psychological assessments of management candidates • Assessment center • Performance management training
Merger, acquisition, or reorganization	• Attitude survey • Teambuilding • Layoffs and reducing management positions • In-house outplacement services
Accidents	• Employee contests • Wellness program

(continued)

(Figure 3-1 continued)

Business Problem	Cost of Business Problem	Solutions to Business Problems (Circle one or more)	Deadline for Implementing Solution	Cost of Solution	$ Improvement Benefit	Cost-Benefit Ratio
		• Employee assistance program • Accident reduction program • Intensive prehiring reference checks				
Recruitment and hiring		• Interns and trainees • Employment tests • Psychological assessments of management candidates • Assessment center • Intensive prehiring reference checks • Reducing recruitment costs				
Compensation		• Incentive compensation • Commissions for —salespeople and —customer service —representatives • Piecework pay • Employee contests • Management bonus				

	• Suggestion system • Interns and trainees • Gainsharing • Prorated merit salary increases following leaves of absence
Benefits costs	• Capitated short-term disability • Quartermaster program • Reducing unemployment insurance costs • Employer-supported child care • Well pay and personal time banks • Containment of health care costs • Wellness program • Employee assistance program • Accident reduction program • Intensive prehiring reference checks
Labor relations	• Attitude survey • Reducing employee grievances
Equal employment opportunity	• Training to avoid expensive equal employment opportunity problems

Also, these organizational research methods address a number of concerns, including the following:

☐ Uncovering business problems and opportunities that can be turned into profit improvement projects for the human resources staff
☐ Revealing solutions to some of these business problems
☐ Helping to enlist support, ownership and involvement by non-human-resources staff for the solutions implemented by the human resources department; without such management and employee commitment, carrying out the solutions indeed would prove hard, if not impossible, to accomplish

All of those important concerns can be answered with these four action-oriented organizational research methods:

1. Interviews
2. Questionnaires
3. Observations
4. Investigation of records

These four methods can be used in a number of ways. For instance, interviews can be conducted to uncover business problems that may yield to human resources-type solutions. Also, interviews help pinpoint exactly what problems or opportunities might exist.

If many people are involved in a business problem, then it generally is unwieldy to interview every one of them. A quicker method is to first interview a small but representative sample of the people who have knowledge of the problem and then, based on the interviews to create a questionnaire or survey that can be filled out by everyone else involved in the problem. One type of questionnaire is the attitude survey, which often proves useful for questioning a large number of people on problems that may be occurring.

Another method is observations. To do this, the human resources manager must keep his or her eyes and ears open. Since human resources managers interact with people in all departments of a company, they often are in a great position to observe problems that affect profitability or productivity. Also, the human resources manager could interview non-human-resources executives and staffs to determine what sorts of problems they notice which, if solved, could result in an improved bottom line.

Finally, investigation of records is another method for spotting business problems. It also is useful for measuring improvements stemming from solutions implemented by the human resources staff. For example, if productivity is a problem in a company, then probably productivity figures that show the extent of the problem are available. Or, if turnover is a thorn in the company's side, then turnover records most likely are available for the human resources staff to examine.

Here is a description of how the four research methods can be put to use. Suppose, for instance, that productivity is a problem in a particular department. One of the company's human resources managers decides to tackle it. First, he or she would probably interview selected managers and other employees to discover the extent of the problem as well as its possible causes and even potential solutions. Then the human resources manager would examine the interview data and devise a brief, easy-to-complete questionnaire or survey to enable the other employees to comment on the problem, its causes, and possible solutions.

At the same time, the human resources manager may frequent the department with the productivity problem. While there, he or she would be wise to observe how the department operates. In these "inspections," the observer should take special note of any human resources problems that may contribute to the productivity problem. For instance, he or she may notice that supervisors fail to reinforce highly productive employee behavior and instead just criticize unproductive behavior; or that employees are not trained to do their jobs as productively as possible.

At the same time that interviews, questionnaires and observations are proceeding, the human resources manager also can check records related to productivity in this particular department, as well as comparisons to the productivity of similar departments. Furthermore, the human resources manager also would do well to check into other records that may yield clues to the productivity problem's cause. These records may include performance appraisals and training records of employees in that department.

These four methods—interviews, questionnaires, observations, and investigation of records—provide a well-rounded and on-target gauge of the department's productivity problem. They provide an action-oriented approach to discover the extent of the productivity problem, the causes of the problem, plus ideas for solving the problem. Most likely, the Planning Schedule lists one or more solutions that can be set in motion to solve the problems revealed using the four research methods. The following chapters describe how to implement these profit-improvement solutions.

PART II
APPLYING SPECIFIC HUMAN RESOURCES-ORIENTED TECHNIQUES TO IMPROVING CORPORATE PROFITABILITY

Part II of this book considers specific techniques that human resources managers can apply to help *measurably* improve corporate profitability. Each technique presented here helps solve one or more business problems typically confronted by an organization. These business problems are pinpointed in the Planning Schedule shown in Chapter 3 (Figure 3-1).

The solutions embodied in these techniques are arranged according to usual activities carried out by human resources professionals. Human resources executives readily can decide which staff member may be best suited to solve which business problem faced by the company. Each technique or solution is discussed in terms of the same half dozen issues, namely:

1. *Business problems addressed*. This is important because some human resources techniques can be used to solve more than one business problem.

2. *Overview of solution*. Here a concise sketch of the solution is given.

3. *How to implement solution*. This discusses the how-to methods that need to be followed to effect a solution.

4. *Deadline for implementing solution*. This information lets you know approximately how long it might take to effect the solution. With this information, it is possible to determine which solutions might be feasible timewise and which may just take too long to achieve the desired results.

5. *Deadline for measuring profit improvement*. Sometimes a company wants profit improvement techniques to show measurable benefits right away, and other times a company feels comfortable carrying out a solution that may not show any measurable profit improvement for a year or longer. This information helps you determine if the solution under consideration falls within an acceptable timeframe for measuring profit improvement.

6. *Case example of profit improvement*. This section under each solution describes a business problem that was solved using a particular human resources-oriented technique. Each example is laid out using the six-part Planning Model.

Most of the case examples are drawn from the experiences of corporations. Some descriptions explain how one company solved a business problem in a profit center manner. In other instances, the examples are composites of how a number of organizations solved a particular problem. Finally, a few examples are hypothetical and are described as such.

The key purpose of the case examples is to show how to use the Planning Model. While each example may prove useful or interesting in itself, the main goal is to help you grasp how to put a human resources profit center into action when tackling crucial business problems. For this reason, numbers usually are rounded off. For instance, an example may actually refer to a problem involving 123 managers. However, for the sake of simplicity and reading ease, the example may state that the problem entailed 100 managers.

Also, some organizations that provided examples did not calculate the various costs and benefits of what it did. That is to be expected in most human resources departments at this point in management history, since they tend not to bother much with how they measurably affect profitability. Also, some companies understandably felt hesitant to divulge the dollar figures entailed in their solutions to business problems. When an organization did not provide specific dollar figures for what it did, the dollar amounts cited in the case examples were calculated based on what seemed realistic in the situation.

Chapter 4
Incentive Pay and Other
Compensation Techniques

This chapter describes how to use incentive compensation or pay plans to *measurably* improve corporate profitability. The strategies covered include the following:

☐ Commissions
  —Salespeople
  —Customer service representatives
☐ Piecework pay
☐ Employee contests
☐ Management bonus
☐ Suggestion system
☐ Free (or Almost Free) Labor
  —Interns
  —Trainees
☐ Gainsharing
☐ Prorated merit salary increases following leaves of absence

WHY INCENTIVE PAY ACCOMPLISHES MORE THAN MERIT PAY

When a human resources professional looks into what sort of pay plan will result in the most productivity, the two main choices wind up being incentive pay plans versus so-called merit pay plans. *Both* types of pay plans claim to pay for performance.

However, one enormous difference exists: Incentive plans pay employees only for *measurable* productivity, while, in sharp contrast, merit pay plans generally pay a straight salary with increases at the judgment or whim of the employee's supervisor. That is, incentive pay plans compensate employees for what they actually produce, while merit pay plans do not as clearly pay people for their real contribution to the organization's bottom line. That is a significant difference.

Almost all companies claim that they want to pay for performance, yet they often do not practice what they preach. An example may be derived from a Conference Board examination of compensation practices at about 500 companies.[1] Slightly over half of the companies studied used executive bonus plans, but only 11 percent used profit sharing plans of one type or another, 8 percent offered potential bonuses to *all* nonexecutive employees, 3 percent implemented group productivity incentives, and just 1 percent gave financial incentives for group cost control endeavors.

Incentive-type pay plans are used by a growing number of companies, but there is a lot of room for further growth in this practice. No wonder so many managers wonder about how to make employees more productive. They do not seem to realize that "You get what you pay for." Most companies simply have not yet wanted to pay for the high level of productivity they desire to obtain from their employees. These companies offer little monetary motivation for employees to turn in a highly productive performance.

Indeed, a typical so-called merit pay plan (in which employees get increases based on their supervisor's judgment) often gives practically the same increase to a highly productive employee as it grants to the employee's less productive peers. For example, let's say that a highly productive employee is appraised at the end of a 12-month period. His supervisor thinks the employee did a superb, highly productive job. In that case, the employee might receive a 6 percent "merit" pay increase for his work. At the same time, a moderately productive employee in the same job might well be given a 3 percent "merit" pay increase.

The difference in wage increases is comparatively small. Also, the difference probably will not seem large enough to motivate the superb employee to work really hard for the next 12 months. For example, if both employees earn $25,000 per year, then the superior employee will receive a 6 percent increase, or $1,500, during the next year, while his less productive counterpart with the 3 percent will be granted a $750 raise.

It is doubtful that the difference in the two employees' productivity amounted to only a $750 difference in the company's bottom line. It is almost an insult to pay the hard worker only $750 more for his outstanding work. After all, he could have worked at a much more leisurely pace and ended up with virtually the same so-called merit salary increase.

Now, let's look at the same situation from the incentive pay point of view. Using an incentive system, employees are paid for how much they produce. Their pay in some way reflects how much they contribute to their employer's success. That accomplishes three key goals:

1. *It makes employees entrepreneurial.* When employees know that they will make more money only when they contribute to bettering the employer, then suddenly the employees have a personal and financial stake in making sure that the company makes more money. After all, the employees' incentive pay is directly related to how much the *employee* helps the employer forge ahead.

2. *It reinforces productive behavior.* Reinforcement refers to rewarding a person for what he or she does. It is part of human nature to repeat behavior that is positively rewarded. It also is part of human nature not to repeat behavior that is not positively rewarded. For instance, if employees work long and hard to turn in a good performance

and are suitably rewarded for the results, then there is quite a good chance that the employees will continue to work hard for the company. In contrast, if employees are not rewarded for their tremendous productivity, then they are much more likely to feel little urge to exert themselves too strenuously on the company's behalf. After all, they will not be paid for what they really produce for the company.

3. *It allows employees to perceive a sense of fairness.* Most people continually make mental notes about whether or not they feel their employer treats them fairly or equitably. People very much want to feel that the respect, recognition, status, prestige, and compensation they receive is based on a fair system that takes their contribution into account. When someone is paid commensurate with how much he or she produces, then that seems fair and equitable. However, the same person paid with only limited regard for how much he or she produces may feel he or she is not really being treated fairly and squarely. Incentive pay plans help ensure that employees feel they are paid in a fair and equitable fashion.

These three points encompass the reasons why this chapter focuses on incentive pay methods much more than on the merit pay plans that are common in most companies.

■ COMMISSIONS

Business Problems Addressed

Sales Force Performance
Compensation

Overview of Solution

A commission boils down to paying a person a percentage of the amount the person sells. For example, if a salesperson earns a 10 percent commission, that means that for every $100 the salesperson sells, he earns $10 in commission. Or, if a bank teller receives one percent of all new account deposits the teller "sells" for the bank, then the teller receives $1 for every $100 of deposits into new accounts.

Interestingly, not every company pays commission to its sales force, although a majority do. A study sponsored by the American Productivity and Quality Center of Houston and the American Compensation Association found that 30 percent of the companies they surveyed paid salespeople only a salary.[2] Seventy percent used salaries *plus* commissions. The same survey showed that only about 23 percent of sales support staff can earn any commission for their endeavors. These figures point to the opportunities available to companies to expand the use of commissions as a means of motivating and rewarding their employees involved in the bread-and-butter of their companies—the sales force.

How to Implement Solution

1. *Ensure organizational commitment.* First, the company management must make a commitment to pay its sales force for what it sells. That is, the company has to believe that sales should be encouraged through paying commissions rather than a straight salary.

2. *Determine commission amount*. The next step is to decide what commission or commission plus base salary might prove best. One consideration to take into account is the profit margin on the goods sold. For instance, if a product has a 50 percent profit margin, that means that half of each dollar of that product's sales is profit. If another product has a five percent profit margin, then a nickel of each dollar sold is profit for the company. The company must decide how much of this profit it is willing to part with in the form of commissions, or commissions and salary, paid to the sales force.

3. *Communicate commission plan to sales force*. The company must *clearly* convey the commission system to the sales force. No commission method can succeed if the salespeople do not understand exactly how much they might earn for selling a certain amount of goods or services. For this reason, it generally proves best to keep the commission plan very simple and easy to understand.

4. *Pay commissions promptly*. The company must set up a bookkeeping system to keep track of how much commission each sales employee earned. Few things could deflate an otherwise motivated salesperson more than having to argue, fight or otherwise run after the commission he or she rightfully earned.

The payment system should follow one of the basic laws of pragmatic reinforcement. Specifically, the sales employee ought to receive the commission *as soon as possible* after earning the commission. Reinforcement or rewards, such as pay, have the greatest effect when the person receives the reward immediately after earning it. So, twice monthly pay is better than monthly pay. Weekly payment of commissions could work even more effectively.

Deadline for Implementing Solution

Commission plans can be implemented fairly quickly. The main time considerations are in planning what sort of commission arrangement to use and communicating the plan to the employees in an easy-to-grasp manner.

Deadline for Measuring Profit Improvement

Bottom-line enhancements from commissions generally come fairly quickly. However, a commission plan may need to be updated and modified as time passes. For instance, after awhile, sales personnel may get so used to the commission arrangement that they almost consider it as a regular salary in a certain respect. In such a case, the company may want to lower the commission rate a bit on the average sales volume, but add an even higher commission percentage for sales *over* a certain amount.

For example, let's say that a sales force builds up to an average of $100,000 per year in sales per salesperson. The commission rate is 25 percent. So, each salesperson averages $25,000 in earnings based on commission. The company wants to increase the sales, but the sales force has become too complacent earning $25,000 per year. This amount seems almost like a regular salary to them.

In this situation, the commission may be changed so that salespeople earn 20 percent on their first $100,000 in sales, and 30 percent on anything they sell over $100,000 per year. This sort of "tweaking" of the commission system should foster greater sales effort, so that the salespeople can get back up to the $25,000 average personal earnings they grew accustomed to collecting.

Case Examples of Using Commissions to Improve Profits

Two examples of profit improvement through commissions are presented here. The first one deals with the most common use of commissions, namely, commissions paid to salespeople. The second example considers a comparatively untapped area of using commissions to spark profit improvements, that is, paying commissions to customer service staff.

USING SALES COMMISSIONS TO SPUR INCREASED PERFORMANCE BY SALESPEOPLE

This case focuses on a steel products firm that compensated its sales force the old-fashioned way: It paid salespeople a salary only, with no possibility of commission. The firm's salespeople lived in their sales regions and operated out of their own homes. National sales managers supervised the sales staff and helped them out when they could.

Over a period of several years, sales declined steadily. It is important to note that the problem did not stem solely from the fact that many traditional steel companies are having a harder time in the marketplace. The problem and the solution are outlined in the *Planning Model* shown in Figure 4-1.

To begin with, the *business problem* centered on the company's dwindling sales. Its products and their pricing were competitive with other firms in its market niche. The company's distribution system and quality also were competitive. Nevertheless, the company's sales continued their downward spiral. The *cost of this business problem* was a decline in sales at an average of about 10 percent fewer sales per year over a period of years. The year-to-year comparisons for the most recent period showed that sales went from $100 million down to $90 million. Furthermore, the company saw no immediate way to turn the situation around.

At this point the company's human resources managers made key recommendations for the company's future. As a *solution to the problem*, they recommended that the company enhance its salary-only salesperson compensation method by turning it into a salary-plus-commission plan. The company's 100 salespeople earned an average of $40,000 a year, and their average sales were around $1 million each. Since their salary alone equaled 4 percent of their average yearly sales, it was decided that allowing the salespeople to earn a 5 percent commission on all sales over $1 million seemed quite fair to the salespeople and to the company. The sales force could earn more money, at a higher percentage than it usually earned, which should prove motivating. At the same time, the company could sell more and probably enjoy lower production costs per unit it manufactured because of the projected increase in volume.

The possible inducements created by adding a commission poten-

Figure 4-1. Planning Model for using commission to increase sales force performance.

BUSINESS PROBLEM

Decreasing sales at a steel products company

COST OF BUSINESS PROBLEM

Sales dropping 10%/year
Most recent year's sales: $90 million, down from the previous year's $100 million

SOLUTION TO BUSINESS PROBLEM

Change salespeople's compensation from salary-only to salary-plus-commission
Commission = 5% of each salesperson's sales over $1,000,000/year

COST OF SOLUTION

$250,000

Cost = Number of salespeople × Average commission paid/salesperson
     = 100 salespeople × $25,000/salesperson
     = $250,000

$ IMPROVEMENT BENEFIT

$14.75 million/year

Improvement benefit
     = Sales increase − Commissions paid
     = $15 million/year − $250,000/year
     = $14.75 million/year

COST-BENEFIT RATIO

60:1

$14,750,000:$250,000

tial to the sales staff's salaries were studied in a survey of the salespeople. The survey uncovered a fact that the company already suspected, namely, that the salespeople were not overly motivated to begin with. The comment of one salesperson summed up the survey's findings: "When a salesman gets a straight salary—no matter how much he sells—it's pretty hard to get up in the morning." It was assumed that the addition of the commission would give the salespeople a good reason to get up in the morning and feel motivated to sell more.

This assumption proved correct. During the first year of the salary-plus-commission compensation plan, sales increased $15 million, or around 17 percent, to $105 million annually. The main *cost of the solution* was the five percent commission on each salesperson's annual sales over $1 million. Since there were 100 salespeople, average sales of $1 million each amounted to the first $100 million in sales. So, in effect, the sales force earned its five percent commission on the last $5 million of the company's sales. The company paid $250,000 in commissions.

For this quarter of a million dollars, the company experienced a $14.75 million *improvement benefit*. This improvement is from the $15 million sales increase ($90 million per year up to $105 million per year) minus the $250,000 paid in commissions.

Given this situation, the company's *cost-benefit ratio* was 60:1. This was calculated by comparing the $14.75 million improvement in sales to the cost of that improvement, or $250,000. That certainly is a fine return on the company's investment of putting a salary-plus-commission compensation plan into operation.

COMMISSIONS FOR CUSTOMER SERVICE REPRESENTATIVES LEAD TO INCREASED SALES

Customer service representatives often are in a perfect position to talk customers into buying more goods or services, because customer service representatives of all types often have a good deal of interaction with customers or clients. They easily can "pitch" to the customer the virtues of buying more than the customer otherwise would purchase. However, despite this tremendous potential, only about 23 percent of American companies pay commissions to sales support employees.[3] There is a huge vacuum that many companies can fill by motivating such employees with a commission in return for selling their employer's wares.

Just such an opportunity is transforming a small but enlightened portion of the banking industry, for instance. Previously, banks viewed their tellers as service providers. Bank tellers merely used to take depositors' money and perhaps add a "Thank you" or "Good-bye" at the end of the transaction.

Now, more and more banks are changing all that. They now consider their bank tellers as the front line of their sales offense. Why? Because more bank depositors interact with tellers than interact with bank salespeople (conventionally called loan officers or personal bankers, rather than what bankers would consider crass sounding, namely, the title salesperson). Tellers are in a perfect position to put in a sales plug for depositors to use the bank more.

For instance, after depositing a check, a bank customer now might receive a deposit slip, a smile, and a sales question such as "I notice that you have only a regular checking account and savings account here. Would you be interested in a higher paying money market account? You'll make even more money on it." Or, a depositor may hear, "You know, our bank offers a fine array of opportunities for your Individual Retirement Account. I notice that you usually keep more than enough money in your account to open up an IRA with us. How would you like me to get an IRA specialist to talk with you about how you can invest your IRA contribution?"

Companies in many industries are turning their customer service employees into a whole new, exciting, and certainly profitable sort of sales force. This new wave of customer service employee is likely to continue to increase in number and in effectiveness.

The following example occurred in a direct mail company that sold goods through brochures it mailed out quarterly to over 150,000 customers or potential customers. The *Planning Model* for this case example appears in Figure 4-2.

Figure 4-2. Planning Model for increasing sales by paying commission to customer service representatives.

BUSINESS PROBLEM

A direct mail company has difficulty increasing the dollar amount its customers spend on orders they phone in to the company.

COST OF BUSINESS PROBLEM

Average orders taken per order taker = $3,600/day
There are 16 order takers
Company's total phoned in orders = $14.4 million/year
($3,600 × 16 order takers × 250 business days/year = $14.4 million)

SOLUTION TO BUSINESS PROBLEM

Transform the order takers into a commissioned inside sales force. Offer them a commission of 3% of all orders they take in over their average daily sales of $3,600.

COST OF SOLUTION

$96,440

Costs included:

A. Training costs
B. Commissions paid

A. Training costs

    = (Number of order takers × Average hourly salary and benefits × Hours of customer service sales seminar) + (Number of managers training order takers × Average hourly salary and benefits × Hours of customer service seminar)

    = (16 order takers × $10/hour × 2 hours) + (2 managers × $30/hour × 2 hours)

    = $320 + $120

    = $440

B. Commissions paid

    = Number of order takers × Average order takers sales amount over $3,600/day × 3% commission × Number of work days/year

    = 16 order takers × $800 × .03 × 250 days/year

    = $96,000/year

Cost of solution

    = $440 + $96,000/year

    = $96,440/year

$ IMPROVEMENT BENEFIT

$3,103,560/year

Improvement Benefit

    = Increased Sales − Cost of Solution Increased Sales

    = This Year's Sales − Last Year's Sales

    = This Year's Sales

    = Number of order takers × Average sales/order taker × Number of work days/year
    16 order takers × $4,400/day/order taker × 250 days/year

    = $17.6 million/year

Last year's sales

    = Number of order takers × Average sales/order taker × Number of work days/year

    = 16 order takers × $3,600/day/order taker × 250 days/year

    = $14.4 million/year

Increased sales

    = $17.6 million/year − $14.4 million/year

    = $3.2 million/year

Cost of solution

    = $96,440/year

Improvement benefit

    = $3.2 million/year − $96,440/year

    = $3,103,560/year

COST-BENEFIT RATIO

32:1

$3,103,560:$96,440

Essentially, the *business problem* was sales. The company chose the right mailing lists. It tested dozens and dozens of mailing lists to determine which ones held the best potential customers. The company also did superb marketing research to find out which products its target market most wanted to purchase. However, even after all this marketing work, the ultimate lifeblood of the company rested on how much money was taken in through the orders mailed and phoned in to the company's order takers. Customers placed a good many orders through the mail. However, the vast majority of orders arrived through the company's 800 phone number. In fact, the company sold $14.4 million each year over the phone. The average phone order taker racked up $3,600 a day in orders, and there were 16 order takers, each working an average of 250 days per year.

The company executives did not feel they could affect the amount of orders mailed in, except by changing the mailings, products offered, and pricing. However, a more immediate opportunity struck them as quite feasible and relatively quick to implement. Specifically, they felt quite confident that they could take more control over increasing the over-the-phone orders. To do so, they reasoned that the *solution to the business problem* lay in turning the phone order takers into "polite yet aggressive" sales agents.

This solution would entail a major change in how the company conceptualized and used its customer service representatives who took the orders over the phone. The company no longer could consider them to be mainly pleasant, well-organized people who were capable of writing and properly routing orders, while they acted nice to the customers who phoned the company. Instead, the order takers needed to become salespeople.

The two sales managers devised a two-hour seminar to teach the order takers how to sell over the phone. The workshop conveyed a number of key areas the order takers needed to look at to develop their skills. These included the following:

☐ Viewing themselves as salespeople, not just as order takers.
☐ *Always* suggesting that the customer buy more products during each phone contact.
☐ Focusing on how the customer can spend less money, in a sense, if the customer purchases in greater quantity. That way, the total order may cost more to the customer, but the per unit cost would be less. For example, if a customer ordered 15 cases of file folders, then the cost would be less per case than if the customer bought only the 10 cases that the customer originally called to order.
☐ *Pushing* the customer on the sale items described in the special center insert in the brochure. These sale items were profitable to sell. These items also always appeared to be great buys, and a little coaxing could induce customers to purchase them.
☐ Selling "specials." As part of its new over-the-phone sales campaign

method, the company instituted different unadvertised specials every day. These so-called specials were items that the company could buy in huge quantities, for example, from overstocks that their suppliers held in their warehouses that they wanted to get rid of. These specials were bought by this direct-mail marketing firm at prices lower than their suppliers normally would charge. There was one problem, though, with the specials. They typically were items that were in relatively low demand, or they were items that were no longer going to be produced. Therefore the normal market demand for these products was rather limited—but they could be sold at the *right* price with a bit of coaxing by the phone order takers.

☐ Acting as the customer's friend. The order takers learned the importance of making the customers *enjoy* calling to place their orders. To do so, the order takers were instructed to call the customers by their first names, as though they were friends. Also, the order takers were instructed on how to act cheerful and gracious on the phone. Many of the people calling to place orders were secretaries. They were used to serving their bosses, so they particularly cherished talking to a friendly person who clearly wanted to serve them.

With the added incentive of a 3 percent commission on all sales over the average daily order of $3,600, the order takers felt more than happy to learn the skills taught in the brief workshop. They also felt good using these skills on the job. Their main reinforcement proved to be the extra $24 per day they typically earned using their new salary-plus-commission compensation system. Most of the order takers earned a salary of $7 an hour, or $56 per day. The extra $24 per day meant a 43 percent boost in their average daily earnings.

The results certainly proved quite satisfying to both the company and the order takers. From the company's perspective, the newly commissioned order takers helped haul in over $3 million in new sales over the first year of the commission system, about a 20 percent increase in sales. At the same time, the new compensation system cost the company barely anything, since the order takers earned commission on a gainsharing basis. Under such plans, employees earn more money when they produce (in this case the "production" is selling) more than they previously produced in a baseline period. In this case, the baseline was the previous year's average phone order of $3,600. The company could decide if it wanted to keep the baseline at $3,600 in average daily sales in future years. Or, if it so desired, the company could increase—or even decrease—the baseline rate that the order takers had to beat in order to earn their commission.

The *cost of the solution* was $96,440. During the first year of this solution, the company realized an *improvement benefit* of about $3.1 million. These results yielded a handsome *cost-benefit ratio* of 32:1. In other words, after only its first year, turning phone order takers into a commissioned inside sales force proved quite profitable to the company.

■ PIECEWORK PAY

Business Problems Addressed

Productivity
Turnover, Absenteeism, and Tardiness
Work-Group Effectiveness
Compensation

Overview of Solution

A piecework compensation system pays production employees based on the quantity of *quality* goods or services that they produce. The more goods or services of acceptable quality that they produce, the more money they earn.

This overview of piecework pay requires definitions of two key terms: "quality" and "production employees." The proper use of these terms is crucial to the successful implementation of any piecework pay system. To begin with, the focus on quality is quite important, because it is one thing for someone to produce a lot of something. It is quite another thing for the same person to produce it of a quality that the enterprise can sell and expect to be accepted—and, hopefully, even appreciated—by the firm's customers. The company would be foolish, indeed, to have high production levels if the goods or services produced prove to be of low or unacceptable quality. That is why a piecework compensation system definitely pays employees *only* for goods or services they produce that prove suitable in quality.

The next definition of utmost importance in a piecework compensation system is that of production worker. For our purposes, the term production worker must be viewed in the broadest manner possible. Specifically, anyone who produces goods or services that can be *measured* is a production worker in this regard. Given this definition, the first type of production worker most people think of is a manufacturing employee on an assembly line. These people certainly do production work. They produce x number of widgets per hour or per day, whether the widgets are books coming off a printing press, cars rolling off an assembly line, metal products, or whatever else their company may manufacture.

But the identification of who is a production worker needs to be even broader than that. Many other people literally are production workers in the truest sense of the term. For example, many types of professionals are production workers. Despite their advanced degrees, physcians, accountants, lawyers, clinical psychologists, and veterinarians are production workers. How can that be? The bottom line (figuratively and financially) is that these professionals bring in money based on how much they produce. They manufacture services, such as patient care or accounting, and, in doing so, they are production workers. These professionals can be paid on a piecework basis just like an assembly line employee, because both professionals and assembly line workers are production employees whose work output can be *measured*.

How to Implement Solution

A piecework incentive system is an outgrowth of the scientific management movement spearheaded by Frederick Winslow Taylor. Taylor was the first industrial engineer. He perfected the use of time-and-motion studies to determine how a job could be performed most efficiently and effectively. He also proposed that production employees should be paid based on the amount of useable goods they produce. (The comic movie *Cheaper by The Dozen* is about Frederick Taylor and his family. The movie portrays how Frederick Taylor and his wife, who was one of the first industrial psychologists, used time-and-motion studies at home to "scientifically manage" their 12 children.)

The main steps for creating a piecework incentive pay system generally are the following:

1. *Guarantee a base, or minimum, pay*. By doing this, a company assures its employees that they *will* earn something for their labors. Without such a guarantee, it may prove difficult to recruit or retain good employees.

2. *Set production standards*. Determine how much production employees reasonably can produce. Such baseline data may come from a number of sources, such as

☐ Previous 12 months' production records
☐ Longer term production records
☐ Standards determined by industrial engineers

At future dates, the baseline can be changed as needed. These changes could take place every year, based on the latest production figures. Another option is to change baseline production rates after new machinery or other efficiency-enhancing devices are installed.

3. *Determine piecework pay*. A company often bases piecework pay on either (1) each product or service an employee produces or (2) the percentage that production output exceeds the baseline.

4. *Communicate piecework pay plan to employees*. Any change in how employees are treated, including how they are paid, may disrupt the status quo in the workplace. Piecework pay is no different. As with any compensation technique, it proves best for the organization to make sure that each and every employee affected by the piecework pay plan knows precisely how his or her wages will be determined. It also would be useful for the company to publicize its production figures. Such information lets employees know exactly how well they are doing. Good places to publicize production records are at work stations, bulletin boards, and in the cafeteria. The watchword here is to freely and extensively give employees all the data they need to determine how well they are performing. Then, they can make informed decisions about how much harder they need to work to earn what they want.

Nucor Corporation, a highly successful steel company headquartered in Charlotte, North Carolina, has used a piecework incentive system for over 20 years. Let's look at how Nucor uses piecework pay for its steel-straightening department. Historically, in the steel industry, an average of about 10 tons per hour can be straightened. With this data in mind, Nucor decided that the baseline for its steel-straightening department would be eight tons an hour. For producing eight tons per hour, employees are paid their hourly base pay of about seven dollars.

However, for every ton this department straightens over eight tons per hour, the department's employees earn a five percent bonus. Note that the piecework pay, which Nucor calls a production bonus plan, is earned by a work group, such as a production department. Individual production employees cannot earn a bonus. This certainly gives employees a financial stake in working together as a team to increase productivity.

Nucor also makes two crucial assurances to its employees. First, Nucor will never change the baseline (for example, eight tons per hour in the steel-straightening department) unless a revolutionary new technology is installed which greatly improves production speed. The second promise employees receive is "We'll let you earn as much as you can earn," explains Jim Coblin, Nucor's manager of personnel services.[4] That is, the more the employees produce, the more money they can earn. The obvious kicker is that the company first must have the sales to justify the output. But, if the sales have been made or are expected, the only limit on how much Nucor's production employees make is the quantity of quality products they manufacture.

How well does Nucor's piecework system work? Production figures tell the story. In the steel-straightening department alone, Nucor produces an average of about 20 tons per hour. That is twice the steel industry's average production rate. Because of their production efficiency, Nucor's employees can earn a fine bonus over their base salary. In 1986, the average steel worker at a major steel company earned $27,500. In contrast, Nucor's steel workers earned about $30,000 on average. At Nucor's Darlington, South Carolina, plant, the average production worker earned over $30,000 in 1986. During the same year, the average Darlington County high school graduate who held a manufacturing job earned about $14,000. Needless to say, Nucor never goes begging when it needs to fill a production job in its plants.

Nucor's system throws in a number of other production requirements, too. First, bonus money is paid only on *quality* tons produced. Work-group members do not receive a single penny of bonus money on any goods they produce that are of unsuitable quality. So, the employees have a huge financial stake in making sure they do top-notch work. Also, if an employee is late to work, he loses his entire *daily* bonus, regardless of how productive his department is that day. If an employee is absent even one day, he loses his entire *weekly* bonus. The result is that in Nucor's plants, absenteeism stands at less than one percent. Tardiness is virtually nonexistent.

In addition to the incredibly strong production-oriented atmosphere Nucor creates, these production figures also mean a good deal to Nucor's marketing efforts. "When people ask why Nucor can sell steel so cheaply and still make a nice profit, it's because we produce so very much per man per year," comments Mr. Coblin. The statistics of tons produced per man per year reveal a lot. The five largest integrated steel mills in the United States produce 347 tons per man per year. Japan's largest integrated steel mills manufactured 550 tons per man per year. In sharp contrast, Nucor's average is 960 tons per man per year.

These statistics may not be totally comparable, since Nucor uses steel mini-mills that are in some ways different than the mills used by many large steel companies. Nevertheless, the differences certainly are startling. They also consistently occur at a company like Nucor that knows how to motivate its hourly steel workers to continually keep production *and quality* running high. This information sheds light on why Nucor may be the only steel company in the world that has never had to lay off anyone.

Deadline for Implementing Solution

Two ways exist for determining the timeframe to implement a piecework pay system. At a brand new plant or facility, a company can implement piecework pay as soon as the plant or facility begins operation. In such situations, this incentive compensation approach readily becomes the status quo for the company's pay system.

However, according to Vincent J. McNamara, a compensation consultant with VJ Associates in Northbrook, Illinois, piecework pay could become more time consuming to implement at an existing plant or facility that possesses a history of using a nonpiecework pay system. At such locations, it takes three to six months to fully explain the system to affected employees, to show employees how they should earn as much or potentially even more than they previously earned, plus to allay employees' other concerns about the new compensation system.

Deadline for Measuring Profit Improvement

Profit improvement can be measured shortly after the piecework system is put into place, sometimes as soon as a week or a month, because the entire piecework system is based on the *measurable* productivity of employees. So, as soon as employees' productivity in producing quality goods or services is measured, both the piecework compensation and the realization of productivity improvements can begin.

MAKING PIECEWORK PAY IMPROVE THE BOTTOM LINE

Piecework incentive compensation works quite well in manufacturing companies. It is a logical and extremely pragmatic way to motivate and reward high levels of productivity when it comes to making goods.

However, now, as an increasing percentage of the economy revolves around service industries, it is time to begin using piecework pay plans even more in service industries. After all, many of the jobs carried out by service workers are *measurable* and they do require a noticeable level of *quality* at the same time. The only difference is that service employees "manufacture" services, while manufacturing workers produce tangible goods. So, why not compensate service industry employees in the same manner as their fellow workers in manufacturing jobs? Doing so calls for instituting piecework incentive plans.

This case example presents one such pay plan which did a great job of increasing the billings (that is, sales) of a certain type of service employee, namely, general practice physicians at a private health clinic. The *Planning Model* for this endeavor is shown in Figure 4-3.

The owner of this clinic, a physician herself, saw a tremendous opportunity in a *business problem* her clinic faced. Her clinic had more than enough demand for its services. So, getting patients was not a problem. In fact, the problem was one that most organizations wish they had—the clinic had too many patients calling in to receive its services. It could not see them as quickly as the patients would like. As a result, some patients went elsewhere to receive prompter attention.

Figure 4-3. Planning Model of piecework incentive pay plan for health clinic general practice physicians.

BUSINESS PROBLEM

Desire to increase billings 20% in a private health clinic

COST OF BUSINESS PROBLEM

The clinic's *salaried* physicians saw an average of 5 patients/hour or 40 patients/day. With this level of productivity, billings ran $150/hour or $1,200/day for each physician. For this amount of work, each physician earned $100,000/year, which is $50/hour or $400/day. The clinic wanted to get the billings up 20%, which translates into physicians seeing an average of 6 patients/hour or 48 patients/day.

SOLUTION TO BUSINESS PROBLEM

A. Take physicians off straight salary
B. Start piecework incentive pay system by paying physicians $11/patient that they see
C. Continue the quality control procedures to monitor patient care

COST OF SOLUTION

$320,000/year

Cost of solution
    = Piecework Pay Total − Previous Salary Total
Cost for each physician's pay jumped to $132,000/year from the previous $100,000/year salary that each physician received.
Piecework pay total
    = Number of physicians × Pay/patient seen × Number of patients seen/hour × Number of work hours/day × Number of work days/year
    = 10 physicians × $11/patient × 6 patients/hour × 8 hours/day × 250 days/year
    = $1,320,000/year
Previous salary total
    = Number of physicians × Annual salary/physician
    = 10 physicians × $100,000/year
    = $1,000,000/year
Cost of solution
    = $1,320,000/year − $1,000,000/year
    = $320,000/year

$ IMPROVEMENT BENEFIT

$600,000/year increased billings

Improvement benefit
   = Current year's billings using piecework incentive pay − previous year's billings using salaried pay
Current year's billings
   = Number of physicians × Average number of patients seen/hour/physician × Number of work hours/day × Number of work days/year × Average fee/patient
   = 10 physicians × 6 patients/hour/physician × 8 hours/day × 250 days/year × $30 patient
   = $3,600,000/year
Previous year's billings
   = Number of physicians × Average number of patients seen/hour/physician × Number of work hours/day × Number of work days/year × Average fee/patient
   = 10 physicians × 5 patients/hour/physician × 8 hours/day × 250 days/year × $30/ patient
   = $3,000,000/year
Improvement benefit
   = $3,600,000/year − $3,000,000/year
   = $600,000/year

COST-BENEFIT RATIO

1.88:1

$600,000:$320,000

But the clinic owner realized there was a strong need for her clinic to treat more patients. For a *solution to the business problem,* her human resources management consultant hit upon a sound idea. He pointed out that the general practice physicians developed a habit of seeing an average of about five patients per hour. If they could maintain high quality standards and see an average of six patients per hour, then the clinic's billings for the general practice physicians' work would increase 20 percent.

This increase would stop a percentage of patients from going elsewhere for medical care. Also, the improved patient service would enhance the clinic's word-of-mouth reputation as a medical facility that provided quick, convenient, and good quality care. A more active clinic could make more efficient and profitable use of diagnostic tests, pharmacy services and the expertise of the clinic's specialists, who would have more patients referred to them by the general practitioners.

In order to reap these benefits, the consultant suggested that the clinic cease paying the general practice physicians a straight salary. In its place, he suggested that the clinic pay these physicians on a piecework basis while employing quality control standards. But, he added, the physicians should be able to earn *more* money using the piecework incentive pay plan than they could under their salaried pay status.

With this in mind, a piecework pay plan was established. It was announced to the physicians that the piecework plan was an experiment and would be called off unless their billings went up by 20 percent or more.

This plan greatly appealed to the physicians since their additional efforts could bring them an immediate 10 percent boost. They could have continued to see five patients per hour while making more than before. But, as expected, the per patient piecework pay, along with the promise that the incentive pay would be scrapped unless billings increased, catalyzed a lot more energy and efficiency among the general medical staff.

As a result, the number of patients they saw increased to an average of six patients per hour. That was the 20 percent increase in billings that the clinic owner wanted. However, that was not a "free" 20 percent billings increase because the 10 physicians each earned an average of $132,000 per year under the piecework plan, $32,000 per year more than they earned with their previous $100,000 annual salary.

But the cost of the solution certainly was more than worth the added expense in wages, because the *improvement benefit* totaled $600,000 annually in increased billings by the general practice physicians, a 20 percent increase over the same physicians' previous year's billings. Other benefits accrued to the clinic. Because of the increased flow of patients through the clinic, the use of other clinic services such as diagnostic testing, pharmacy, and medical specialist services expanded.

All in all, the piecework incentive pay plan was effective. Patient service was improved and quality standards were maintained. The *cost-benefit ratio* was 1.88:1. That is not a startling cost-benefit ratio; however, it shows that this incentive plan did what it was intended to do. Also, if the billings from the increased use of other clinic services were added in, then the cost-benefit ratio would have been a good deal more than its approximate 2:1.

■ EMPLOYEE CONTESTS

Business Problems Addressed

Productivity
Work-Group Effectiveness
Sales Force Performance
Accidents
Compensation

Overview of Solution

Employee contests or, as they sometimes are called, competitive games, often provide a dramatic way to help improve company profitability. Such contests usually are thought to be the sole province of the sales department. But actually almost every department can devise some sort of competitive games to improve sales, increase productivity, decrease costs and, at the same time, increase the bank accounts of the highest performing employees who win the contests.

Managers can be endlessly creative when devising various contests. In fact, it often proves best to change the contests fairly frequently to add excitement and test out new approaches.

Essentially, an employee contest pits work groups or teams against each other, or sometimes individuals compete to see who can turn in the best performance on some measurable work activities. The important point here is that the contest must focus employees' energy on *measurable* outcomes over which they can exert a good deal of control. For instance, a contest over which department exhibits the "most winning" attitudes would seem patently ridiculous. In contrast, a contest to see which department can produce the most widgets, sell the most products, or have the fewest accidents is vastly more measurable and greatly more in line with the goal of improving corporate profitability. Gimmicky contests for nontangible end results will gain very little. But contests concerning measurable activities and quantifiable end results fulfill the organization's mission of increasing its output, selling more, spending less, and altogether becoming increasingly effective in the work it rewards.

Examples of employee contests abound. For example, in a manufacturing environment, the plant manager could set up a contest among the work crews to see which group produces the most. The competitors could be work groups on the day shift, evening shift, and night shift for instance. Or, work teams that perform similar tasks could compete against each other. Teams that use similar machines and manufacture the same products could compete against each other for which team produces the most useable goods during a given amount of time.

Sales staffs frequently get involved in employee contests. For example, one company found that the amount of new or repeat business it obtained depended on the season of the year. During nice, warm summer weather, the company landed lots of new business. However, during the cold winters, the company's main income came from repeat business from existing customers, with only a minimal amount of new business.

What accounted for the difference? The answer proved rather simple to pinpoint. During the warm months, the company's salespeople felt more than happy to get out in the sunshine and call on potential new accounts. But in the harsh winters experienced in this company's region, salespeople avoided going out to call on potential new customers. Instead, the salespeople stayed inside where it was warm and comfortable and only called their existing accounts to drum up repeat business.

To counter this trend, the company instituted a series of contests. In the summer, the company created a contest for who could obtain the most repeat business while still bringing in more than a predetermined amount of new business. Then, during the winter, the company reversed the contest. It rewarded salespeople who ventured out in the cold weather to pick up new business while still pulling in over a certain amount of repeat business over the phones. The contest worked quite well. It helped even out the new business-repeat business cycles the company had experienced for quite a few years, resulting in steadier year-round business and increased profitability.

The restaurant industry also puts contests to great use. Some successful restaurants regularly hold contests. They will, for example, offer a reward to the waiter or waitress who sells the most of some particularly high-profit food or drink. For instance, many restaurants regularly mark up alcoholic beverages by about 1,700 percent, yielding a hefty profit for each drink sold. No wonder some restaurants offer rewards to the waitperson who sells the most alcoholic drinks.

How to Implement Solution

1. *Announce that a contest will be held.* This step needs to be carried out with a good deal of gusto, enthusiasm, and fanfare. Employees can read just how committed management is to holding a real honest-to-goodness contest that really means something to the company and—most of all—to the employees who can win something in the process.

2. *Describe what will be measured.* The end result that the contest seeks to reinforce or reward needs to be totally clear. All employees involved in the contest need to know exactly what they must do well. Also, management must announce to everyone involved how the measurements will be made, as well as how disputes will be settled. Participants need to know that the entire contest is fair and that everybody involved possesses an equal chance to win.

3. *Tell who the competitors are.* Here, a number of possibilities exist. Perhaps individual employees can compete against each of their peers. Or, workgroups can compete. Another way to proceed is to form teams of people from whom management wants better cooperation for the sake of the company; joining people together as colleagues in a contest is a superb way to promote rather quick, and sometimes startling, teamwork and positive peer pressure to turn in a good performance.

4. *Give the time frame of the contest.* Let everyone know just how long they must compete before an employee or a team of employees is declared the winner. The time frame could be as short as one day or it could last a year. In general, the shorter the interval, the better. The reason lies in the theory of behavioral reinforcement. Essentially, people prefer to receive a reward (or at least have the possibility of winning a reward) over short periods of time. A short-term contest could generate loads of spark, enthusiasm, and drive among employees. In contrast, with a much longer contest of, say, a year or so, many employees may well wait until the tenth or eleventh month of the contest to really start plugging away like wildfire. Certainly, most companies prefer a short burst of energy among their employees to a longer term fizzle that contains minimal sizzle.

5. *Tell employees what the rewards are.* Two main types of rewards exist—monetary and nonmonetary. The monetary type of reward is easy enough to define. It amounts to a check given to the employee or employees who win the contest. The nonmonetary reward could take quite a few different forms. It could be tangible or intangible. Certain intangible rewards such as praise or recognition are nice, but tangible rewards usually linger longer in an employee's memory. For example, if an employee wins a television set, then every time that employee watches television, he or she will remember how his or her effort resulted in winning the television that can be appreciated everyday. Other types of nonmonetary, tangible rewards include trips to locations both near and far or even engraved plaques announcing the accomplishments of the winners.

Deadline for Implementing Solution

It usually does not take too long to design and implement an employee contest. However, all participants must be thoroughly briefed on the goals of the contest, and how they can win, *before* the contest can commence. Adequate time must be spent communicating this crucial information to all contest participants.

Deadline for Measuring Profit Improvement

This factor depends on the sort of performance the contest seeks to encourage. For example, a contest on daily sales of a certain product has a very short time frame to measure its effectiveness. On the other hand, a contest on sales of a particularly expensive and hard-to-sell product would take much longer before profit improvement could be measured and rewards given to contest winners.

REDUCING PAST-DUE ACCOUNTS RECEIVABLE USING A CONTEST

One specialty products distribution company put employee contests to very profitable use. This firm's staff included a dozen people who handled accounts receivable, that is, bills the company mailed but for which it had not yet received payments. The *business problem* developed because this staff proved lethargic about running after customers who did not bother to pay their accounts in a timely fashion, specifically, within 30 days. Overall, it seemed that the staff felt very minimal urgency when it came to collecting the money customers neglected to pay on time. No amount of prodding, snappy motivational messages, or verbal encouragement could convince the staff to run after the company's debtors. The result was that the company usually had an average of half a million dollars in past-due bills outstanding. Given the way the company financed its distribution business, the *cost of this business problem* amounted to around $60,000 annually.

So, a new tactic was instituted with fine, cost-beneficial results. This *solution to the business problem* involved a competition. Each week, the accounts receivable staff member who collected the most overdue account money earned a $200 reward. The person who collected the second highest dollar amount of past-due bills earned a $100 bonus. These rewards certainly provided a suitable inducement, because the accounts receivable clerks earned an average of $12,000 a year. That comes to $240 per week, assuming a 50-week work-year with two weeks off for vacation. These staff members were offered the opportunity to make 83 percent more money than their weekly pay when they came in first. And the person who came in second could pull in about 42 percent more than the usual weekly wages. The *cost of the solution* was $15,600 ($300 in weekly prize money being paid out 52 weeks per year).

The company discovered that this inducement proved irresistible to the accounts receivable staff. As can be seen from Figure 4-4, the *Planning Model,* this innovative compensation technique *measurably* motivated otherwise typically rather lackadaisical employees. In fact, they reduced the accounts receivable by 60 percent, from an average of $500,000 outstanding down to $200,000 within the first year that the contest operated. This is even more remarkable, since prior to the contest the amount of past-due bills had remained relatively stable for quite a long time with no previously recognized way to reduce it.

The reduction of past-due bills yielded a fine *improvement benefit.* With the company paying 12 percent interest on past-due bills, its new $200,000 amount of overdue accounts receivable cost it around $24,000 per year in interest charges. That was $36,000 per year less than the firm paid when it had a half million dollars overdue. This improvement benefit means that the company contest netted it a 2.3:1 *cost-benefit ratio.* That certainly is a fine payback for the company in dollars and cents. Also, the solution catalyzed staff members to reach levels of performance that no one in the company had previously imagined possible.

Figure 4-4. Planning Model for competitive contest that reduced past-due accounts.

BUSINESS PROBLEM

A company wants its accounts receivable department to speed up collections of past-due bills owed to company in order to reduce the costly interest charges the company owes on its unpaid bills.

COST OF BUSINESS PROBLEM

$60,000/year

Cost
    = Average amount of past-due bills throughout year $\times$ 12% interest
    = $500,000/year $\times$ .12 = $60,000/year

SOLUTION TO BUSINESS PROBLEM

Employee Contest

Each week, a $200 reward is given to the accounts receivable clerk who collects the greatest amount of past-due bills. A $100 reward goes to the clerk who collects the second largest amount.

COST OF SOLUTION

$15,600/year

Cost
    = Amount paid in weekly contest × Number of weeks per year
    = $300/week × 52 weeks/year
    = $15,600/year

$ IMPROVEMENT BENEFIT

$36,000/year

Improvement benefit
    = Annual cost of business problem before implementing contests − Annual cost after implementing contests
Cost before implementing contests = $60,000/year
Cost after implementing contests
    = Average amount of past-due bills throughout year × 12% interest
    = $200,000/year × .12
    = $24,000/year
Improvement benefit
    = $60,000/year − $24,000/year
    = $36,000/year

COST-BENEFIT RATIO

2.3:1

$36,000/year:$15,600/year

■ MANAGEMENT BONUS

Business Problems Addressed

Productivity
Manager and Executive Effectiveness
Compensation

Overview of Solution

Management bonuses sometimes are referred to as the proverbial donkey-and-carrot approach to compensation. The carrot is the monetary bonus a manager can earn *if* the manager runs hard and fast enough *and* accomplishes certain preset goals. When used effectively, the bonus is made to look juicier and more delectable each year. Thus, the bonus system continually keeps a manager coming back year after year, always yearning for more and bigger "carrots."

Management bonuses focus attention: They reward managers or executives for accomplishing certain preset goals. Usually, but not always, these goals are measurable, often in financial terms. In addition to base compensation, managers have the opportunity to earn even more money through accomplishing what is necessary to win a bonus.

Bonuses can be given for a variety of reasons. The may be given to a manager who completes certain tasks, such as opening up a new plant under estimated costs. Or, a manager may earn a bonus for ensuring that much equipment or many programs were installed in a timely and cost-effective manner. The possibilities for how and why a manager can receive a bonus are endless.

However, the bonus should be meaningful. For example, one major company in the health care industry inappropriately awards bonus dollars essentially based on a manager's job title. This is portrayed in Table 4-1.

Table 4-1 implies that this company's bonus system does not really reward levels of performance. All managers with each job title receive essentially the exact same bonus, with only minor differences. The lowest performers were separated from the top performers in each job title classification by a mere $2,000. When asked why the bonus system was so narrow and so lockstep, the firm's chief executive officer and chairman of the board replied, "Two reasons. First, we only have good management personnel, so it's hard to distinguish among them. So, why shouldn't we give everyone basically the same bonus. Secondly, we don't want to get any manager upset. They talk about who got what size bonus, and if one of them found out that one of his peers got a greater bonus, we'd have a huge uproar and turnover around here. We'd rather avoid those nasty things."

Actually, what that company really avoided is having to make distinctions among different levels of productivity. When a creative, productive manager doesn't receive a fatter, sweeter "carrot" than a less productive peer, something is amiss. This bonus system does not *really* reward productivity; it merely acts as a way for the company to give every manager some money over and above the manager's regular salary, which is a far cry from the incentive compensation technique that management bonuses are supposed to be.

How to Implement Solution

1. *Set measurable goals*. Here, a management-by-objectives (MBO), method works quite well. Each goal must include a measure, such as a certain level of profitability, sales, or productivity; a deadline to complete the goal, investment or cost to complete goal; and steps that must be taken to reach the goal. Every goal set by a manager as part of an MBO-oriented bonus system must receive the approval of the manager's own supervisor.

2. *Determine bonus criteria*. Managers, just as anyone else, feel more motivated when they know the rewards for their labors than when they have only vague ideas as to how to earn a bonus. So, it is important to let all managers in the bonus program know

Table 4-1. Inappropriate bonus system used at a large health care company.

Management Title	Base Compensation	Bonus
Manager	$ 53,000	$ 9,000–$11,000
Director	76,000	14,000– 16,000
Division vice-president	93,000	24,000– 26,000
Division president	112,000	34,000– 36,000

exactly what they must do to receive a bonus. The more clearly the bonus criteria are explained, the better the program works for everyone involved. Managers will feel it is fair and above board; the company will know exactly what benefits it will gain *before* it must spend money for financial or other bonus awards.

3. *Assess how well the criteria were met*. At the end of set time periods—perhaps a quarter, a year, three years, or five years—the manager's performance must be evaluated. The appraisal must zero in on how well the manager met or exceeded the goals necessary to earn a bonus. This appraisal could use the company's normal performance appraisal process, with one significant addition. Specifically, with a bonus system, managers know that not only can their performance appraisals affect their base salary, but appraisals also can determine the amount a manager can expect to receive as a bonus. This fact underscores the importance of focusing bonus criteria on *measurable* performance.

For example, one large bank (which is not faring too well financially) gives managers a bonus based partly on how well they write their annual goals or objectives. While it is important for managers to write down their goals, such work should be considered part of their normal managerial duties. To award a bonus to a manager just for doing his or her regular job makes a joke out of the MBO-type process by which most well-organized businesses operate. In contrast, awarding bonus dollars for a manager meeting *measurable* productivity or financial goals certainly sets the right businesslike tone for the proceedings and simultaneously rewards superior performance for what shows up on a firm's bottom line.

4. *Pay bonus promptly*. A basic tenet of optimally using any sort of reward, such as a bonus or other type of incentive pay, is to give the award *immediately* after it is earned. For instance, one natural resources company could not understand why its bonus system did not seem to motivate continual strong performance among its managers. The company complained that it paid handsome bonuses. Why, then, was the costly bonus system ineffective?

The cause of the problem boiled down to when the bonuses were paid to managers. This company paid bonuses to managers in April for work that had been completed during the previous January–December calendar year. In other words, this organization paid bonuses four months—a third of a year—*after* the managers completed the work for which they were being rewarded! Small wonder that managers saw little connection between the goals they accomplished and the bonus check they received four months later. One manager put it this way: "By the time I got my bonus, I forgot what I did to deserve getting a bonus in the first place."

To correct the situation, this natural resources company changed its bonus payment timetable. It began paying bonuses in January for work completed during the previous 12 months. Managers responded well to this needed change. They began consciously linking their performance to the bonus they could pocket after they reached or surpassed their preset goals.

Deadline for Implementing Solution

Generally, a management bonus system can be thought out and planned within a couple of months. After this development phase, the considerable aspects of implementing a management bonus system begin. This phase includes logistical items such as budgeting for the bonuses, incorporating the bonus system into the organization's regular compensation procedures, plus communicating the bonus criteria to everyone involved.

Also, the political aspects of the bonus system need to be addressed to some degree. An organization implementing a management bonus system must devise and articulate a clear rationale concerning who is eligible for bonuses and why they are eligible while others are not. Mending hurt feelings takes some time.

Such logistical ingredients entailed in implementing a bonus system generally take 6 to 12 months. Furthermore, periodically, the bonus method must be reconsidered and modified to reflect new business, economic, and marketplace conditions.

Deadline for Measuring Profit Improvement

Bonuses usually are given out annually. At the end of a year (fiscal or calendar, whichever the company decides to use), managers' performances can be measured and bonuses calculated. However, an even better method is to pay different types of bonuses at different intervals. For instance, bonuses can be paid out quarterly for meeting predetermined, very short-term productivity quotas and annually for accomplishing somewhat longer-term productivity goals. Certain bonuses may be paid once every 2, 3, or even 5 years for reaching much longer-term goals. The key point is that no matter what timeframe is used to measure managerial performance and award concommitant bonuses, the bonus must be awarded based on the manager achieving *measurable* goals that the company finds valuable.

SUCCESSFUL PLANT START-UP
USING A MANAGEMENT BONUS PLAN

This *business problem* occurred in a very large printing company that was building a huge, state-of-the-art printing plant in the South. The firm wanted its new plant to cost less than projected to start and it wanted to have the plant producing salable printing in less than four weeks.

Much of the company's future success depended on this plant because, in its northern plants, the company had experienced extremely costly trouble with unions, including strikes, work slowdowns, restrictive work rules that prevented introducing innovative work procedures and methods, and overly costly wage pacts. The increasingly obsolete technology of the firm's existing plants, combined with the less-than-optimally productive labor force, made it practically impossible for this printing company to compete in bids for large, long-term printing contracts with major magazines, book publishers, and catalog producers. Building a plant with state-of-the-art technology in a right-to-work state was this company's best hope. Figure 4-5 is the *Planning Model* for tackling this business problem.

Further adding to the company's concerns were its previous failings in opening two southern printing plants. In both cases, the company proved colossally adept at "saving a nickel and then losing a dime," explained the firm's new vice president of manufacturing. Both plants were designed to take work from the company's northern plants, as well as to offer additional capacity so that new printing contracts could be handled. However, the results in terms of productive capacity fell far short of expectations.

Why did this occur? Simple. For the first plant, the company did not install the latest printing equipment, so its machines were not competitive. Although the plant was new and in an overwhelmingly nonunion region, it still could not compete with other large printing firms.

The second plant the company opened presented a new opportunity for the company to do things the right way. However, the company blundered at this plant start-up, too. The latest printing equipment was installed. This was a high-tech, state-of-the-art plant. However, in an effort to keep costs down, the company decided to staff the manufacturing operations almost solely with low-wage, inexperienced people. Although these people were willing to work hard and motivation was no problem, they simply did not possess the necessary technical skills to make a large printing plant run smoothly and profitably. As the situation deteriorated at this plant, union organizing drives became common at the plant—even though it was located in an area of anti-union sentiment.

Given these problems, the company decided that its third southern plant needed to work well, with no hitches, and certainly no repetition of its two previous southern fiascos. The *business problem* focused on how this large printing company could (1) build the plant under its $100 million budget, and (2) have the plant producing usable printing with minimal waste within four weeks of the plant start-up.

The *cost of this business problem* certainly looked formidable. First, the plant was estimated to cost $100 million to open, definitely one of the most expensive printing plants ever built. Second, experienced engineers and printing production experts determined that it probably would take the plant at least four weeks of operation before it would manufacture an adequate ratio of usable printing product (such as magazines and catalogs) compared to unusable product or waste.

To assure that these two main goals were met, the company instituted a *solution to the business problem* consisting of a management bonus plan. The plan offered tremendous financial rewards to the plant manager and his direct-reports, that is, the four managers who reported directly to the plant manager. These four managers included the plant's director of manufacturing, chief engineer, director of personnel, and controller.

The company also made sure that it did not repeat the problems it created at its two previous southern plants. To do so, at the new plant, the company took the following shape:

1. Properly and thoroughly trained employees in the many very technical printing skills they needed to use each day.
2. Hired some production employees who already possessed cru-

Figure 4-5. Planning Model for management bonuses for starting a new plant ahead of schedule.

BUSINESS PROBLEM

A large printing company is building a new plant. It wants the plant (1) built under budget and (2) producing usable printing with minimal waste within four weeks after start-up.

COST OF BUSINESS PROBLEM

Here are the estimates of how much the new plant was expected to cost:

A. Plant budget for construction, machinery, initial staffing and training is $100 million.
B. Such plants at best generally take four weeks of operation before they produce usable printing with minimal waste. Expected waste per week during start-up is $400,000 ($100,000/week × 4 weeks = $400,000).

SOLUTION TO BUSINESS PROBLEM

Management bonus plan

COST OF SOLUTION

$194,000

Bonus plan worked as follows:

Bonus for:	For Plant Manager	For Each Manager Reporting to Plant Manager
Every million dollars plant costs under $100 million	$10,000	$3,000
Every week under 4 weeks that it takes plant to produce useable printing	$ 3,000	$1,500

Cost of solution included:

    A. Bonuses for starting plant under budget
    B. Bonuses for producing usable printing in less than 4 weeks

A. Start-up bonus
    = (Millions plant started under budget × $10,000) + (Number of managers reporting to plant manager × Millions plant started under budget × $3,000)
    = (8 × $10,000) + (4 × 8 × $3,000)
    = $80,000 + $96,000
    = $176,000
B. Production bonus
    = (Number of weeks less than 4 weeks that it took plant to produce usable printing × $3,000/week) + (Number of managers reporting to plant manager × Number of

weeks less than 4 weeks that it took plant to produce usable printing × $1,500/
manager)

= (2 weeks × $3,000/week) + (4 managers × 2 weeks × $1,500/week)

= $6,000 + $12,000

= $18,000

Cost of solution

= $176,000 + $18,000

= $194,000

$ IMPROVEMENT BENEFIT

$8,200,000

Improvement benefit

= Amount plant cost under budget + Amount not spent on predicted printing waste

Amount plant cost under budget

= Budget to open plant − Actual cost to open plant

= $100 million − $92 million

= $8 million

Amount not spent on predicted printing waste

= Amount expected to be spent on printing waste − Actual amount spent on printing
waste

= $400,000 − $200,000 = $200,000

Improvement benefit

= $8,000,000 + $200,000

= $8,200,000

COST-BENEFIT RATIO

42:1

$8,200,000:$194,000

---

cial technical skills, so they could "hit the ground running" as soon as the plant's production operations began.

3. Avoided union organizing drives. This was accomplished by hiring very people-oriented supervisors and then heavily training them in the supervisory skills that play an important part in making unions unnecessary.

The *cost of the solution* totaled $194,000. This derived from the plant manager receiving $10,000 and his direct-reports earning $3,000 for every million dollars the plant came in under its $100 million budget. Since the plant cost $92 million to start, or $8 million under budget, these 5 people earned a total of $176,000 in bonus money for bringing the plant in below budget. Also, the plant manager earned $3,000 and his direct-reports earned $1,500 for every week less than four weeks that it took the plant to produce an acceptable level of usable, quality printing product. Since the plant took only two weeks to produce usable printing, this management bonus totaled $18,000.

The *improvement benefit* resulted from the plant costing the company $8,200,000 under expected start-up costs. The plant cost $92 million to open, which is $8 million less than the budgeted $100 million. Also, the plant's initial manufacturing waste totaled about $200,000 less than the expected $400,000 in waste. Given the excellent results achieved by this plant's top management team, the company realized a superb 42:1 *cost-benefit ratio*. This ratio is derived from the plant's start-up costing the company $8,200,000 less than expected, with the main expense needed to achieve this under-budget start-up being the $194,000 in management bonuses paid to the plant manager and the four managers who reported directly to him.

■ SUGGESTION SYSTEM

Business Problems Addressed

Productivity
Incentive Compensation

Overview of Solution

Modern corporations have replaced the old-fashioned suggestion box with the more modern suggestion system. General Motors, Northern Telecom, Eli Lilly, Unisys, American Airlines and American Telephone & Telegraph count themselves among the over one thousand companies and government agencies that use suggestion systems. These companies found that this technique offers a relatively straightforward means to tap employees' ideas for improving company profitability while rewarding participating employees for their ingenuity.

A survey of about 1,000 companies using suggestion programs, conducted by the National Association of Suggestion Systems (NASS), found that companies saved $1.82 billion via their suggestion systems.[5,6] The survey also turned up other interesting data. For instance, about 26 percent of all suggestions are adopted. Over nine million employees are eligible to participate in suggestion programs. The net savings per 100 eligible employees is around $20,000. The average award is $416, and the highest award given was $150,000. In general, NASS recommends that an award be approximately 15 percent of the first year net savings from a suggestion.

Some detractors put down suggestion systems. A major reason given is that companies already pay their employees to think up ways to profitably run their organizations. So, their reasoning goes, why should any organization give special awards for employees doing what they already get paid to do? An organization needs to resolve many concerns prior to implementing a suggestion system.

Companies that use suggestion systems consider them valuable from a dollars-and-cents perspective. Unisys Corporation is one such company. As shown in Figure 4-6, during approximately the first six years of Unisys' suggestion system, the company saved over $14.3 million. It also rewarded suggesters to the tune of around $2.9 million for their effort making over $11.4 million for the corporation.

How to Implement Solution

1. *Appoint a suggestion system coordinator.* The coordinator often works in the human resources department, but may work in the engineering department or finance department, depending on how the company prefers to operate.

2. *Set ground rules.* A suggestion system, despite its simple sounding concept, really can become complex. Also, any organization implementing a suggestion system needs to take many legal and employee relations concerns into account. For example, the company must clearly delineate who owns the suggestions after they are made (usually the company does, not the employee who made the suggestion). Such decisions can hold legal implications for the company. They also potentially open up the company for employee disgruntlement. For instance, an employee whose idea is rejected (about 74 percent of all suggestions are rejected) may feel hurt, misunderstood or—especially since the company may later implement a similar idea—cheated. All of these concerns make it imperative that the company set clear, *written* ground rules and procedures. These items should include the following:

- *Policy manual.* This should be quite detailed and cover every combination and permutation of what could occur while operating the suggestion system.
- *Employee handbook.* The employee handbook summarizes in simple, everyday language the policies detailed in the policy manual. Each employee who is eligible to participate in the suggestion system either should have a copy of this handbook or one should be readily available. Possible suggestion system rules appear in Figure 4-7.
- *Forms.* The main form needed is the suggestion form itself. The suggestion form might include a very brief summary of the program's basic ground rules, as well as space for writing a suggestion and signing the form. Figure 4-8 is a sample suggestion form.

Figure 4-6. Statistical highlights from Unisys Corporation's employee suggestion program from October 1981 to July 1987.

Number of eligible employees	150,741
Number of suggestions received	52,736
Number of suggestions received per 100 eligible employees	35
Number of suggestions decided	50,777
Number of suggestions adopted	8,596
Adoption rate	17%
Net savings for first 12 months following implementation of each adopted suggestion	$14,306,177
Total award dollars paid to employees	$2,864,669

Figure 4-7. Sample employee suggestion program rules.

EMPLOYEE SUGGESTION PROGRAM RULES

Employee Eligibility

Employees at the   (either on paid or non-paid appointments) are eligible to submit suggestions. Employees who are on personal leave, on long-term disability or are retired are also eligible to submit suggestions.

Two or more eligible employees may submit a suggestion, defined as a **joint** suggestion.

Suggestion Eligibility

For a suggestion to be considered eligible for a cash award it must:

- be written or typed on the ESP form
- be signed by an eligible employee(s)
- be received in the ESP Office where it will be date and time stamped and given a number
- recommend a specific action
- directly affect an operation or procedure of the

- be original (if the suggestion is a duplicate of one already received, the suggestion received first will be the one considered)

If the person evaluating the eligible suggestion is able to improve on the original idea, find a different or better application of it, or takes any action leading to an improvement as a result of his or her evaluation, the original suggestion will still be eligible for a cash award.

Subjects Not Eligible

A suggestion will not be considered eligible for a cash award if:

- it is an idea within the scope of the suggester's job where he or she could implement the idea without further approval
- it addresses policy including conditions of employment and/or benefits or policies or procedures which may be legally required
- it is a problem already under study and assigned to someone who is working on a solution

Cash Awards

Cash will be awarded for those suggestions which are reviewed and approved. (The ESP Brochure outlines review and approval process.)

The minimum cash award is $15.00. The maximum cash award is $100.00 for **intangible** suggestions and $5,000 for **tangible** suggestions (see definitions below). All awards are subject to federal and state tax and FICA deductions.

When two or more employees have submitted a **joint** suggestion which qualifies for a cash award, the award amount will be divided equally among all the eligible employees who signed the suggestion form.

If the employee was eligible at the time of submission but the status of that employee changed prior to approval of the suggestion, the employee is eligible to receive a cash award if the suggestion is approved.

Change in status includes the following: leave of absence; termination (voluntary or involuntary); layoff (definite or indefinite); retirement; and/or death. (In case of death, the award will be paid to the estate.)

For Tangible Suggestions—(When cost savings can be calculated)—For approved suggestions the award will be 15% of the first year's net savings. Net savings is defined as the difference between the present and proposed method minus the costs to implement the suggestion.

For Intangible Suggestions—(When cost savings cannot be calculated)—Approved intangible suggestions will be assigned points by the Committee. Awards will be determined by the number of points assigned.

Time Limits, Duplicate Suggestions and Requests for Re-evaluation

All suggestions will be kept on file for six years from the date of original receipt in the Suggestion Program Office. Duplicate suggestions will not be considered for one year from the date of the letter of final notification.

If within the year, the original suggester can demonstrate that methods, procedures or operations have changed, the employee may request reevaluation of the original suggestion. The employee should resubmit the suggestion form, attach a request for re-evaluation and include details of how conditions have changed. The Committee will determine whether conditions **have** changed and whether the suggestion should be reevaluated.

Requests for Reconsideration

An employee may request a review by the Suggestion Program Administrator of determinations made by the Suggestion Program Committee. Within thirty (30) days of the date of the letter of notification of suggestion approval status to the employee, the employee should write the Suggestion Program Administrator requesting reconsideration of the decision.

The request should outline reasons why the Committee's determinations may be inappropriate. The Suggestion Program Administrator will meet with the employee to discuss the concerns and issues raised. The Suggestion Program Administrator will determine final action.

This process is the exclusive, final and binding procedure for resolving any disputes arising under the Employee Suggestion Program. Disputes will not be subject to any other grievance process.

General

Participation in the Employee Suggestion Program is voluntary.

The   reserves the right to use the approved adopted idea that has been awarded in any manner it sees fit for its own internal purposes. The suggester however, under the guidelines of the   Patent Policy may seek patent and/or property rights. If the suggester obtains such rights, suggester agrees that the   will have royalty-free use of the suggestion within the

The eligibility of the suggestion or the suggester, the amount and type of award and any or all policies or procedures pertaining to the Employee Suggestion program are determined within the guidelines and procedures established by the   . The   has the exclusive authority to determine policies and procedures and reserves the right to terminate, amend or modify the Employee Suggestion Program at any time.

Employee Suggestion Program
Personnel Department

(From National Association of Suggestion Systems, Legal Guidelines. Chicago: National Association of Suggestion Systems, 1986, p. 23.)

3. *Appoint suggestion committees.* Often two types of suggestion program committees exist. The first type is close to the action. It often is composed of employees in the department where suggestions come from, such as, production workers, as well as a member of management or a member of the suggestion system coordinating committee. The second type of committee is an oversight committee. This committee may hold final approval over many suggestions. Or, sometimes this committee must approve all suggestions that require more than a certain amount of money or involve organizing activities of a number of departments or divisions.

4. *Encourage suggestions.* Everyone involved in the suggestion program needs to encourage employees to submit their ideas. Many companies have actual suggestion boxes into which employees can drop their completed suggestion forms. Other publicity also helps draw ideas from eligible employees.

5. *Grant awards.* According to the National Association of Suggestion Systems' research of its member companies, most suggestions are processed by the appropriate committees within 90 days of submission. A little less than half (44 percent) of the awards are granted based on *estimated* savings that could result from the suggestion. Slightly over half (56 percent) of the awards are based on a later evaluation of *actual* savings stemming from the suggestion.

Regardless of which way awards are granted, the quicker and more frequently suggesters receive awards, the more likely employees are to think up useful ideas and submit these ideas to improve company profitability. As for the awards, they typically are cash. Noncash awards often include bonds, merchandise, or tickets to special events. The company usually takes out various taxes and related fees before giving the award. Also, suggesters who win a noncash award must pay similar expenses.

6. *Publicize successes.* It is important to publicize success. Obviously, the best publicity is word of mouth, especially after suggesters receive cash or noncash awards. However, other publicity outlets also exist. These include company newsletters, bulletin boards, award ceremonies officiated by members of top management, and announcements in local newspapers. Publicity keeps up the excitement of the suggestion system and encourages employees to come up with ideas that enhance their employer's bottom line.

Deadline for Implementing Solution

A number of administrative procedures, committees, forms, and policy manuals need to be created before a suggestion system can be put into action. Also, all employees

Figure 4-8. Sample suggestion form.

EMPLOYEE SUGGESTION PROGRAM

SUGGESTION FORM		FOR OFFICE USE ONLY
		Suggestion # _____
		Subject _____
		Comm. Action _____
		Date Closed _____

DIRECTIONS:

1. Complete the form by typing or printing with a black ballpoint pen.

2. Attach any applicable diagram or sketches or additional sheets if necessary.

3. Sign the form and detach the employee copy for your records.

4. Return the first 3 copies to the Suggestion Program Office by folding and stapling so the address appears on the outside.

If you need assistance, please see your supervisor or call the ESP Office at

x _____

PRESENT:

The present situation, method, procedure or service is as follows:
(Tell us what is done now and where it is done)

_____

_____

_____

PROPOSED:

My idea for changing or improving the situation, method, procedure or service is:
(Include the areas that would be affected by the change)

_____

_____

_____

BENEFIT:
(Please check appropriate items)

My idea will:
☐ Increase productivity
☐ Improve service
☐ Reduce costs
☐ Prevent waste
☐ Improve quality
☐ Other _____

Please explain the advantages and benefits of your suggestion:

_____

_____

Estimated savings: _____

Are there any other ways you know of to change the situation, method, procedure or service?
☐ Yes ☐ No If yes, give details of alternatives:

_____

_____

Is there someone else familiar with this situation who might help evaluate the suggestion?

☐ Yes   ☐ No

If yes, please give name _____ Title _____ Phone _____

SUGGESTER IDENTIFICATION   ## JOINT SUGGESTERS

| Last name | First | Initial | Soc. Soc. # | | Last name | First | Initial |

| Job Title | Department | Phone Ext. | | Last name | First | Initial |

Dept. Mailing Address/Location   Suprv.
Name

I/We have read, understood and agree to the rules as set out on the reverse side of form governing the
Employee Suggestion Program as established by the   and agree that if the suggestion is
approved, and I/We obtain patent rights, that the   has royalty-free use of the suggestion within the

Note: All unsigned suggestions will be returned. They will not be eligible for consideration until signed.   (All
joint suggesters must sign)

Signature   Signature

Send form to: Suggestion Program Office
               Personnel Dept., PO Box   Signature

URPO
9/83
SS#100

(From: National Association of Suggestion Systems, Legal Guidelines. *Chicago: National Association of Suggestion Systems, 1986, p. 22.)*

involved must be made aware of the essentials of how the program operates. All this takes
time. An organization planning to start a suggestion system needs to allocate about half a
year to a year for its implementation.

Deadline for Measuring Profit Improvement

There are two parts to this concern. First, suggestion advisory committees need to
estimate how much money will be saved from each suggestion it accepts. Then, a
percentage of the net savings may be paid to the suggester for his or her idea. So, a fairly
quick prediction is made of how much profits might improve.

The real test comes when the suggestion actually is implemented. Some suggestions
quickly result in enhanced profits or lower costs. Other suggestions can take a good deal
of time before they are implemented and yielding more money for the company. The
suggestion system offers a quick means of acquiring ideas for how much profit improvement will come about. However, only time will tell if the *real* savings or profit projections
turn out to be accurate.

BENEFITING FROM A SUGGESTION SYSTEM PROGRAM

A plastics manufacturing company decided that it needed to get
more ideas from its shop floor employees. The *business problem* was

reducing costs and improving manufacturing efficiency. Unfortunately, the company had long been operated in a rather autocratic manner by an extraordinarily bright multimillionaire entrepreneur who owned most of the company's shares. However, after the company was sold, the acquiring company installed its own management. The new management was appalled by how few suggestions for improvements came from the production departments. Instead, most efficiency improving ideas emanated from engineers, vendors, and the former owner of this company. Figure 4-9 depicts the *Planning Model* for handling this business problem.

Since the problem was not clearly defined, the company could not come up with any definite *cost of the problem*. All the company knew was that it wanted to reduce costs and increase manufacturing efficiency, but it did not know by exactly how much.

The new top management team met with the plant managers and the production supervisors to discuss how to tackle the problem. The *solution to the business problem* that most appealed to them was implementing a suggestion program. So, a committee was formed to start this program. A rather energetic quality assurance supervisor was given the responsibility of coordinating this program as half of her duties, and she was allowed to cut back on her quality assurance supervising time.

The program took about two months to plan. During that time, the program's coordinator attended a training program on how to set up suggestion systems. She developed and distributed a program manual, employee handbook for the program, and also suggestion forms. Employees were informed about the program during brief meetings, and also via the company newsletter and bulletin boards. Also, members of the suggestion program committee spread excitement about the program by word of mouth.

One particularly sticky question arose before the program started. Specifically, a rumor started that employees would lose their jobs because of suggestions the company implemented. This certainly was a potentially valid concern. The president of the company was approached about how to handle this matter. He absolutely wanted the program to work well, and he did not want it to result in any job losses. So, he issued a letter to all employees clearly stating, "No one will lose a job because of any suggestion submitted to our suggestion program. Absolutely no one. That's a promise, and I always keep my promises. You have my word." He signed the letter which was included in each employee's paycheck envelope and also tacked to all company bulletin boards.

Shortly after the suggestion program started, suggestions began flowing in. The suggestion review committees responded to each suggester within 45 days. Of the few hundred suggestions received, 63 ideas were implemented. Each suggestion resulted in an average of

Figure 4-9. Planning Model for a manufacturing company's successful suggestion system.

BUSINESS PROBLEM

A company desires to reduce its manufacturing costs and increase its efficiency

COST OF BUSINESS PROBLEM

N/A

SOLUTION TO BUSINESS PROBLEM

Suggestion system program

COST OF SOLUTION

$140,000 for first year

Costs included:

    A. Awards to suggesters
    B. Suggestion program operating expense

A. Awards
    = 15% of annual net savings resulting from suggestions
    = .15 × $500,000 for first year
    = $75,000 for first year
B. Operating expenses
    = 13% of annual net savings
    = .13 × $500,000 for first year
    = $65,000 for first year

Cost of solution
    = $75,000 + $65,000
    = $140,000 for first year

$ IMPROVEMENT BENEFIT

$500,000

COST-BENEFIT RATIO

3.6:1

$500,000:$140,000

$8,000 net savings to the company, after all costs (including awards) were deducted, or a total of about half a million dollars.

Interestingly, the suggester whose ideas netted the company the most money (and earned the suggester the highest dollar amount of awards) was a janitor in one of the manufacturing plants. This man had dropped out of grammar school many years before. He spoke little while at work, except when someone asked him a question. No one expected him to have any ideas to submit to the suggestion program, but he came up with several useful suggestions.

It seems that this man was mechanically minded. While he swept the floors and cleaned up around the machines, he would notice how the machines operated in minute detail. He came up with ways to reduce machine breakdowns and reduce machine-caused waste. Since he could not write much more than his name, he had his daughter write his ideas on suggestion program forms at home. Then, the man would bring the completed suggestion forms to the plant.

After he submitted his fourth accepted suggestion, the president of the company called this janitor into his office. The president asked him, "Why didn't you ever give the company any of these great suggestions before?"

The man replied, "Well, no one ever asked me. And now I can make some more money from it, also."

Given the benefits the company enjoyed, the *cost of the solution* seemed like a comparatively paltry $140,000. This included the 15 percent award given to each suggester whose suggestion was implemented. That meant a total of $75,000 in awards. For example, a suggestion that netted the company $10,000 earned its suggester a check for $1,500 before taxes were deducted. Also, the company figured that it cost about $65,000 to operate the suggestion program for its first year, or about 13 percent of the net savings. Thus the $75,000 in awards and the $65,000 in administrative costs meant that the Suggestion Program cost the company $140,000.

However, the program much more than paid for itself. The *improvement benefit* totaled $500,000. With these results, the *cost-benefit ratio* ended up at a nice 3.6:1.

■ FREE (OR ALMOST FREE) LABOR: INTERNS AND TRAINEES

Business Problems Addressed

Productivity
Employment
Compensation

Overview of Solution

For a great many people who want and need work experiences, serving internships for the employer, practica, or traineeships offer a promising opportunity.

These people provide a fairly large supply of free or inexpensive labor. And, quite often if they are students, their professors will advise them on how to handle many work situations. So, an organization with interns often receives free consulting from knowledgeable professors, in addition to the brainpower and labor of the intern. Fortunately, there are interns interested in gaining experience in a wide variety of fields: marketing research, production planning, engineering, human resources management, public relations, advertising, data processing, and a host of other specialties.

Most interns are extremely anxious to please their managers, and motivation is usually not a problem. Also, the intern knows from the start that by turning in a good performance, a good recommendation for regular employment will be forthcoming. Sometimes an intern works out so well that the organization may offer the intern a regular job. When an intern works out so well, it also reduces an organization's need to search for people to fill certain jobs. In fact, an internship provides an organization with a free or very low cost way to check out the quality of a potential employee.

How to Implement the Solution

1. *Determine the business problems an intern could help solve.* The first step is to decide exactly what sort of problems or opportunities the intern could work on. Be sure that the desired outcome is clearly understood by the intern and everyone who will work with the intern.

2. *Locate intern sources.* The company should consider a wide range of sources in seeking out appropriate interns. For example, if a company wants an intern to help do marketing research that is statistical in nature, then a university's math or statistics department may provide viable candidates. Also, the psychology department could offer candidates, especially from the pool of doctoral students specializing in statistically-oriented experimental or industrial psychology.

Faculty members are another potential source. For example, one nonprofit organization wanted an intern to help devise its marketing plan. Fortunately, one nearby business school had a professor who had written books and many articles on how nonprofit organizations can succeed at marketing themselves and their services. This organization called that professor. The professor provided a superb student intern. Also, the professor took a good deal of personal interest in the intern's project. So, she spent many, many hours conferring with the intern about how to complete the project successfully.

The outcome was threefold: The organization developed its marketing plan and it worked very well. The intern did a fine job, including the indirect consultation the professor provided (such consultation otherwise could have cost the organization thousands of dollars). And, finally, since the marketing project worked so well the professor described it in a journal article. In the end, everyone ended up benefiting.

3. *Review applicants' résumés.* An organization cannot evaluate interns as it would regular employees. Instead, look for *potential*.

4. *Interview candidates.* Two main questions need to be answered during the interview. First, can the intern *potentially* complete the project the organization has in mind? Second, is the intern the sort of person the company wants to have around its offices for three to nine months?

During the interview, the intern must be told about the project the organization has in mind. The intern needs to hear as many details as possible about the work he or she will perform. Only then can the intern decide if the project is right for the sort of experience being sought.

5. *Orient and train the intern.* Never expect an intern to start immediately doing a fantastic job. As with most employees, it will take the intern some time to get used to the organization, how things are done, and the context in which the project will be carried out. Encourage staff members to interact with the intern and teach the intern about what they do.

Importantly, the intern usually likes to feel as though he or she is part of an ongoing team or workgroup.[7] Do not separate the intern from others in the department. Instead, show the intern how his or her endeavors help the department and the organization as a whole.

6. *Supervise the intern.* Interns need attention, advice, coaching, training, and counseling. Those activities take time. A lot of attention should be given to the intern, however, the intern should more than pay for the time with the results of the project. So, the time and effort should prove worth it—if handled properly by both the intern and the intern's supervisor in the company.

7. *Appraise the intern frequently.* It often proves helpful to evaluate an intern once per month on how well the intern is proceeding on his or her projects. Also, at the end of the internship period, the intern needs a very thorough performance appraisal. Sometimes the school the intern attends provides an appraisal or evaluation form for the intern's supervisor to complete. However, the organization's typical performance appraisal form could add to the realism of the internship experience.

Deadline for Implementing Solution

Finding a good quality intern usually is not a quick proposition. A number of steps must be carried out to locate an intern who has the potential to work out well. It is comparable to hiring an employee, except the intern will not be as qualified and may well need more supervision and on-the-job training to complete the work successfully. An organization that wants to take interns on board should begin looking for them three to six months before they are needed.

Most student internships last one-half school year to one full school year. Often the students look for internship sites during the school year preceding the internship. For instance, a student who wants to start an internship at the beginning of the school year, in September, may best find one during the end of the previous school year, around March, April, or May.

Deadline for Measuring Profit Improvement

Before an intern begins, the organization *must* determine exactly what projects it will have the intern carry out. Based on these projects, the organization can make predictions of how long it might take for the intern's work to result in corporate profit improvement. How long it may take to measure the profit improvement remains for the organization to determine.

REAPING REWARDS FROM NEARLY FREE LABOR

This *business problem* centers on interns used by an advertising company. The company was a small but growing concern. Its partners were long on ideas but short on funds to capitalize on many of their brainstorms. Because of this shortage of funds, the firm could not afford to conduct some extensive marketing research to gauge the potential of a new advertising approach dreamed up by the partners. The *Planning Model* for overcoming this problem appears as Figure 4-10.

The *cost of the business problem* would be hard to calculate in this case example because this situation was not so much a costly business problem as it was a lost opportunity to cash in on a seemingly profitable new market. However, the firm could not afford to hire fulltime employees to carry out the needed marketing research. Also, the cost of market research consulting services looked prohibitive to the firm's partners.

So, the *solution to the business problem* was to hire two interns to carry out the marketing research project. These interns were graduate students obtaining their MBA degrees from a well-known local business school. It was not at all an accident that the interns' academic advisor was a marketing wizard who possessed a fine reputation as a marketing researcher. This was the key to the success of this internship, since the parnters hoped to benefit from some of the professor's wisdom for free while they provided an internship site, along with an intriguing marketing research opportunity for the two MBA students.

The students did a thorough job of researching this marketing opportunity. The concept involved selling ads for display in retail stores, such as supermarkets and other stores that commanded a high volume of business.

The *cost of the solution* was $37,200. This amount covered the $100 stipend paid to each of the two interns during their 36-week internship. It also included expenses related to the interns' work. These expenses included phone charges, secretarial assistance, typing, transportation while in the field collecting marketing research data, computer use to crunch the research data, plus the time spent by company staff to supervise the interns and monitor their progress.

The interns researched a number of key areas, including types of ads that could be sold to specific retail stores and potential selling methods. They drew up a detailed marketing plan with heavy input from their marketing professor. The interns also went so far as to write job descriptions of potential salespeople who might sell advertising for retail store display. To streamline the recruiting process, they pinpointed where potential salespeople were working so they could be easily located. They even devised a commission-based incentive compensation plan for salespeople.

The *improvement benefit* turned out to be $600,000 in new profits

Figure 4-10. Planning Model for using low-cost interns.

BUSINESS PROBLEM

Shortage of funds to conduct marketing research needed to investigate a potentially lucrative new market niche.

COST OF BUSINESS PROBLEM

N/A

The firm did not so much have a costly problem as it had a possibly highly profitable idea that would prove risky to start implementing without suitable marketing research.

SOLUTION TO BUSINESS PROBLEM

2 marketing research interns for a 9-month period

COST OF SOLUTION

$37,200

Costs included:

    A. Interns' stipends
    B. Interns' work-related expenses

A. Stipends
    = Number of interns $\times$ Wages per week per intern $\times$ Number of weeks of internship
    = 2 interns $\times$ $10/week/intern $\times$ 36 weeks
    = $7,200
B. Work-related expenses, such as phones, secretarial assistance, typing, computer use, and company staff time to supervise = $30,000

Cost of solution
    = $7,200 + $30,000
    = $37,200

$ IMPROVEMENT BENEFIT

$600,000 profit/year

$4 million sales/year with a 15% profit margin = $600,000/year

COST-BENEFIT RATIO

16:1

$600,000:$37,200

---

per year because the firm enjoyed $4 million per year in new sales that had a 15 percent profit margin. This new profit would not have been possible without the interns' work. From taking the opportunity of using interns, the company enjoyed a 16:1 *cost-benefit ratio.*

■ GAINSHARING

Business Problems Addressed

Productivity
Work Group Effectiveness
Interdepartmental Collaboration
Incentive Compensation

Overview of Solution

Gainsharing, or productivity gainsharing as it sometimes is called, simply is a way to share a portion of productivity improvements (or gains) with the employees responsible for the improvements. According to the United States General Accounting Office, over 1,000 companies use gainsharing in one form or another. This number keeps growing as more companies realize the power of the results of gainsharing. Also, research on group gainsharing programs consistently indicates that gainsharing works. In fact, the average labor savings amounts to 29 percent.[8] Productivity increases average 16.5 percent.[9] For this reason, gainsharing is a compensation and management technique that builds productivity improvements directly into the reward system a company uses.

A gainsharing system motivates employees to improve efficiency and decrease costs. Why? Because in a gainsharing plan, employees get to keep a percentage of the gain in productivity, sometimes as high as 50 percent. Thus, for example, if according to the conditions of a gainsharing plan employees decrease costs by $1 million, the company keeps $500,000, and the employees divide a bonus amount totaling half a million dollars.

Gainsharing plan development allows for a lot of creativity on the part of the plan's directors, as well as employees affected by the plan's bonus system. For instance, after the first year of a gainsharing program, Dana Corporation's Spicer Heavy Axle Division decreased waste and rework costs by 50 percent compared to the year before the gainsharing program began.[10]

Another successful gainsharing plan was implemented at a crushed stone plant of Vulcan Materials Company, Southern Division, headquartered in Birmingham, Alabama. According to the company's report on the plan,

The first year of implementation was an overwhelming success. As a result of gainsharing, productivity at the plant for 1986 soared 31.3% over the previous year's level. Total variable costs were reduced 13.7%, although the overall cost of the materials and supplies had actually increased during the year. Employees received bonuses of 22% of their annual earnings, giving the average employee over $4,000 in extra pay for the year. In addition, the plant's excellent safety record was maintained and absenteeism was reduced 26% from the previous year. Finally, a survey on employee relations measured a 13% improvement from the beginning of the year to *the end of the year, reflecting an excellent employee relations climate. By every measure, the results of the gainsharing program exceeded expectations and met all of its objectives.*[11]

These examples highlight the tremendous results gainsharing can achieve for companies and their employees. A great deal of work goes into operating a successful gainsharing plan. Fortunately, the outcomes can make it worthwhile for everyone involved.

How to Implement Solution

1. *Develop gainsharing plan guidelines.* These guidelines must list all the rules of the game for a gainsharing program. These guidelines must be readily available to all employees involved in the gainsharing program. All employees should be encouraged to familiarize themselves with the guidelines. They include such items as:

- ☐ How the plan works
- ☐ What baseline productivity measures will be used
- ☐ How bonus percentages will be determined
- ☐ When and how bonuses will be paid
- ☐ How productivity gains will or will not affect job security

2. *Decide how productivity will be measured.* A myriad of options exists for determining exactly what productivity measures will be used. For example, Dana Corporation's Spicer Heavy Axle Division defines productivity as the ratio of labor costs to output. McDonnell Douglass Electronics in St. Charles, Missouri, a division of McDonnell Douglas Corporation, uses a return on investment (ROI) method to measure productivity improvements.[12] ROI is calculated as earnings divided by investment in the division. No one productivity measure is right for every organization; each must decide which measure best suits its purposes.

3. *Determine baseline historical level of performance.* Gains can only exist when compared to historical or baseline levels of performance. For example, perhaps historically it used to cost a company one dollar to manufacture a widget. Following implementation of a gainsharing plan, employees devised ingenious ways to decrease that cost, let's say to 90 cents per widget. This 10 cent per widget productivity gain only exists when compared to the baseline or historical information that widgets used to cost a dollar to produce. With such information, baselines and bonuses can be calculated. Without such historical data, companies cannot know how much productivity increased. Companies often determine baseline data from the previous year's productivity statistics. Or, a company could use performance data from a 2-, 3-, 4-, or 5-year history.

4. *Inform employees of gainsharing program rules.* Gainsharing plans cannot just be announced in memos and company newsletters. Most employees will be unfamiliar with what a gainsharing plan is and they will not appreciate how gainsharing plans can produce win-win outcomes for both employees and employer. So, employees need to have question-and-answer sessions to introduce the concept and groundrules for the gainsharing system.

Another type of training may also prove worthwhile, namely, training in how to use group problem solving and decision making. Most employees are relatively adept at carrying out their own jobs. However, they often do not know how to collaborate and solve productivity problems with their colleagues in a participative manner. Brief training in group problem solving and decision making can help employees. It also helps ensure that the plan will have a greater likelihood of success for all parties.

5. *Encourage productivity problem solving.* Management must encourage ideas from employees as to how to upgrade productivity. Since some productivity improvement ideas involve spending money or changing procedures, a mechanism must be in place to handle decisions on such matters. Often this mechanism is a committee in a plant, office, work group, or division. This committee reviews ideas submitted by employees. It then decides whether the idea can be funded and implemented. Also, the faster productivity ideas are acted on, the better. In general, it is best for any decision-making committee to announce its thoughts on ideas submitted within 30 days of the submission. This fast turnaround time quickly gets new ideas implemented and demonstrates management's commitment to making the gainsharing system work well.

6. *Communicate performance data frequently.* Productivity gains do not occur in a vacuum. Employees need and want to know how they are doing. Any company operating with a gainsharing system needs to tell employees how productive they are frequently. For instance, the company may tell employees weekly, biweekly or monthly how much they are producing compared to the baseline or historical rate of production. This information lets everyone know whether they are on track in productivity improvement or if they are just spinning their wheels. It allows work groups, departments, or plants to know when to adjust their methods of operation. If productivity is on the upswing, they can keep doing whatever it is that helped increase productivity. If productivity is merely flat or decreasing, then they know that they must change course and try different ways to enhance performance.

7. *Pay monthly, quarterly, or annual bonuses.* Most gainsharing programs pay bonuses at least once per year. To do so, they take thorough stock of how much productivity has increased during the period compared to the baseline term. If productivity did not improve, then employees do not receive any bonus. If productivity improved, then employees receive a bonus based on this improvement. For example, if a company uses a 50–50 bonus arrangement, then a company that has a $1 million productivity gain would pay out half of it to employees and keep half of it for itself.

Each employee's bonus can be calculated in a number of ways. Some companies pay each employee the exact same bonus. Other companies pay employees a prorated percentage based on how many hours the employee worked. In this circumstance, an employee who worked an average of 40 hours per week would earn a bigger bonus than another employee who worked an average of 35 hours per week. Still other companies divide gainsharing bonuses by the level of the employee in the organization's hierarchy. The rationale here is that it may take more money to motivate an already highly paid executive than it might take to motivate a much lower paid line employee.

8. *Recalculate baseline level of performance.* An ongoing gainsharing plan requires periodic updating of the baseline against which productivity gains are measured. This usually is done once per year, at the same time that the bonuses are calculated. Since hopefully productivity gains were made, employees already increased productivity to a new baseline level. So, for the following year that increase in productivity is considered a given. All new productivity gains are then determined against the new baseline or historical level of performance.

Deadline for Implementing Solution

It may take 6 to 12 months to implement a gainsharing plan. First, company management must decide that it not only can live with gainsharing but also that it will act in an open, participative manner to make the gainsharing plan successful. Next, it often proves useful for managers and, if possible, line employees, to visit organizations that already operate a gainsharing plan so that people can learn what sorts of assets and liabilities a gainsharing plan could offer. After that, the company must decide on the guidelines for calculating the rewards, and these guidelines must be conveyed to all employees in the plan.

Deadline for Measuring Profit Improvement

Companies take major measure of productivity improvements at least annually. However, measures need to be taken more than only annually. Throughout the year, employees need to know how well they are doing at improving productivity. With such information, they can continue to use productivity improvement techniques that prove measurably useful. They also can eliminate or change techniques that do not lead to productivity gains.

GAINSHARING HELPS PROFITS RISE

This example occurred in a large baking company. The company produced huge quantities of baked goods that supermarkets sell each day. It had automated its bakeries as much as possible over the last half dozen years. The employees were mostly old-timers who knew the ins and outs of producing the company's assorted breads, cakes, pies, and rolls.

Management thought that it had the basis for operating smoothly. However, management identified one expensive *business problem* as the labor costs involved in the baking. By decreasing labor costs, the company could run a more efficient and thus more profitable operation. The *cost of the business problem* was indeterminant. The company just knew that it wanted more profit from its present operations. Figure 4-11 shows the *Planning Model* for this case example.

Management decided that a cost-effective way to increase profits was to implement a gainsharing program as the *solution to the business problem.* The gainsharing plan would pay bonuses to employees if the ratio of labor costs to output decreased. If the ratio stayed the same or increased, the company would not pay any bonus to its employees. Management defined labor costs to include both direct and indirect costs, such as salaries, absenteeism, and waste caused by human (not machine) error. The productivity baseline was the previous 12 months' ratio of labor costs to output. Bonuses were paid quarterly, with the company and employees dividing the productivity gain 50-50.

Almost every employee contributed to the effort to improve productivity. On the factory floor, employees worked hard to decrease mis-

Figure 4-11. Planning Model for baking company's successful gainsharing plan.

BUSINESS PROBLEM

Decreasing labor expenses and thereby increasing profits

COST OF BUSINESS PROBLEM

No actual cost can be calculated for such a problem

SOLUTION TO BUSINESS PROBLEM

Gainsharing Program

A. Productivity defined as ratio of labor costs to output
B. Baseline is previous 12-month period's productivity
C. 50-50 split of productivity gains between employees and company

COST OF SOLUTION

$1.25 million

This represents half of the productivity gains which, in accordance with the gainsharing plan, were paid out as bonuses to the employees

$ IMPROVEMENT BENEFITS

$2.5 million

This is the productivity gain during the first year of operating the gainsharing plan

COST-BENEFIT RATIO

2:1

$2.5 million: $1.25 million

---

takes. Maintenance employees decided to work during certain non-production hours to keep the machines in tip-top running order. By doing so, fewer breakdowns would occur during production runs and financially valuable production time would not be lost. In the factory offices, people even stopped throwing away paperclips in attempts to keep down costs. Heavy peer pressure built up to keep employees from being absent or tardy, since such expenses lowered their potential bonuses. In fact, employees even informally decided to shorten their break periods so bakers would spend more time producing baked goods. This sort of decision worked through peer pressure among the employees.

The gainsharing program worked well. During its first year, the *cost of the solution* was $1.25 million. That represents the money paid to employees in bonus checks. At the same time, the *improvement benefit* to the company also was $2.5 million. This was the value of the productivity improvement. The company could keep half of this amount, since employees and the company evenly split the dollar value of the productivity gain. As a result of this gainsharing plan, the solution turned out to yield a 2:1 *cost-benefit ratio.*

This gainsharing program carried no major risk for the company. After all, it was operated with a "no gain, no bonus pay" philosophy. Both the company and its employees had nothing to lose and a lot to gain.

■ PRORATED MERIT SALARY INCREASES FOLLOWING LEAVES OF ABSENCE

Business Problems Addressed

Productivity
Absenteeism
Compensation

Overview of Solution

Companies that use merit pay plans typically grant an employee a percentage salary increase each year. This increased percentage is determined by how well the employee's performance is evaluated by his or her immediate supervisor. Someone who is viewed as having done a great job may receive a comparatively high percentage increase. Someone else who turned in a less capable performance would receive a smaller increase. During periods of heavy inflation, percentage increases often range from 2 percent to 12 percent. At times of low inflation, these increases generally cover a range of 1 percent to 5 percent.

It is quite possible for companies to decrease the costs of their merit pay plans. How? One quite promising method is prorating merit increases following leaves of absence. Depending on how many employees take leaves of absence, a company can avoid spending a good deal of money it otherwise would have earmarked for merit pay increases.

However, a number of problems arise when determining what percentage of salary increase an employee deserves when the employee has been on leave of absence during the year. For our purposes here, the leave of absence of most concern occurs when the employee is away for 30 days or longer. The problems that occur include the following:

1. *Employee is paid for days not worked.* During the year, the company already may have paid the employee for days during which the employee did not work.

2. *Time period covered by performance appraisal is decreased.* Supervisors generally appraise performance once every 12 months. This performance evaluation usually forms the basis of the employee's overall performance rating. But when an employee is away

from work for an extended period of time, the employee is not really appraised for actually working a full 12 months. Despite this fact, the percentage pay increase almost invariably derives from the appraisal covering the previous 12 months.

3. *It is unfair to most other employees.* An organization creates a sense of inequity when two employees are rated the same and granted the same percentage raise when one of the two employees worked a full 12 months while the other worked less than the full 12 months. For example, let's say that two employees both are rated "Excellent" on their annual performance appraisals. One of these employees worked a full 12 months during the year. The other employee took a three month leave of absence, thus working only 75 percent of the 12 month period. Perhaps their employer gives a 10 percent merit increase to employees who receive a rating of "Excellent."

If both of these employees receive the exact same 10 percent merit increase, that readily would appear unfair. After all, one of these employees worked 100 percent of the 12 month period, while the other only worked 75 percent (9 out of 12 months) during the same review cycle. A more fair and equal treatment would be to give the entire 10 percent increase to the employee who worked 12 months and give a 7.5 percent increase (75 percent of a 10 percent salary increase) to the employee who took a three month leave of absence.

4. *It is unfair to the company.* Why should a company increase the salary of an employee as though the employee had worked an entire 12 month period when, in reality, that employee worked less than a full 12 months? Companies are wise to avoid basing any part of their pay system on rewarding employees for not working.

How to Implement Solution

1. *Decide what leave of absence is too long.* The company may decide that anyone taking a leave of absence over 30 days should not receive the full merit salary increase that their performance level normally would dictate.

2. *Write and communicate proration policy.* This new policy must be applied consistently to everyone involved. A formal, written policy statement helps do just that. Also, employees must be aware that a leave of absence they may take can affect any salary increase they could be eligible to receive. The policy statement used by one firm appears in Figure 4-12.

3. *Implement proration policy.* Some questions may arise. Certain employees may not readily understand why they are not, in effect, paid for not working. Nevertheless, the innate logic and fairness of this proration approach makes it easy for most employees to understand and accept.

Deadline for Implementing Solution

This solution can be implemented quickly, probably within one or two months. Management just must make a commitment to cease rewarding people for *not* working. A policy statement must be made, and it should be communicated to employees. After that, this policy can be put in effect for all affected employees.

Deadline for Measuring Profit Improvement

Cost savings will be realized as soon as one merit increase is prorated because an employee took a leave of absence. Many companies budget a certain amount of money for

Figure 4-12. Company policy statement on prorating merit increases following leaves of absence.

OBJECTIVE: To establish a company-wide policy for defining the effect of a leave of absence on merit increases.

BACKGROUND:

- The philosophy of our company's merit increase program is based on the concept of a 12 month review or appraisal period.
- The program is designed for a supervisor to have adequate opportunity to accurately and objectively assess performance.
- The merit increase guidelines (increase percentages) are developed and targeted based on this premise, i.e., an employee has been working for a full 12 months.
- A 12 month interval is a common practice in a majority of industries, including our industry.

RATIONALE: A leave of absence, personal as well as medical, interrupts and shortens the length of time over which performance is being assessed. A leave of absence decreases the amount of working time being applied to the merit increase guidelines.

The company recognizes that employees may be ill for a lengthy period and also understands that due to various legitimate reasons, a personal leave is necessary. Thus, a 30 day period is established as the timeframe within which a leave of absence does not affect the merit increase percentage.

In order to ensure equity and consistency and to establish specific criteria under which leaves of absence affect the merit increase program, the following policy applies:

POLICY: No pay increases may be granted to employees during a leave of absence. Leave of absence includes both personal and medical (short-term disability or STD). For a leave of absence that exceeds 30 days, the salary increase percentage will be prorated by the amount of time equal to the length of the leave of absence.

> FOR EXAMPLE: An employee has been on a leave of absence for 2 months. This employee, on the basis of performance, is eligible for a 6.0% merit increase. Since the employee has worked for 10 of the 12 months, the increase percentage is prorated (6.0% × 10/12 = 5.0%). Thus, the employee receives a 5.0% merit increase.

---

merit salary increases. Such budgets generally do not take into account the fact that not all employees will work a full 12 months before they are eligible for potential salary raises. By paying only prorated increases to employees who take leaves of absence, the company ought to spend less on salary increases than it budgeted. While that is not profit improvement in the usual sense of the term, it does represent human resource management intelligently conserving the company's money in a measurable way.

SAVING CORPORATE CASH THROUGH PRORATED MERIT INCREASES FOLLOWING LEAVES OF ABSENCE

A compensation manager at a medium-sized electronics company spotted a way to conserve his company's cash. Historically, of this company's 5,000 employees, 5.2 percent, or 260 employees, would take a 30 day or longer leave of absence during a given 12-month timeframe. The manager realized that this all-too-common situation posed a *business problem* that he could solve. The problem focused on how to reduce the dollar amount the company paid out in salary increases. Figure 4-13 shows the *Planning Model* used in solving this business problem.

Figure 4-13. Planning Model for prorating merit increases following a long leave of absence.

BUSINESS-PROBLEM

Reducing dollar amount paid for salary increases, focusing on employees who take leaves of absence of 30 days or longer

COST OF BUSINESS PROBLEM

$260,000/year

This 5,000 employee company historically has 5.2% of its workforce take leaves of absence of 30 days or longer. That is 260 employees. The average salary at the company is $20,000/year. The typical salary increase planned for the coming year is 5%, or $1,000 per employee. The 260 employees expected to take extended leaves of absence would pocket $260,000 in salary increases under the previous salary administration system that did not prorate for leaves of absence.

SOLUTION TO BUSUNESS PROBLEM

Prorate merit salary increases following leaves of absence of 30 days or longer.

COST OF SOLUTION

$5,250

Costs included:

A. Brief survey of employees' potential reactions to proration policy
B. Writing and communicating proration policy
C. Changing procedures in the compensation and payroll departments to implement new policy.

(continued)

(Figure 4-13 continued)

A. Survey = $2,000
B. Policy writing and communicating = $3,000
C. Changing procedures = $250

Cost of solution
    = $2,000 + $3,000 + $250
    = $5,250

$ IMPROVEMENT BENEFIT

$44,200 for first year of new policy

Improvement benefit
    = Pre-proration salary increases paid to employees with extended leaves of absence
    − Prorated amount paid to employees with extended leaves of absence
Pre-proration amount = $260,000/year
Prorated amount
    = Number of employees affected by proration policy × Average annual non-prorated salary increase × Prorated percentage of average salary increase earned by affected employees
    = 260 employees × $1,000/year × (10 months worked out of 12 months)
    = 260 employees × $1,000/employee/year × .83
    = Improvement benefit
    = $260,000 − $215,800
    = $44,200

COST-BENEFIT RATIO

8.4:1

$44,200:$5,250

Since the average salary in the company was $20,000, and the average salary increase was expected to be 5 percent, or $1,000, the *cost of this problem* would amount to $260,000 for the coming year. The *solution to the business problem* was to prorate the salary increases of employees who took leaves of absence for over 30 days during a 12 month period of time. Thirty days was decided upon as the cut-off point, since it represented a relatively sizeable portion of a work year. It also allowed seemingly adequate time for an employee to recover from most illnesses or complete a personal, nonillness-related leave of absence.

The *cost of the solution* was $5,250. This included an informal survey of employees' possible reaction to a proration policy; writing and communicating a new policy concerning prorating merit increases; and changing administrative procedures in the compensation and payroll departments. The informal survey was an interesting and useful twist. The vice president of human resources felt concerned that such prorations might lower employee morale or seem discriminatory against people who were sick for extended periods of time. So, the compensation manager conducted brief interviews of employees at various levels of the organization. He interviewed a representative sample of senior level managers, middle level managers, supervisors, and line employees from a number of departments. Based on the interview responses, a brief questionnaire was developed. This questionnaire was given to several hundred employees to complete. Figure 4-14 shows the survey questions he used.

Figure 4-14. Questions for informal survey about employees' reactions to prorated merit increases following leaves of absence.

1. Imagine you took a leave of absence for more than 30 days. When you came back to work and received your merit salary increase, do you think you would deserve the same salary increase given to an employee who worked as hard and as productively as you did for the entire 12 months without any long leave of absence?

   Yes _____   No _____

   Comments: _____

   _____

   _____

2. If someone took a 30 day or longer leave of absence, but then received the same merit salary increase as someone who did just as good a job—but did *not* take a leave of absence—would you consider that fair treatment?

   Yes _____   No _____

   Comments: _____

   _____

   _____

3. When considering leaves of absence that might affect salary increases, do you consider 30 days enough time for most leaves of absence?

   Yes _____   No _____

   Comments: _____

   _____

   _____

4. Would it affect most employees' productivity if they knew that the company would prorate their merit increases if they took a 30 day or longer leave of absence?

   Yes _____   No _____

   Comments: _____

   _____

   _____

The survey's responses overwhelmingly indicated that employees in all levels of the company and of both genders considered a proration policy fair and reasonable. Also, employees did not think that a proration policy would affect productivity. As one employee put it, "It sure is more than fair that the company would allow even 30 days, especially since we're supposed to be here working during even those days."

The solution resulted in an *improvement benefit* of $44,200 during its first year of use. This improvement takes into account reducing the $260,000 that normally would have been paid to employees with extended leaves of absence to $215,800. Since the average leave of absence was about 60 days, or two months, the employees with long leaves were granted 83 percent of the salary increase they would have received if they had not taken a leave of absence, or $215,800. The 83 percent figure represents these employees working an average of 10 months out of 12. Thus, instead of the average five percent increase, these employees typically received a 4.2 percent increase. While the difference is not huge, it does account for a 17 percent decrease in salary raises granted to employees who were away from work for long periods of time.

That is a good payback for a quick $5,250 project. For the first year of this proration policy, the *cost-benefit ratio* was 8.4:1. That is because the first year's $44,200 improvement benefit came from an investment of $5,250 in this solution. Over a period of five years, taking into account inflation and higher average salary, this proration policy easily could reduce salary increases by over a quarter of a million dollars per year. In that case, the long lasting benefits of proration would have an even more outstanding effect on the company's bottom line.

Chapter 5
Employee Benefits Programs

Normally, benefits are thought of as a cost of doing business. In actuality, there are a number creative plans that human resources managers can use to decrease benefit costs (which adds up to improving the bottom line) and even some benefit plans to help improve employee productivity.

In this chapter, a number of these cost-beneficial benefit plans are discussed. These include:

- ☐ Containment of health care costs
- ☐ Well pay and personal time banks
- ☐ Capping short-term disability benefits
- ☐ Reducing unemployment insurance costs
- ☐ Employer-supported child care
- ☐ Quartermaster program

■ CONTAINMENT OF HEALTH CARE COSTS

Business Problem Addressed

Benefits Costs

Overview of Solution

As every human resources professional knows, health care benefits cost companies huge sums of money. In 1986, American companies spent $1,857 per employee on health benefits. This figure grows at least six percent per year.[1]

Given the enormous size and complexity of this costly business problem, this book can only touch on some of the main techniques that companies need to explore. The examination and recommendations offered here are by no means intended as a complete discussion of this problem.

To tackle rising health care costs, organizations can stop or at least stem this huge expense in a number of ways. These methods take the form of changing the ways employees perceive and use the health care marketplace. Figure 5-1 lists some of the methods, along with estimates of cost savings gained by implementing each method. These estimates are based on the benefits-consulting experience of Hewitt Associates.

Some ways to decrease, or at least contain, health insurance-related costs include requiring:

☐ Increase in deductible
☐ Second surgical opinion
☐ Preferred provider organization (PPO) enrollment
☐ Health maintenance organization (HMO) enrollment
☐ Preadmission testing
☐ Preadmission certification
☐ Coordination of benefits when a married couple both work and have separate insurance coverage (to make sure no one gets reimbursed more than 100% of health care expenses)
☐ Hospital bill audit
☐ Retrospective hospital review

For instance, an increasingly used health care cost containment method relates to requiring second surgical opinions. An employee who is told by a physician that surgery is needed first must obtain approval for the surgery from his or her employer's insurance carrier. Without such approval, the employee risks not being reimbursed for the surgery's expenses. Generally, minor, inexpensive surgery is approved with little fuss.

However, when an employee seeks approval for more costly surgery, the insurance

Figure 5-1. Estimated health care savings using various cost containment methods.

Cost Containment Method	Estimated Cost Savings*
Second surgical opinion	0–2%
PPO enrollment	1–8%
HMO enrollment	± 5%
Preadmission certification	1–7%
Coordination of benefits	0–10%

*These estimates vary according to benefit plan design, employee demographics, health care providers, claims experience, and the length of time the health cost management program has been in place.

(From information provided by Hewitt Associates, Lincolnshire, Ill. August 5, 1988.)

carrier often requires a second surgical opinion. Often, the insurance carrier pays 100 percent of the cost of the second opinion. If the second surgical opinion agrees with the first opinion, then the carrier approves the surgery. If the second opinion disagrees with the first opinion, then the carrier may not approve the surgery for reimbursement, or the carrier might allow (and even pay for) a third opinion to be rendered.

More and more companies find that second surgical opinions and other health care cost containment methods work to their advantage. For instance, International Business Machines Corporation (IBM) started a special 40 percent deductible on costs for its employees' first day of hospital care. This act significantly decreased short-term hospital stays by IBM employees, according to the company.[2] Another example comes from a Rand Corporation study of deductibles that showed that medical care expenses declined 20 percent when employees had to pay 25 percent of their health care costs.[3]

Health benefit expert Bernard Handel proposes that companies adopt what he calls first generation and then second generation health care cost containment strategies.[4] The first generation strategies include:

□ Administrative controls
□ Basic cost management programs
□ Basic health promotion and education
□ Alternative delivery systems
□ External activities
□ Communication with participants and providers

A checklist of these strategies appears as Figure 5-2.

Second-generation cost-containment strategies suggested by Handel include the following:

□ Expansion of database collection (in conjunction with other benefit plans in area and insurers)
□ Expanded cost-management programs
□ Expand health risk behavior-modification programs
□ Alternative delivery systems

Figure 5-3 presents these strategies in somewhat greater detail.

One of the most striking examples of health-care cost reduction took place at Chrysler Corporation.[5] The car maker reported decreasing its insurance costs by $300 per employee through instituting precertification of elective surgery, using utilization reviews, requiring the use of generic drugs, creating PPOs with hospitals and physician groups, and restricting the use of select procedures, such as tests, hospitals, and physicians not approved by Chrysler. Prior to installing this cost-containment program, about $500 of health insurance costs went into each car manufactured by Chrysler. In contrast, about $150 in health insurance costs were expended to produce the average Japanese car. The decrease in health-care expenditures helped Chrysler lift itself out of the severe financial straits it suffered during the early 1980s.

Companies and the health insurance industry seldom use only one health care cost containment technique in isolation from other techniques. Instead, they group a number of cost containment methods together so that a number of techniques can play roles in

Figure 5-2. Checklist of cost containment strategies implemented.

First Generation Cost Containment

	Yes	No
1. Administrative Controls		
Collection of meaningful claim data	[ ]	[ ]
Plan redesign	[ ]	[ ]
Review of funding method	[ ]	[ ]
Eligibility controls	[ ]	[ ]
Claim controls (general)	[ ]	[ ]
Subrogation/coordination of benefits	[ ]	[ ]
Hospital bill audits	[ ]	[ ]
Weekend hospital admissions	[ ]	[ ]
Flexible benefits	[ ]	[ ]
2. Basic Cost Management Programs		
Utilization review	[ ]	[ ]
Mandatory second surgical opinion program	[ ]	[ ]
Preadmission testing program	[ ]	[ ]
Ambulatory surgical incentives	[ ]	[ ]
Birthing centers	[ ]	[ ]
Home care	[ ]	[ ]
Hospice care	[ ]	[ ]
Urgent care	[ ]	[ ]
3. Basic Health Promotion and Education		
Employee assistance programs	[ ]	[ ]
Wellness programs	[ ]	[ ]
Physical fitness and general health promotion	[ ]	[ ]
Weight, smoking, and stress management	[ ]	[ ]
Alcoholism programs	[ ]	[ ]
Safety programs	[ ]	[ ]
4. Alternative Delivery Systems		
Health maintenance organizations and IPAs	[ ]	[ ]
Preferred provider organizations	[ ]	[ ]
Other alternatives	[ ]	[ ]
5. External Activities		
Coalition efforts	[ ]	[ ]
Group buying	[ ]	[ ]
Regional data collection	[ ]	[ ]
Health planning participation	[ ]	[ ]
Participation in administration of health providers	[ ]	[ ]
Regulation and lobbying	[ ]	[ ]
Consumer information	[ ]	[ ]

6. Communication With Participants and Providers

| Organized programs | [ ] | [ ] |
| Seminars and meetings with participants and families | [ ] | [ ] |

(From Handel, B., "Dealing with the Medical Revolution-Health Care Cost Containment in a Changing Health Environment" in Employee Benefits Annual 1986. *Brookfield, Wis.: International Foundation of Employee Benefit Plans, 1987, p. 42.)*

decreasing or containing expenses. Chrysler is one example of this grouping. The outcome proved more beneficial than if the auto maker had simply implemented one technique at a time.

How to Implement Solution

1. *Determine current health insurance benefit costs.* This determination pinpoints the baseline. For example, the problem may be quite different for a company that annually spends $1,800 per employee compared to another company that annually spends $900 per employee.

2. *Choose health insurance cost containment alternatives.* Figures 5-2 and 5-3 give an extensive list of choices for controlling health expenses. Each organization must decide which ones might work best for its particular situation. For example, in regions with a good supply of hospitals and physicians, a company probably can negotiate charges that are 20 percent or more below the usual and customary rates charged in the region. Such PPOs can help cut costs. However, a company located in an area with a shortage of health care facilities or professionals may not find such negotiating as fruitful.

3. *Let employees know why and how their benefits are being changed.* Most employees feel scared about possibly losing any of their health insurance benefits. Indeed, many employees consider health insurance as a right that is owed to them, rather than a benefit that their employer provides for them. It is thus critically important to inform employees about the changes. They may need extra help and advice until they learn how to make better educated choices about how to plan and allot their health care dollars.

Deadline for Implementing Solution

It often takes an organization a year or longer to examine its current health insurance situation and alternatives. Then, a good deal of planning and employee education need to be conducted. Whereas the payback can be great, the effort also will need to be carried out over a lengthy period of time.

Deadline for Measuring Profit Improvement

An organization may begin to notice cost decreases a year or longer after it has implemented cost containment techniques. Such cost containment is an ongoing strategy. It is not a one-time venture. To begin, an organization may provide some rather simple cost containment approaches, such as offering HMO or PPO options. After that, it could try more complicated cost containment alternatives. Each technique could yield savings.

Figure 5-3. Second generation advanced cost containment strategies.

1. <u>Expansion of Database Collection</u> (in conjunction with other benefit plans in area and insurers)

    a. Specific data by providers
    b. Specific data by location
    c. Specific data by medical procedures
    d. Data for dental, vision and all benefit programs

2. <u>Expanded Cost Management Programs</u>

    a. Preadmission certification
    b. Extended care/discharge planning
    c. Less costly alternatives
    d. Individual case management
    e. Use of medical/dental consultants

3. <u>Expand Health Risk Behavior Modification Programs</u>

    a. Counseling program
    b. Chemical abuse program
    c. Psychological and psychiatric counseling, and alcoholism prevention programs
    d. Rehabilitation program
    e. Nutrition education

4. <u>Alternative Delivery Systems</u>

    a. Specific data collection by provider
    b. Identification of efficient providers
    c. Consumer education as to efficient providers
    d. Experience rating of alternative plans
    e. Maintaining quality and accessibility

(From Handel, B., "Dealing with the Medical Revolution—Health Care Cost Containment in a Changing Health Environment" in Employee Benefits Annual 1986. *Brookfield, Wis.: International Foundation of Employee Benefit Plans, 1987, p. 43.)*

Also, a company may want to implement wellness and employee assistance programs, as discussed in Chapter 6. Such programs, combined with health insurance programs, can further lower insurance costs while improving employee health.

REDUCTION OF HEALTH CARE COSTS

Let's look at the hypothetical example of how a 5,000-employee company faced the *business problem* of constantly rising medical coverage costs. This self-insured firm realized that no relief would be in sight if its medical insurance practices continued. Figure 5-4 shows the *Planning Model* the company used to change this business problem for the better.

Figure 5-4. Planning Model for reducing health care costs.

BUSINESS PROBLEM

Constantly rising medical coverage costs, with no relief in sight if current insurance practices continue

COST OF BUSINESS PROBLEM

$9,000,000/year

Cost
  = Number of employees × Annual cost per employee for health benefits
  = 5,000 employees × $1,800/year/employee
  = $9,000,000/year

SOLUTION TO BUSINESS PROBLEM

Health care cost containment program

The company implemented a program similar to that used by Chrysler.

COST OF SOLUTION

$730,000

Costs included:

  A. Planning cost containment program
  B. Educating employees on programs
  C. Cost of certain components of program

A. Planning = $100,000 for benefits staff time and consultant usage
B. Educating employees
    = Number of employees × Time of group meetings to present and discuss program
      × Average wages and benefits of employees
    = 5,000 employees × 2 hours × $13/hour
    = $130,000
C. Component costs
    = Number of employees × Cost of components per employee
    = 5,000 employees × $100/employee
    = $500,000

Cost of solution
    = $100,000 + $130,000 + $500,000
    = $730,000

(continued)

(Figure 5-4 continued)

$ IMPROVEMENT BENEFIT

$1,500,000/year

Improvement benefit
    = Cost under previous program − Cost under cost containment program.
Cost under previous program = $9,000,000/year
Cost under cost containment program
    = Number of employees × Annual cost per employee for health benefits
    = 5,000 employees × $1,500/employee/year
    = $7,500,000/year
Improvement benefit
    = $9,000,000/year, $7,500,000/year
    = $1,500,000/year

COST-BENEFIT RATIO

2.1:1

$1,500,000:$730,000

If the company paid the average amount per employee for health care costs, then it spent about $1,800 annually for each of its 5,000 employees, meaning that the *cost of the business problem* was $9,000,000. The *solution* could be a cost containment program similar to the one implemented by Chrysler. That program enabled Chrysler to reduce its annual health care costs by $300 per employee. The program components are shown in Figure 5-5 also shows the percentage of decrease in health care costs attributed to each program component as estimated by health care economist Edward R. Stasica of Stasica & Associates in Mount Prospect, Illinois.

The company would spend around $730,000 as the *cost of the solution.* While that may seem like a hefty figure, it could be quite worth it. If this company realizes an annual $300 per employee cost reduction, an approximately 17 percent decrease, then its *improvement benefit* would amount to $1,500,000. This figure is how much less the company would spend under the new cost containment program.

Comparing the improvement benefit to the company to the cost of the solution generates a 2.1:1 *cost-benetfit ratio.* This certainly would be a fine use of company funds to reduce costs.

■ WELL PAY AND PERSONAL TIME BANKS
Business Problems Addressed

Absenteeism
Benefits Costs

Figure 5-5. Health care cost containment program components and resulting cost decreases.

Program Component	Percentage Health Care Cost Decrease
Utilization review	6%
Precertification of surgery	2
Medical consultant use	1
Requiring generic drug use	1
Negotiated reduction in fees from physicians and hospitals	3
Refusal to use many physicians and hospitals that did not grant reduced fees	3
Constricting the options available for certain medical care procedures	1

Overview of Solution

One of the most easily abused and costly personnel policies is paid sick leave, or sick pay. Sick pay policies begin with a sound basis: They are *meant* to provide employees with pay in case an illness prevents them from working. However, research indicates that companies with sick pay actually may promote and reward absenteeism.[6] Other research shows that companies with paid sick leave have up to twice the amount of employees calling in sick as organizations without a paid sick leave program.[7]

Such studies and the growing first-hand experience of human resources managers of this problem point out the need to pay employees for being well, rather than for sickness that keeps them home and to encourage employees to act responsibly when it comes to using their *paid* time away from their jobs.

This twofold need is answered by well pay and personal time banks.[8] Well pay focuses on motivating employees to stay well. It rewards employees for coming to work rather than staying home with real or pretend illnesses. With well pay, employees could earn money for *not* using sick leave.

Personal time banks encourage employees to behave responsibly in regard to scheduling the time their employer pays them to be away from work, such as for sickness, vacations, and holidays. This technique grants each employee a set number of paid days during which the employee does not have to show up at work. For example, an employee may be given 15 days to use for sickness, vacations, or personal holidays, as the employee desires. Thus, one person may use all 15 days to go on a vacation. Another person might take 10 vacation days and 5 sick days. The choice is up to the individual employee. Sometimes an organization specifies that at least some of the days off must be preapproved, so the company can control work schedules better. Figure 5-6 shows one firm's personal time bank policy.

Both programs seek to motivate employees to:

☐ Decrease absences
☐ Stay well or at least more carefully evaluate when they are too sick to come to work

Figure 5-6. Sample personal time bank policy.

OVERVIEW

Each employee is given a set number of paid days he or she can take off. These days may be used for any purpose the employee desires, such as vacations, sick days, or personal days.

PROCEDURE

1. A new employee can take off up to 7 business days with pay after he or she works for the company for 6 months, but before the employee works for the company for 12 months. For instance, if an employee starts working for the company on January 1, 1987, then the employee can take off up to 7 business days between June 1, 1987–December 31, 1987. If these 7 days are not taken during the 6-month period, then they are forfeited.
2. After an employee works for the company for 12 months, the employee can take off up to 15 business days during each 12-month period. Each 12-month period begins on the anniversary of the date the employee started working for the company. For example, if an employee started working for the company on January 1, 1987, then the employee would be eligible for 15 paid business days off between January 1, 1988–December 31, 1988. If these 15 days are not taken during the 12-month period, then the days are forfeited.
3. Any time an employee wants to take off 3 or more business days in a row, the employee must obtain the approval of his or her manager *at least 30 days in advance*.

Also, from the company's perspective, absences caused by employees calling in sick produce a number of costly problems, including:

- ☐ Payments to employees for saying they are sick
- ☐ Overtime when some absent employees must be replaced by others who often earn time-and-a-half overtime pay
- ☐ Absence tracking system needed to make sure that employees do not take more sick days than they are allowed
- ☐ Extra management time to handle problems catalyzed by employees calling in sick
- ☐ Productivity decreases caused by missing employees or people working overtime who may not be as productive as the employees they are replacing

However, *caveat emptor*. Three issues related to implementing well pay and personal time banks must be taken into account by any organization considering these approaches:

1. These two approaches work best when the organization *really* experiences excessive absenteeism. As an ancient truism explains: "If it ain't broke, don't fix it." The same holds true with well pay and personal time banks. Specifically, if absenteeism is not a major problem, then an organization would be better off if it did not change its absenteeism policies.

2. If a company is unionized, then the new policies need to be negotiated into the labor contract.

3. If the new policy reduces the total days employees can take off, then it is wise to offer employees extra pay for *not* being absent.

How to Implement Solution

1. *Create and communicate new policy.* A well pay policy needs to state that employees will be paid a certain amount of money if they do not use sick leave. A personal time bank policy needs to outline how many business days an employee may take off but still be paid. These days typically include time employees might use for vacations, sick days, and holidays. An example of a combined well pay-personal time bank policy appears in the upcoming case example. A company may wish to continue to allot the same number of paid days away from work that it previously allotted to employees. Or, the organization might decide to decrease the number of paid days.

In either case, employees need to learn about the new policy one to three months before it takes effect to give them time to adust to the fact that "the game will be played by different rules from now on." It also allows them enough time to begin thinking about paid time away from work in a new and more responsible light. At first some employees may feel that their "right" to call in sick is being violated. However, by explaining the rationale behind the new policy, most employees will acknowledge the logic of changing the policy.

2. *Set up administrative procedures.* This new policy requires some modification in the usual absence tracking mechanism. Also, the benefits and payroll departments need to begin new procedures for matters such as paying employees for not being sick over a period of time.

Deadline for Implementing Solution

It takes three to six months to implement a well pay or personal time bank program. This includes planning, policy writing, communicating the new policy, and setting up the administrative functions needed to support the new policy.

Deadline for Measuring Profit Improvement

Such measurement may best be carried out after a year with the new program. By that time, employees should be used to living with the new system. Also, after a year of a well pay or personal time bank plan, the company should have an adequate amount of data to evaluate the program's effects on:

- ☐ Absenteeism
- ☐ Overtime caused by absenteeism
- ☐ Absence tracking system
- ☐ Management time spent on problems caused by absenteeism

BENEFITING FROM A PERSONAL TIME BANK AND WELL PAY PROGRAM

A service company faced a costly *business problem.* It found that employees used too many sick days, resulting in the company paying people quite a lot of money for *not* working. While the company professed to "pay for performance," the firm disliked paying people who did not even show up to work, especially those who called in sick. The problem occurred all days of the week, however, it seemed more pronounced on Mondays and Fridays. Also, the company noticed that employees tended to take practically all of the sick days the company was willing to pay for.

Company officials were astonished to discover that the *cost of this business problem* was $584,375. This amounted to an average of $1,169 annually for each of the company's 500 employees.

The cost derived from:

1. $332,500 paid out in wages to people who called in sick
2. $196,875 in overtime pay (about half the absences required a replacement who was paid time-and-a-half overtime pay)
3. $5,000 for the company's absence tracking system
4. $50,000 in management time spent handling absence-related problems, such as juggling work schedules, arranging replacements, and supervising these needed changes

So, the company embarked on its chosen *solution to the business problem:* a combined personal time bank and well pay program. Figure 5-7 is the *Planning Model* for carrying out this solution.

Figure 5-7. Planning Model for personal time bank and well pay program.

BUSINESS PROBLEM

Employees using too many sick days, resulting in company paying a lot of money for employees not to work

COST OF BUSINESS PROBLEM

$584,375/year

Costs included:

A. Payment to employees sick pay for not working
B. Overtime for replacements required to cover half of the absences
C. Absence tracking system
D. Extra management time to handle problems associated with absences

A. Sick pay
    = number of employees X Average number of sick days taken X average wages and
      benefits of people calling in sick
    = 500 employees × 7 sick days/year × $95/day
    = $332,500/year
B. Overtime
    = Number of employees × Average number of overtime days each employee's
      absences caused × Average daily wage paid to people working overtime × time-
      and-a-half for overtime wage premium
    = 500 × 3.5 days/year × $75/day × 1.5 overtime premium
    = $196,875/year
C. Absence tracking system = $5,000/year
D. Management time = $50,000/year

Cost of problem
    = $332,500/year + $196,875/year + $5,000/year + $50,000/year
    = $584,375/year

SOLUTION TO BUSINESS PROBLEM

Personal Time Bank and Well Pay Program

COST OF SOLUTION

$18,440

Costs included:

A. Communicating new policy to all 500 employees during 1-hour meetings
B. Paying $100 award to 100 employees who did not take sick days for a year
C. Administrative expenses to install personal time bank and well pay program

A. Communications
    = Number of employees × 1 hour meetings to communicate new program × Average
      hourly wages and benefits
    = 500 employees × 1 hour × $11.88/hour
    = $5,940
B. Well pay awards
    = Number of employees earning award × $100 award
    = 100 employees × $100 award
    = $10,000
C. Administrative expenses = $2,500

Cost of solution
    = $5,940 + $10,000 + $2,500
    = $18,440

$ IMPROVEMENT BENEFIT

$256,875/year

(continued)

(Figure 5-7 continued)

Improvement benefit = Cost of problem before implementing personal time bank and well pay program − Cost of problem after implementing program

Costs after implementing program included:

    A. Paying employees sick pay for not working
    B. Overtime for replacements required to cover half of the absences
    C. Absence tracking system
    D. Extra management time to handle problems associated with absences

A. Sick pay
    = Number of employees × Average number of sick days taken × average wages and benefits of people calling in sick
    = 500 employees × 3 sick days/year × $95/day
    = $142,500/year
B. Overtime
    = Number of employees × Average number of overtime days each employee's absences caused × Average daily wage paid to people working overtime × Time-and-a-half overtime wage premium
    = 500 employees × 1.5 days/year × $75/day × 1.5 overtime premium
    = $84,375/year
C. Absence tracking system = $5,000/year
D. Management time = $25,000/year

Total cost after implementing program
    = $142,500/year + $84,375/year + $5,000/year + $25,000/year
    = $256,875/year improvement benefit
    = $584,375/year − $256,875/year
    = $327,500/year

COST-BENEFIT RATIO

18:1

$327,500: $18,440

Prior to implementing the personal time bank and well pay programs, employees could take a total of 28 paid days off from work; 10 vacation days, 10 holidays, and 8 sick days. Also, employees received no award if they did not use their sick days. In contrast, the new program allots a total of 24 days that employees can take off with pay: 10 vacation days, 10 holidays, and 4 sick days. Employees who do not use sick days earn a $100 bonus after 12 months of perfect attendance. Table 5-1 compares the previous paid time off program with the company's new personal time bank and well pay program.

The program also gives employees some new freedom in using

Table 5-1. Comparison of company's previous paid time off program with new personal time bank and well pay program.

	Previous Paid Time Off Program	New Personal Time Bank and Well Pay Program
Vacation days	10 days/year	10 days/year
Holidays	10 days/year	10 days/year
Sick days	8 days/year	4 days/year
Money for not using sick days	0	$100/year

their vacation and sick days. For example, one employee may take 14 vacation days during a year. Another employee may need to take 10 sick days due to illness and then would have four days left to use for vacation time. This program puts the employees in a situation in which they must take responsibility for how they use their paid time away from their jobs. Another feature of the new program is that the company will monitor sick days taken on Fridays and Mondays and days before and after a holiday. These two new rules make it harder for employees to exploit sickness as an excuse for taking a company-paid extended weekend or holiday. Another alternative would be to reduce the number of sick days. Employees could retain their full leave, but the personal time bank and a modified well pay program could be implemented.

The *cost of the solution* came to $18,440. This cost included communicating the new policy to all 500 employees in meetings lasting up to one hour each, paying the $100 award to employees demonstrating perfect attendance for a year, and various administrative expenses.

The cost certainly proved well worth it. A year later, the company reported a $256,875 annual *improvement benefit* resulting from the company's paying less sick pay and overtime premium pay. Also, the decreased absences enabled the company's supervisors and managers to spend more time doing their regular duties and less time handling problems caused by absences.

All in all, the company realized an 18:1 *cost-benefit ratio* from this solution to a costly and troublesome business problem. The ratio probably would have wound up even higher if the company had included productivity measures in the equation. After all, absences tend to cause drops in productivity. So, decreasing absences should help keep productivity around normal levels.

Another intangible but important benefit is that the company is forcing its employees to take personal responsibility for how they use their paid time away from work, since employees can decide how to gauge their vacation and sick days.

■ CAPPING SHORT-TERM DISABILITY BENEFITS

Business Problems Addressed

Absenteeism
Benefits Costs

Overview of Solution

Many companies use a disability policy that pays employees their full wage or a percentage of full wage when they are absent for a prolonged illness. By doing so, companies provide a financial cushion for employees suffering from lengthy illnesses. Unfortunately, such a well-meaning policy can leave a company vulnerable to employees who want to abuse their employer's good intentions. For instance, employees can feign illnesses to stay away from work longer. They can complain to their physicians that they need extra time to recuperate so that their physicians write letters to the company suggesting that the employee should be able to stay away from work longer.

Unfortunately, most companies have not taken steps to protect themselves from such abuses of short-term disability benefits. However, there is a way that employers can avoid such abuses, while still looking after the health and welfare of their ill employees. This method is, in effect, putting a lid on the amount of time that a company will pay an employee to stay home while suffering from certain illnesses. This is a variation of the diagnostic related groups (DRG) method of handling insurance or Medicare claims. With the DRG approach, the cost of reimbursed treatment is capped. That is, a treatment provider receives only up to the amount that the DRG method deems usual and customary to treat a particular illness. Any cost over that DRG amount must be borne by the treatment provider or passed on to the patient.

Companies can implement a variation of DRGs in their short-term disability benefits. For example, a company's medical department may determine that most employees suffering from a broken leg should be able to return to work within two weeks. So, the company pays the employee with a broken leg up to two weeks of short-term disability benefits while the employee is recuperating. But if the employee stays away from work for over two weeks, then the employee may need to use vacation days in order to collect wages.

Or, the employee could take an unpaid leave of absence if more than two weeks are used. Either way, this method puts the burden of responsibility on the employee to get back on the job within whatever time period is reasonable for adequately healing from a specific illness. Employers also may want to build into this system a second opinion program in which specialists other than the employee's own physician examine the employee to determine whether more time off the job is warranted.

How to Implement Solution

1. *Determine extent of short-term disability problem.* A company that wants to implement this method probably suspects that it has a problem with abuse of short-term disability benefits. That may or may not be true. To find out for sure, the company's

benefits department needs to decide how long a person may suffer from various illnesses before the person *probably* is well enough to return to work. Then, the medical department can sift through records of what illnesses employees had, as well as whether or not employees stayed out longer than the usual and customary time it should have taken them to heal from the sickness. If this study uncovers that employees are staying away from work longer than they may need, then a capitated, short-term disability policy could produce bottom-line enhancements.

2. *Write and distribute new policy*. To do this, a medical consultant or the company's medical director (if there is one), a benefits consultant, and other human resources managers need to formulate a policy for the company. As with most company policies, this policy needs to be distributed to all appropriate managers and departments.

3. *Inform managers and supervisors*. Managers and supervisors must be aware of all aspects of the new policy because such a policy markedly changes the way the company handles employees' wages during short-term disabilities. Employee morale could be lowered if some employees were to go on short-term disability and *then* discover that they would not receive pay if they stayed out longer than a specified period of time. To avoid this possible morale deflater, managers and supervisors need to be able to:

☐ Explain the new policy and its rationale to their employees.
☐ Tell employees basically how the policy would affect them when they suffer lengthy illnesses.

4. *Develop procedures to handle capitated short-term disability benefits*. Under traditional short-term disability benefit plans, payroll and benefits clerks need to do minimal checking into whether or not a sick employee earns wages while away from work. However, with this new system, the company may need a list of hundreds of illnesses, along with a table showing how long a person with each illness probably deserves to receive pay. To avert possible overpayment or underpayment, benefits and payroll clerks need to learn how to use these tables in their daily jobs.

Deadline for Implementing Solution

This solution can be implemented within a few months. It requires some research on the severity of the short-term disability benefit abuse. Then, a policy and guidelines need to be established and approved by top management. If a union is involved, then use of this short-term disability benefit policy must be written into the labor contract. If this step must be taken, then implementing this policy in the unionized portion of the workforce could take considerably longer, depending upon how the union negotiations proceed.

Deadline for Measuring Profit Improvement

Profit improvements usually can be seen after the policy is used for one quarter. A more thorough evaluation of the effectiveness of this policy occurs after it is in effect and consistently followed for a year or longer.

SAVING CORPORATE CASH USING CAPITATED SHORT-TERM DISABILITY BENEFITS

The disability benefits coordinator at a chemical company continually noticed that quite a few employees who received wages during a short-term disability stayed away from work for a seemingly long time. As a registered nurse, she had a fairly good sense of how long most people need to recover from various ailments. She sensed that such timeframes were being over extended by all too many employees. That is, she perceived a *business problem* existed in the form of employees' abusing the company's short-term disability benefits and, in effect, squandering company funds. The *Planning Model* she used to work out this business problem appears as Figure 5-8.

Figure 5-8. Planning Model for implementing capitated short-term disability benefits.

___

BUSINESS PROBLEM

Abuse of company's short-term disability policy. These probable abuses of short-term disability benefits result in the company paying employees disability pay even after the employees should have been healthy enough to return to work.

COST OF BUSINESS PROBLEM

$1,500,000/year

Cost
- = Annual hours of short-term disability wages paid by the company × Average wages per hour
- = 150,000 hours/year × $10/hour
- = $1,500,000/year

SOLUTION TO BUSINESS PROBLEM

Capitate or limit the number of days an employee receives wages when suffering from a lengthy illness. A specified number of days will be allowed for each type of illness. Employees staying away from work for a greater number of days will not receive disability pay for the extra days.

COST OF SOLUTION

$20,000

Costs included:

A. Writing and distributing new short-term disability policy
B. Training managers and supervisors to carry out new policy

    C. Developing procedures for benefits and payroll departments to use in administering new policy

A. Writing and distributing new policy = $5,000
B. Training = $10,000
C. Developing procedures = $5,000

Cost of solution
    = $5,000 + $10,000 + $5,000
    = $20,000

$ IMPROVEMENT BENEFIT

$300,000/year

Improvement benefit = Annual amount of short-term disability wages paid before new policy − Amount paid after implementing new policy
Amount before new policy = $1,500,000/year
Amount after implementing new policy
    = Annual hours of short-term disability wages paid by the company × Average wages per hour
    = 120,000 hours × $10/hour
    = $1,200,000/year
Improvement benefit
    = $1,500,000/year − $1,200,000/year
    = $300,000/year

COST-BENEFIT RATIO

15:1

$300,000:$20,000

First, she calculated the *cost of the business problem,* which was the amount of short-term disability wages paid out during the previous 12 months. It turned out to be pay for 150,000 hours of short-term disability, with an average wage of $10 per hour, adding up to 1.5 million dollars per year.

Given this problem, she thought that a good *solution* would be to determine how many days it normally might take to recover from each particular illness enough to return to work, which evolved into a policy that would pay wages to employees if they returned within the specified number of days. If they required longer to recuperate, employees would be allowed to use their paid vacation days, or they could take an unpaid leave of absence.

The *cost of the solution* amounted to $20,000. In this amount were expenses for formulating and distributing a new short-term disability policy; training managers and supervisors in how to carry out the new policy; and developing systems to track and properly pay employees for their legitimate short-term disability needs. The new policy resulted in paying employees for 20 percent less time than they previously had been paid during their short-term disabilities. The *improvement benefit* came to a $300,000-per-year reduction in wages paid to recipients of short-term disability benefits. Given the costs and benefits of carrying out this innovative benefits technique, the short-term disability coordinator could proudly show that her innovative solution to a business problem produced a 15:1 *cost-benefit ratio* for her employer.

■ REDUCING UNEMPLOYMENT INSURANCE COSTS

Business Problems Addressed

Turnover
Benefits Costs

Overview of Solution

The FUTA tax (Federal Unemployment Tax Act) generally becomes one of the so-called hidden costs of doing business. Yet, it is a cost that companies can control in a number of ways, so it can be reduced to enhance the bottom line.

The key to this cost reduction is the intricate reserve ratio formula that determines each firm's rate of taxable contribution to the unemployment insurance fund. A major factor determining this rate is the amount an organization uses the unemployment insurance fund: An organization that has a great many unemployment insurance claims paid out of the fund pays a higher tax ratio than an organization that has very few, if any, unemployment insurance claims against it.

The taxable wage limitation is the first $7,000 of pay that an employee receives. If an organization's tax ratio is 3.0, then the company pays $210 per employee ($7,000 × .03 = $210). If a company has 100 employees, then it pays a total of $21,000 per year. A one-thousand-employee company pays $210,000 annually.

If, by better human resources management, the tax ratio can be lowered to 2.0, then the organization can cut its per employee costs to $140 (see Table 5-2). That is a one-third decrease in costs.

Some of the techniques available to help lower unemployment insurance tax liabilities include:

☐ Lessening layoffs through better human resource planning
☐ Better documenting why each employee leaves the organization
☐ Fighting claims that the company should not legally pay

If a claim is filed, the organization *definitely should* appeal the claim if there is any chance of winning. Some valuable techniques for winning the appeal appear in *Twenty-*

Table 5-2. Examples of unemployment insurance costs at various taxable contribution rates.

| | Taxable Contribution Rate* | | |
	1%	2%	3%
Per employee	$70	$140	$210
Per 100 employees	$7,000	$14,000	$21,000
Per 1,000 employees	$70,000	$140,000	$210,000

*On first $7,000 of wages

Seven Ways To Avoid Losing Your Unemployment Appeal, published by the California Unemployment Appeals Board in Sacramento, California.[9] This booklet is available for the asking.

How to Implement Solution

1. *Train all management staff in basic unemployment law.* The first line of defense against unemployment tax expenses rests with an organization's managers. These people need to know how their hiring, lay-off and terminating actions affect the bottom line in terms of unemployment costs. Such training should make them aware that each time they hire a potentially unnecessary employee, they risk laying off the employee and then forcing the company to pay on-going, increased unemployment tax.

They also must know that while their lay-off or termination decisions may be quite sound, such decisions nevertheless can cause a ripple effect in terms of unemployment tax expenses. Finally, the supervisors and managers need to know that they need to *document* why they de-employ any employee. Such documentation must be signed and dated. The human resource department should be contacted when questions arise on this documentation, because such reports can be used in the company's favor when it appeals potentially unjustified unemployment claims.*

2. *Conduct and document each exit interview.* Whenever an employee leaves the organization, he or she should receive an exit interview. Such interviews need to delve into *specific* reasons why the employee is leaving the company. It is absolutely crucial to note why an employee is resigning, because the reason for a resignation could come up in an unemployment hearing. For instance, if a person resigns to attend school, then that person typically cannot collect unemployment insurance benefits.[10] In contrast, if an employee's job requires transfer to a distant location, and the employee cannot travel or move that far away, then the employee may possess ample reason to collect unemployment insurance. It is the responsibility of the employee's supervisor *and* the human resources department to obtain such information. With this information, the company knows whether or not it is worthwhile to appeal a former employee's request to obtain unemployment insurance payments.

---

*There are, of course, other reasons to document termination decisions—most notably, to protect the company in the event of a lawsuit for unjust dismissal.

3. *Promptly check each unemployment insurance claim.* Each time an organization receives a notice that a former employee wants to collect unemployment insurance, the company needs to ascertain if the claim is justified. How can this be done? Review the reason for the claim. Does the reason appear to be justified? Also, does it coincide with the *documented* reasons the employee said he or she left, according to the ex-employee's exit interview and supervisor's notes? If it does not, then the claim should be appealed, and it may well be thrown out as an unjustified claim.

4. *Quickly protest questionable claims.* In general, unjustified claims should be appealed within about 10 days after a company receives notification of them. If an organization takes longer, then the wheels of justice may have rolled too far to reverse the claim. Also, it is a good idea for an organization to develop a reputation as a prompt, professional outfit in the eyes of the unemployment appeals board. Such a reputation increases the credibility of the company. Also, unemployment appeals departments often are overworked and understaffed. That makes them all the more appreciative of companies that help make their jobs easier.

5. *Socialize with local unemployment insurance staff.* Here, the term "socialize" does not imply any under-the-table activities. Instead, it merely means that unemployment insurance staffs value a friendly voice on the phone and a friendly face in their offices. They do have rules and guidelines to follow in making their decisions. However, a pleasant human resources official is more likely to have phone calls returned and questions answered than one who deals with unemployment insurance staffs in a curt, gruff, or impersonal businesslike manner.

6. *Audit all statement of unemployment benefit charges.* Every time an organization receives a statement listing the charges against it for unemployment insurance, the statement needs careful auditing. The audit must answer the following questions.

- ☐ Is the statement accurate?
- ☐ Are claims listed for actual past employees, or were some claims for people who never worked for the company? This becomes a more serious question for large organizations, because human resources staffs in large companies probably do not know every past employee's name. In contrast, in small companies, the benefits staff probably at least recognizes whether or not a named person ever was an employee at the organization.
- ☐ Are any charges levied for claims that the company successfully appealed? Perhaps the unemployment insurance department's records do not reflect the fact that some claims were appealed and ruled in favor of the company.

Deadline for Implementing Solution

Steps to reduce unemployment insurance tax take just one to three months to put into action.

Deadline for Measuring Profit Improvement

The tax ratio used to compute an organization's unemployment tax is adjusted periodically. However, it may well take an organization a year or longer before its improved human resources management techniques noticeably reduces its unemployment tax ratio.

An organization aiming to reduce these costs may be able to notice measureable cost reductions (and, therefore, profit improvement) in one to two years if all goes well. However, there are too many variables to predict the exact amount of time needed to produce measureable profit improvements.

REDUCING UNEMPLOYMENT INSURANCE COSTS

A *business problem* spotted by one company's benefits manager was the company's high unemployment tax payments. She reasoned that if the payments could be brought down, then the company would reduce a rather sizeable expense and thus improve its profitability. The *Planning Model* used is shown in Figure 5-9.

Figure 5-9. Planning Model for reducing unemployment insurance costs.

BUSINESS PROBLEM

High unemployment insurance tax payments

COST OF BUSINESS PROBLEM

$210,000/year

Cost

= Number of employees × First $7,000 of each employee's compensation × Unemployment reserve tax ratio

= 1,000 employees × $7,000/employee × .03

= $210,000

SOLUTION TO BUSINESS PROBLEM

Program to trim unemployment insurance costs

COST OF SOLUTION

$11,000

Costs included:

A. Training 50 managers in unemployment law essentials
B. Exit interviews
C. Checking each unemployment claim
D. Protesting each questionable claim
E. Time spent "socializing" with local unemployment officials
F. Auditing unemployment benefit claims statements

(continued)

(Figure 5-9 continued)

A. Training
  = Number of managers trained × Length of training × Average salary and benefits of managers
  = 50 management staff members × 1 hour training × $20/manager
  = $1,000
B. Exit interviews
  = Number of exit interviews × Average salaries and benefits of interviewer and departing employee during interview
  = 100 exit interviews × $30/interview
  = $3,000
C. Checking each unemployment claim
  = Number of claims × Cost to check each claim = 50 claims × $5/claim
  = $250
D. Protesting claims
  = Number of claims protests × Cost per protest
  = 20 protests × $300/protest
  = $6,000
E. Time spent "socializing" with local unemployment officials = $250
F. Auditing unemployment benefit claims statements = $500

Cost of solution
  = $1,000 + $3,000 + $250 + $6,000 + $250 + $500
  = $11,000

$ IMPROVEMENT BENEFIT

$35,000/year

Decreased unemployment tax ratio from 3.0 down to 2.5.
At 3.0, the tax was $210,000/year
At 2.5, the tax is 1,000 employees × $7,000/employee × .025 = $175,000/year
Improvement benefit
  = $210,000/year − $175,000/year
  = $35,000/year

COST-BENEFIT RATIO

3.2:1

$35,000:$11,000

Since the company's unemployment tax ratio was 3.0, the *cost of the problem* was $210,000 in unemployment expenses. The solution the benefits manager implemented focused on the six previously listed steps for paring these costs.

An interesting sidelight of her endeavors was the change in managers' minds toward staffing and human resource planning. Before the effort to trim unemployment expenses, managers often waited until the last possible minute before hiring needed new staff. This sort of rush situation all too often resulted in hiring below-average employees. When these employees were terminated or laid off, they generally added another mark against the company's unemployment insurance record.

Also, prior to the fuss about reducing unemployment insurance costs, managers gave mainly lip service to the concept of human resources planning. However, as the unemployment insurance costs demonstrated, managers needed to pay more attention to planning for their personnel needs and then sticking to their plans. That sort of planned approach would yield employees who were needed and well placed and would avoid the layoffs all too often associated with poor planning for human resource needs.

For $11,000, the *cost of the solution*, the company implemented a good program that generated a $35,000 *improvement benefit*. This benefit came about when the company's unemployment tax ratio decreased from 3.0 to 2.5. This ratio change reduced the organization's unemployment insurance costs from $210,000 a year to $175,000 per year. As a result, the benefits manager's efforts produced a fine 3.2:1 *cost-benefit ratio*. This result does not even include other possible improvements in the company resulting from better hiring and more reliable human resources planning. If the fruits of those improvements were added in, the cost-benefit ratio this benefits manager helped produce could run even higher.

■ EMPLOYER-SUPPORTED CHILD CARE

Business Problems Addressed

Productivity
Turnover, Absenteeism, and Tardiness
Benefits Costs

Overview of Solution

Difficulties with child-care arrangements reputedly lead to increased absenteeism, tardiness, turnover, and stress among parents of young children. For instance, Dominion Bankshares Corporation of Roanoke, Virginia, surveyed employees and found that among parents Dominion employed, slightly over half found it hard to arrange good child care.[11] Over half considered it difficult to reach child-care locations. More than half of the mothers felt extra stress as a result of fretting about child care. And just over half of the parents of children that were eighteen months or younger had difficulty returning to work after childbirth. Also, about one-fourth of the mothers thought about quitting because of their problems arranging child care. These sorts of statistics indicate the problems parents face in combining work with raising children.

Also, the problem seems pretty widespread. The United States Census Bureau, in a 1985 study entitled, *Who's Minding the Kids?*, discovered that around 7.7 million women use child-care arrangements while they work.[12,13] Of these women, 5.9 percent or 454,300 women reported losing some work time in the previous month due to difficulties with their child-care arrangements. Employers are losing out in this child-care problem. They do not get all the attendance, productivity, concentration, brainpower, and energy that they need from their employees who happen to be parents of young children.

One method for handling this problem is for employers to provide monetary assistance to employees who need to arrange child care. This method could take a number of forms. For instance, the company could make a direct payment to the employees to help offset child-care expenses. Or, the organization could offer help as part of a cafeteria-style benefits package. In such a case, the employee might be able to deduct pretax dollars from his or her wages to spend on child-care needs. In some instances, the employer may even reimburse the employee for a portion of this expense. Such an arrangement requires frequent, careful scrutiny by tax advisors to make sure it complies with changing tax laws and guidelines.

Other solutions to this problem are for employers to sponsor or support child-care facilities at or near the worksite. By doing so, working parents have a convenient place to use for day-care, and the firm can help alleviate or avoid some of the work-related problems catalyzed by child-care predicaments. For example, Nyloncraft, Inc. operates Indiana's first 24-hour a day child-care center. The company attributes a three percent decline in absenteeism to the center's existence.[14]

Neuville Industries in North Carolina reports its $22,000 annual subsidy of a child-care center helps it keep turnover at a low four to eight percent.[15] It also helps keep Neuville's absenteeism at only one percent. This absenteeism rate stands a good deal lower than the local industry's average 5 to 10 percent. The company also says its subsidy saves it $20,000–$25,000 each year in taxes. Given these figures, the company-supported child-care center certainly seems to more than pay for itself in a very real dollars-and-cents way.

Other research points out that employer-supported child care also can produce a measurable impact on the bottom line. Testimony before the United States House of Representatives' Select Committee on Children, Youth, and Families revealed that employer-supported child care can have a 4:1 cost-benefit ratio. "In other words," the report states, "for every dollar committed to employer-supported child care, the business would yield four dollars in cost-containment and tax savings."[16] That provides a handsome payback for an altruistic service that simultaneously enhances employee morale, commitment, and the quality of worklife.

How to Implement Solution

1. *Examine company records.* The first step is to determine if child-care problems might affect measurable aspects of job performance. To do this, the records of employees who are parents of young children can be reviewed. Some areas to measure that might prove enlightening include:

☐ Absenteeism
☐ Tardiness

☐ Turnover
☐ Performance appraisal ratings
☐ Number of promotions

Statistics on these measures say nothing in and of themselves. Instead, these figures for parents must be compared to those of employees who are not parents of young children. If there is a difference, then perhaps part of the problem stems from difficulty with child-care arrangements. If that seems to be the case, then the next step may be an employee survey.

2. *Survey parents of young children.* Such a survey should ascertain their concerns and problems associated with obtaining suitable child care while they work. Other matters that the survey should address are the following:

☐ Would they like a child-care facility at or near the worksite?
☐ Would they actually use such a facility?
☐ What hours on what days might they like to use the child-care center?
☐ How much money do they currently pay for child-care arrangements?
☐ What are their feelings about using a company-supported child-care center?

With this sort of information in hand, the company can decide if it should look further into supporting child-care facilities at or near the worksite.

3. *Develop child-care arrangement.* Few companies want to set up their own child-care facility. The costs and potential legal liabilities could prove draining. An alternative is to find a child-care company that would like to serve a relatively captive population composed of the company's employees. A number of national companies exist that do this sort of work. Also, local organizations may want to use this as an opportunity to serve the company's employees.

4. *Company Pays Part of Child-Care Fee.* The idea here is for company-*supported*, not company-*paid* child-care. To do this, the company needs to establish how much money it will chip in to defray child-care costs.

Deadline for Implementing Solution

This is not a quick-fix solution to problems of absenteeism, tardiness, turnover, and productivity. It take a good amount of study and commitment. It may well take a company a year just to develop the arrangement for child-care that its employees could use.

Deadline for Measuring Profit Improvement

The child-care program must be in operation for a year or longer before its measurable effectiveness can be noted. It will take this long for employees to become accustomed to the arrangement, start using it, and begin having it affect their job performance measures.

EMPLOYER-SUPPORTED CHILD-CARE CENTER

A company with a good number of parents of small children experienced certain *business problems.* It noticed that the parents of young children seemed to be absent or resign more than parents of older children or employees who did not have children. The company also suspected that worries about child-care resulted in lowered productivity among these parents. Because of these potentially correctable problems, the company decided to take action using the *Planning Model* displayed in Figure 5-10.

Figure 5-10. Planning Model for employer-supported child-care center.

BUSINESS PROBLEM

Employees who also were parents of young children experienced measureable job performance problems, including comparatively higher absenteeism and turnover, plus lower productivity than employees who did not have young children.

COST OF BUSINESS PROBLEM

$95,000/year

Costs included:

    A. Absenteeism
    B. Turnover
    C. Productivity

A. Absenteeism
    = Number of employees with small children × Number of days per year these parents are absent *more than* employees without small children × Average daily value of an employee at work in this company
    = 100 employees × 3 days/year × $150/day
    = $45,000/year
B. Turnover: The average turnover for the employees without small children was 10%, while the parents of young offspring averaged 20%. Each turnover costs an average of $5,000.
    Turnover
    = Number of turnovers above company average by parents with small children × Average cost per turnover
    = 10 extra turnovers/year × $5,000/turnover
    = $50,000/year
C. Productivity was not measured by the company but, given the higher absenteeism and turnover for parents of young children, it can be assumed that productivity also was lower for this group of employees.
    Productivity = ?

Cost of problem
    = $45,000/year + $50,000/year + ?
    = $95,000/year

SOLUTION TO BUSINESS PROBLEM

Employer-Supported Child Care

COST OF SOLUTION

$27,250

Costs included:

A. Study of employee records to measure absenteeism, tardiness, and other job performance indicators
B. Survey of parents of small children
C. Developing a child-care arrangement with an outside vendor of such services
D. Company payment toward child care

A. Study of employee records = $1,000
B. Survey of parents
   = Questionnaire administration to 100 parents of small children + Interviews of 20 of these parents + Data analysis + Feedback to management
   = $1,000 + $1,000 + $250 + $1,000
   = $3,250
C. Developing Child-Care Arrangement
   = $5,000, mostly for salaries and benefits of employees in these meetings
D. Company payment toward child-care
   = Number of employees' children receiving child-care aid × Annual cost of child-care aid per child
   = 75 children × $240/year
   = $18,000/year

Cost of solution
   = $1,000 + $3,250 + $5,000 + $18,000
   = $27,250

$ IMPROVEMENT BENEFIT

$65,000/year

Improvement benefit
   = Cost of problem before child-care arrangement − Cost of problem a year after implementing child-care arrangement
Cost before child-care arrangement = $95,000/year
Cost after implementing child-care arrangement:

A. Absenteeism
   = Number of employees with small children × Number of days per year these parents were absent *more than* employees without small children × Average daily value of an employee at work in this company

(continued)

(Figure 5-10 continued)

    = 100 employees × 1 day/year × $150/day

    = $15,000/year

B. Turnover

    = Number of turnovers above company average by parents with small children ×
    Average cost per turnover

    = 3 extra turnovers/year × $5,000/turnover

    = $15,000/year

C. Productivity = ?

Cost after implementing child-care arrangement

    = $15,000/year + $15,000/year + ?

    = $30,000/year

Improvement benefit

= $95,000/year − $30,000/year

= $65,000/year

COST-BENEFIT RATIO

2.4:1

$65,000:27,250

First, the company examined the statistics in its personnel records to determine the *cost of the business problem.* Specifically, it appeared important to see if the parents of small children really did cost the company more than employees who did not have small children. The answer turned out to be a resounding Yes, according to the data. The average absenteeism for the parents of small children was over 50 percent higher than for other employees. This higher absenteeism rate cost the company $45,000 annually. Also, their turnover was twice as high as their counterparts who did not have to worry about young offspring, to the tune of $50,000 a year. It was not possible, given the company's records, to pinpoint the cost of the probably lower productivity of these parents compared to the other employees. But, the cost of higher absenteeism and turnover for the 100 parents involved amounted to $95,000 per year. That means that the average parent of a small child cost this employer $9,500 per year more than other employees who did not have children—just in terms of higher absenteeism and turnover, not to mention productivity. This certainly seemed to be an expensive problem.

The company decided that the *solution to the business problem* would be a company-supported child-care center located near the company. The *cost of the solution* was $27,250. This cost included the expenses associated with examining personnel records, surveying parents about child-care needs, developing an arrangement with a child-care facility operator, and kicking in a $240 per year ($20 a month) subsidy for each child in the center.

About a year and a half after the center started operation, the company again examined its records on employee absenteeism and turnover to calculate its *improvement benefit* stemming from the child-care provisions. It was delighted to find that absenteeism among the parents of young children decreased dramatically. It now amounted to $15,000 a year more than the average for the employees who were not parents of small offspring. Turnover also amounted to $15,000 a year more. Taken together, this amounted to the parents of small children costing the company $30,000 per year more than their counterparts without small children. That is $65,000 less than the problem cost prior to starting the child-care arrangement.

Given these improved figures, the company enjoyed a 2.4:1 *cost-benefit ratio*. While this is a commendable return on investment, it actually was higher in all likelihood. If the probably improved productivity were added in, then the cost of the problem would have been higher and improvement benefit would have been even better, resulting in an even higher cost-benefit ratio. Also, the firm could reap certain tax benefits. Taken as a whole, this employer-supported child-care arrangement probably provided the company with an even higher cost-benefit ratio.

■ QUARTERMASTER PROGRAM

Business Problem Addressed

Benefits Costs

Overview of Solution

Many employees are required to wear uniforms during their work day. Employees often pay for their uniforms and replacements. However, some organizations pay employees a set amount of money each year for uniforms. Organizations intend this amount to be spent by the employee *only* for replacing worn or otherwise unusable uniform parts.

Unfortunately, quite a few employees do not spend the entire amount given to them for uniform needs. It is as though the uniform allotment is additional wages. Organizations using this approach may well spend money for uniforms that need not be spent.

A solution to this sort of problem is a quartermaster municipal program. Such programs are becoming more and more popular in municipal police departments. In a quartermaster program, no money is given to any employee for uniform replacements. In place of giving money, the organization has employees turn in worn or unusable uniforms to the company's quartermaster. The quartermaster inspects the garments to determine if they truly need replacement. If replacement is justified, then the quartermaster takes the old uniforms and gives the employee new uniforms in its place. By doing so, the organization spends money only for replacing uniforms that need replacement. Also, the company avoids handing out money that will not go for its intended use.

How to Implement Solution

1. *Estimate true annual uniform replacement costs*. Determine whether or not employees are given an allowance larger than they actually need to replace their worn uniform parts. If so, then granting employees smaller uniform allowances may solve the problem. Or, a quartermaster program could help.

2. *Obtain top management approval*. If a quartermaster program is decided upon, then senior officials need to approve the program. It may work well to survey other organizations that use a quartermaster program to determine how effective their programs are and why they are effective or ineffective. With this data in hand, top management can make an informed decision about this new practice.

3. *Appoint a quartermaster*. If the quartermaster duties can be scheduled into a small portion of a workday, then a current employee can be appointed as quartermaster. The quartermaster must be good at handling small details, keeping records, evaluating whether or not uniform parts need to be replaced, and acting diplomatic when an employee must be told that his or her turned in uniform does not require replacement in its present condition.

4. *Announce and implement quartermaster program*. Affected employees need to know that they will no longer receive a clothing allowance. Interestingly, some employees may feel disgruntled that they no longer receive what they considered part of their regular compensation. Also, guidelines may prove useful to let employees know what sort of wear and tear justifies replacement.

Deadline for Implementing Solution

A quartermaster program can be fully implemented within a month or two. It mainly takes appointment of one employee to act as quartermaster to inspect turned-in uniforms and arrange for replacements. A record-keeping system needs to be set up and maintained. Other than those components of a quartermaster program, not much else should take a tremendous amount of time to implement.

Deadline for Measuring Profit Improvement

In about one year after implementing a quartermaster program, its initial cost effectiveness can be measured. However, an even more accurate gauge may come after a few years. This is especially true in situations in which uniforms tend to wear out over a two or three year period. When that is the case, then it may well take two or three years before the effectiveness of the program can be fully measured.

SAVING MONEY USING A QUARTERMASTER PROGRAM

A police department pinpoints a *business problem* inherent in the way it assures that its officers will have good quality uniforms and equipment. The department gives each of its officers a check for $400 each year to cover replacing and repairing uniforms and other police equipment, such as bulletproof vests, nightsticks, clipboards, guns, flashlights, and aluminum ticket holders. However, the department suspects that actually some officers are spending less than the full $400 and pocketing the remainder. Figure 5-11 presents the *Planning Model* used to examine and correct this costly situation.

The *cost of this business problem* was the $40,000 per year the police department spent each year on new uniforms and equipment. Specifically, the department handed each officer a check for $400 each

Figure 5-11. Planning Model for a police department's quartermaster program.

BUSINESS PROBLEM

A police department thinks it is spending too much on the replacement of its officers' uniforms and police equipment

COST OF BUSINESS PROBLEM

$40,000/year

Cost
   = Number of police officers × Annual uniform and equipment allowance given to each officer
   = 100 officers × $400/officer/year
   = $40,000/year

SOLUTION TO BUSINESS PROBLEM

Quartermaster Program

$ COST OF SOLUTION

$1,000

For administrative expenses and meetings needed to set up the program

$ IMPROVEMENT BENEFIT

$10,000/year

Improvement Benefit
   = Annual cost before quartermaster program − Annual cost one year after implementing quartermaster program
Cost before program = $40,000/year
Cost after implementing program
   = Number of police officers × Annual cost to replace each officer's uniforms and equipment
   = 100 officers × $300/officer/year
   = $30,000/year

(continued)

(Figure 5-11 continued)

Improvement benefit
   = $40,000/year − $30,000/year
   = $10,000/year

<u>COST-BENEFIT RATIO</u>

10:1

$10,000: $1,000

year, earmarked for buying new uniforms and necessary gear. Since the department had 100 officers, the annual cost was $40,000.

The *solution* for handling this problem was a quartermaster program. The quartermaster was a staff sergeant who handled mainly administrative duties in the police department's headquarters. In this program, any officer who wanted a new uniform or piece of equipment needed to present his or her useless item to the quartermaster. The quartermaster inspected the item and determined if it needed replacement. If so, the quartermaster ordered the item from a distributor. The replacement usually arrived at the police department within a few days. Noteable, too, was the fact that the department could negotiate lower costs since it could order a quantity of police goods from one source, thus adding negotiating leverage to help lower the purchase prices.

Given both the lower purchasing price for replaced clothing and gear plus the greater control over how money was spent—or not spent—for replacements, the *improvement benefit* turned out to be $10,000 per year after one year of operating the quartermaster program. This improvement is because the quartermaster was able to lower the per officer cost by 25 percent, a $100 decrease per officer, down to an average of $300 annually for each of the 100 police officers.

The return on investment yielded a respectable 10:1 *cost-benefit* ratio, because a $1,000 investment resulted in a $10,000 annual expense reduction during just the first year of operating the quartermaster program.

Chapter 6
Employee Health and Safety Programs

Many companies complain that they cannot afford to spend money on improving their employees' health. However, in the future, companies will view the situation differently: They will not be able to afford *not* to help their employees improve their health. Employee health pays. In the short term, healthier employees are less likely to be absent, add to turnover, suffer disabilities, have accidents, or die. In the longer term, companies that enhance their employees' health enjoy lower medical costs. Productivity is also an important factor. Healthier employees are more likely to put in a full day's work than their less healthy counterparts.

Three types of programs companies institute to enhance their employees' health—and the corporate bottom line—are:

1. Wellness program
2. Employee assistance program
3. Accident reduction program

■ WELLNESS PROGRAM

Business Problems Addressed

Productivity
Absenteeism
Insurance Costs
Accidents
Benefits Costs

Overview of Solution

More and more people are realizing that they exert a tremendous amount of control over their own health. They know that medical technology, medications, and the art and science of medicine make up only a fraction of their health and well-being. They understand that their behavior plays a key role—if not *the* key role—in how well they feel. Corporate wellness programs help employees take charge of their lives, develop more healthful lifestyles, and reap the benefits of getting into better shape.

Indeed, about half of all causes of premature death are lifestyle rather than environmentally or biologically related, according to the Centers for Disease Control in Atlanta, Georgia, as shown in Table 6-1.

These lifestyle-caused problems are expensive for organizations.[1] For example, American Telephone & Telegraph estimates that it spends approximately $60,000 on health expenses when one employee has a heart attack. Goodyear Tire & Rubber Company claims that the annual cost for each employee who smokes is from $625 to $675 more than for each nonsmoking employee.[2] Control Data Corporation (CDC) found that obese employees spent 11 percent more for health care than did thinner employees.[3] CDC also discovered that employees who did not regularly use seat belts accumulated 54 percent more hospital days than employees who consistently wore them.

The main approach companies use to help employees adopt a health-oriented lifestyle is the corporate wellness program. This program offers a number of services to employees with the intention of enabling them to better their health. From the company's perspective, this type of program offers the opportunity of reducing employee absences, disabilities, health care costs, and turnover, as well as increasing productivity. In one way or another, many wellness programs follow the model used by CDC's Staywell Program, as shown in Figure 6-1.

Common components of a wellness program include the following:

☐ Health assessment questionnaire and/or health tests.
☐ Suggestions individually given to program participants by a wellness nurse improving lifestyle based on questionnaire and/or health test results.
☐ Workshops on health-related topics, such as weight control, smoking cessation, hypertension, and stress management. Figure 6-2 lists classes, usually an hour and a half long, offered by the Plan for Life program sponsored by International Business machines (IBM).
☐ Exercise, either offered at on-site facilities or at nearby gyms or health clubs.
☐ Health-conscious corporate environment that values healthy employees and physical fitness. For example, one major company's wellness program lost its potential effectiveness when its extremely overweight, cigar-chomping, hypertensive chairman of the board wheezed and smoked during a companywide, closed-circuit television broadcast to promote that program. No one watching the program took him seriously. Indeed, division presidents wiped the wellness program expenses out of their next year's budget without hearing any complaints from corporate headquarters. In contrast, other companies, such as PepsiCo, Mesa Petroleum, and Kimberly-Clark, go out of their way to make health an integral and *expected* part of work life.
☐ Evaluation of wellness program effectiveness.

Table 6-1: Proportional allocation of the contributing factors of premature mortality to the four elements of the health field.

Ten Leading Causes of Death Among the Total Population 1 + Years of Age Ranked by Number of Years of Life Lost Before Age 75, U.S.A. 1977

Ten Leading Causes of Death	Years of life <75 lost	Percentage	Health system	Lifestyle	Environment	Human biology
Heart disease	4,295,603	23.4	12	54	9	28
Cancer	3,931,209	21.4	10	37	24	29
Motor vehicle accidents	2,005,688	10.9	12	69	18	0.6
All other accidents	1,442,526	7.9	14	51	31	4
Suicide	898,388	4.9	3	60	35	2
Homicide	780,710	4.3	0	66	41	5
Cerebrovascular disease	775,483	4.2	7	50	22	21
Cirrhosis of liver	559,097	3.0	3	70	9	18
Influenza & pneumonia	309,243	1.7	18	23	20	39
Diabetes	252,566	1.4	6	26	0	68
			10.0	51.5	20.1	19.8

Source: Ten Leading Causes of Death in the United States, 1977, *Centers for Disease Control, U.S. Public Health Service, Atlanta, Georgia, July 1980, p. 45.*

Figure 6-1. CDC's Staywell Process Program Model.

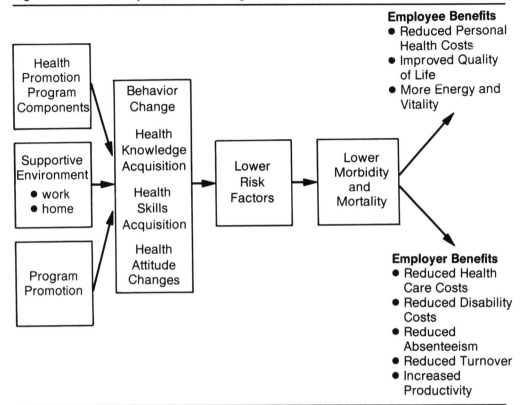

(From Jose, W. S. II, W. R. Williams, and P. E. Keller, "Staywell Program Improves Employee Health and Vitality at Control Data Corp, Wellness Management, Vol. 2, No. 2 (June 1986), p. 2.)

Unfortunately, most companies have not yet evaluated the effectiveness of their wellness programs in measurable terms such as the programs' impact on absenteeism, disability, accidents, turnover, or productivity. As more companies begin evaluating the effectiveness of their wellness endeavors, these companies will need to commit themselves to conducting evaluations over a long period of time, probably for at least five years, because it takes years to notice—and measure—a wellness program's bottom-line effectiveness.

To illustrate the limited amount of time most companies spend on evaluating the effectiveness of their wellness programs, here is a comment from the manager of the wellness program at a huge, extremely profitable major international company. It is concerned with evaluating the cost benefits of his company's wellness program.

[Our company], like most corporations offering wellness programs, thus far has not conducted an extensive formal evaluation in the areas of absenteeism, productivity or cost effectiveness. However, all anecdotal evidence indicates the programs have been far more successful than expected.

Figure 6-2. Courses offered as part of IBM's "Plan for Life" program.

CPR and Obstructive Airway Maneuver
Driver Improvement
Exercise
First Aid
Healthy Back
Nutrition
Risk Factor Management
(looks at connections among smoking, cholesterol,
stress, and obesity to coronary artery disease,
hypertension and diabetes)
Self Care and Family Care
Smoking Cessation
Smoking Cessation Follow-On
Stress Management
Water Safety
Weight Management
Weight Management Follow-On
Weight Management for Adolescents

Fortunately, other companies have evaluated aspects of their wellness programs, and found their fitness programs reduced sickness-caused absenteeism among participants by 22–59 percent, as shown in Figure 6-3.

Such results produce rather impressive cost benefits for organizations running general and specific wellness programs. The cost benefits reaped by some companies range from 1.6:1 up to 6:1. These data are shown in Figure 6-4.

One of the most thoroughly evaluated wellness programs is the LIVE FOR LIFE™ program at Johnson & Johnson. J&J found that:

Cost benefit projections show that the LIVE FOR LIFE™ Program can break even on an operating basis in year 3, with a payout in year 5. These figures have been derived solely from measured reductions in absenteeism and health costs. They do not include the benefits gained from improved morale, satisfaction with supervision, and organizational commitment.[4]

All in all, available statistics show that corporate wellness programs certainly can pay for themselves many times over. Thus, increasing numbers of organizations should soon be implementing them in an effort to get the most out of their employees, for both humanitarian and financial reasons.

How to Implement Solution

1. *Determine potential health problems in organization.* This step allows you to obtain a preliminary idea of what sorts of health-related problems cost your company

Figure 6-3. Sick-leave absenteeism reductions for exercise and fitness program participants.

Company	Percentage Reduction
Prudential Life Insurance	59%
New York Board of Education	55
New York Civil Service	52
Occidental Life Insurance	50
Canada Life Assurance	42
Metropolitan Life Insurance	22

(*From American Heart Association, Greater Boston Division,* The Corporate Heart, *Fall, 1986.*)

Figure 6-4. Cost-benefits reaped by companies' wellness programs.

Company	Cost-Benefit Ratio
General Health Promotion	
General Motors (Pontiac Division)	6.0:1
Pillsbury	3.6:1
Gilette	2.5:1
Intermediate, Inc.	2.0:1
Smoking Cessation	
Toledo Hospital	5.9:1
American Health Foundation	4.0:1
General Motors	2.0:1
High Blood Pressure Control	
National Heart, Lung & Blood Institute	1.6:1
Stress Management	
Equitable Life Assurance	5.5:1

Source: American Heart Association, Greater Boston Division, The Corporate Heart, *Fall 1986.*

money in terms of insurance costs, absenteeism, turnover, accidents, disability, and productivity. For instance, an examination of insurance records may show many claims paid for problems resulting from high blood pressure. Such expenses could indicate the need for an organizational effort to reduce health risks that precipitate hypertension, such as overweight, salt intake, stress, and lack of exercise.

2. *Offer voluntary health evaluations.* Offer employees the chance to answer a health questionnaire and perhaps to take certain medical tests. It is important for these evalua-

tions to be *voluntary* so that no employee feels pressured to do anything he or she does not want to do. A good example of an evaluation method is IBM's Voluntary Health Assessment, described in Figure 6-5. A health questionnaire assesses the sort of health risks that an employee may have in his or her life, such as problems concerning diet, fitness, or seat belt use. Figure 6-6 lists one company's results from its health questionnaire, illustrating the sort of lifestyle problems that such an assessment can uncover.

The health tests often include blood, cholesterol, and fitness exams. These assessments must be followed up with feedback to each employee who takes them. The feedback should include data derived from the health evaluation, along with recommendations on how to improve health. Suggestions may be given for workshops, exercise regimens, and dietary changes.

Figure 6-5. IBM's voluntary health assessment.

The Voluntary Health Assessment

Recent medical advances make it possible to identify an individual's potential risk for developing certain diseases such as heart attack, stroke or cancer. Now information is available on the ways a person can take steps to reduce the risk for these diseases.

Using heart disease as an example, previous screening techniques only identified people who actually had active disease at the time of the examination. The Voluntary Health Assessment (VHA) goes one step further. Based on an analysis of risk factors (e.g., family history, overweight, smoking, etc.), the assessment can identify those individuals who have a high risk of developing heart disease over the next ten years. The VHA also suggests steps which can be taken, such as limiting salt intake, losing ten pounds and exercising regularly, thus significantly lowering the risk for heart disease.

The new Voluntary Health Assessment program is not a substitute for regular checkups by your personal physician. But it is a valuable adjunct because it:

☐ Identifies lifestyles or personal behaviors which can be detrimental to your health.

☐ Suggests measures you can take to improve your health.

☐ Detects chronic ailments at an early stage when treatment is often more effective.

Taking the Voluntary Health Assessment

The VHA is offered at five year intervals to all IBM employees 25 years or older. It is normally given at your IBM Medical Department, or if appropriate, at the office of an IBM-designated physician or medical service organization. Wherever you take the VHA, the examination will be essentially the same. Your IBM-designated physician, however, may ask you to take one or two of your tests at a nearby hospital or laboratory.

The VHA consists of a limited physical examination, laboratory tests, and a questionnaire. Wherever possible the questionnaire portion of the VHA will be taken on the IBM personal computer. Similarly, an IBM nurse or physician will be available to help you complete the questionnaire, review the results with you and also discuss any concerns or questions you may have.

(continued)

(Figure 6-5 continued)

The VHA is tailored to the needs of each age group as follows:

Age 40 and Above	*Age 30 to Age 39*	*Age 25 to Age 29*
• QUESTIONNAIRE* —Health Risk Analysis —Health Status Review	• QUESTIONNAIRE* —Health Risk Analysis	• QUESTIONNAIRE* —Health Risk Analysis
• PHYSICAL EXAMINATION —Height, weight and waistline measurements —Blood pressure —Hearing test —Near and far vision (with and without glasses or contact lenses, if applicable) —Intraocular pressure (eye pressure)	• PHYSICAL EXAMINATION —Height, weight and waistline measurements —Blood Pressure	• PHYSICAL EXAMINATION —Height, weight and waistline measurements —Blood Pressure
• LABORATORY TESTS —Blood work (cholesterol determinations and a blood sugar level) —Electrocardiogram —Routine urinalysis —Hemocult test for blood in the stool	• LABORATORY TESTS —Blood work (cholesterol determinations and a blood sugar level)	

*QUESTIONNAIRE
A computerized *Health Risk Analysis* first determines your overall risk of disease. It then identifies and ranks the major risks to your health. This is done by calculating your risk of coronary heart disease, cerebrovascular disease (stroke), cancer and serious injury from motor vehicle accidents in the next ten years. For example, if you are at risk for lung cancer, the analysis may tell you that one of your specific risk factors for lung cancer is your habit of smoking two and one-half packs of cigarettes per day. It will also provide suggestions for you to stop your smoking habit.

The *Health Status Review* consists of questions about your current health. This section is designed to help identify possible current health problems that require immediate medical or other health related evaluation.

(From Voluntary Health Assessment *IBM).*

Figure 6-6. Statistics from one company's health-lifestyle questionnaire.

- 35% of survey participants do not eat 3 meals a day.
- 35% say they are on a low cholesterol diet.
- 44% are overweight by 10% to 30 + %. However, only 15% are on a weight reduction diet (22% of the women vs. 12% of the men).
- 83% eat more than 12% simple sugars daily.
- 55% say they have a low or very low activity level.
- 88% currently drink alcohol.
- 37% report driving under the influence of alcohol or drugs.
- 25% say they ride with drivers who are under the influence of alcohol (39% of the women do this vs. 19% of the men).
- 27% tend to exceed speed limits.
- 44% use seatbelts less than 25% of the time (only 7% say they use them more than 50% of the time).
- 68% rate themselves as having "good" (highest rating) physical health.
- 57% say they have good emotional health.

3. *Offer selected health-improvement services.* These services could include (1) workshops on health issues, (2) individual or group treatment of unhealthy behaviors, and (3) exercise facilities. Generally, the workshops are provided by local professionals who possess expertise in selected areas of health behavior. For instance, nutrition workshops might be taught by a local dietician or nutritionist, or an on-site aerobics class could be led by an aerobics instructor who lives or works near the company.

Some companies even pay for individual or group treatment. For example, one radio station contracted with a clinical psychologist to provide stop-smoking treatment that combined hypnosis, behavior modification, and personal counseling. This radio station also arranged for the clinical psychologist to provide group treatment to help employees overcome weight problems. That treatment focused on behavior modification plus the use of peer pressure and peer support to help many of the station's employees lose weight.

Finally, wellness programs quite often make exercise and fitness facilities available to employees. Some organizations, such as PepsiCo, erect their own fitness facilities and even staff them with exercise specialists and physicians. However, most companies cannot afford the expense of on-site exercise facilities, so they take other approaches. For instance, a 150-employee financial services firm arranged for reduced membership at a local health club and then paid half of the membership expenses for employees who used it.

4. Evaluate the wellness program's effectiveness. The evaluation could look at a number of measurable items.[5] For example, the program could compare the absenteeism and health-care claims of exercisers versus nonexercisers, as Tenneco did. Table 6-2 presents data from Tenneco's evaluation.[6] This study included a random sample of 273 members of Tenneco's fitness center compared to 249 nonmembers during the first year of the center. The sample included people of both sexes, various age groups, and exercise adherence levels. The evaluation could assess organization-wide measures for improved health to see the impact of the wellness program on the corporate culture. An example of this would be a company that encourages smoking cessation and offers workshops in how

Table 6-2. Tenneco's absenteeism and health care claim costs for its exercisers vs. nonexercisers.

	Absenteeism	Health Care Claims
Women		
Exercisers	47 hours	$639.07
Nonexercisers	70 hours	$1,535.83
Men		
Exercisers	25 hours	$561.68
Nonexercisers	69 hours	$1,003.87

Source: Multifaceted Corporate Medical Services Keep Tenneco 'Building on Quality' Through Good Health. *Houston: American Productivity and Quality Center, April 1985, p. 7.*

to stop smoking. But, there could be employees who never take the workshops but who stop smoking because of peer pressure or the emerging organizational norm that discourages smoking at work. Such information also could prove useful in evaluating the effectiveness of the wellness efforts.

Mesa Limited Partnership provided another example of an evaluation of a wellness program as illustratred in Figure 6-7.

Deadline for Implementing Solution

An organization should spend from 6 to 12 months planning a wellness program. It is best to garner support from top management, develop basic guidelines, and prepare the assessment, services, and evaluation before the program starts. Once the program begins, components of it (such as the services or evaluation) may take too long to begin, causing employee and management support to wane quickly.

Deadline for Measuring Profit Improvement

Measuring profit enhancements takes years. As mentioned earlier, J&J's LIVE FOR LIFE™ wellness program took three years to break even. It helped improve company profitability after five years of operation. This sort of information points out the necessity of companies using wellness programs for *long-term* financial gain, not as quick measures for reducing company costs.

WELLNESS PROGRAM TO IMPROVE THE BOTTOM LINE

This example shows how a wellness program may help improve corporate profitability for a hypothetical 1,000-employee company. It draws on methods used to evaluate various wellness programs. To begin with, the *business problem* is a desire on the part of the corporation to reduce current and potential employee health problems. These problems financially drain the company and cost the employees

Figure 6-7. Mesa Limited Partnership's fitness program general outline.

General Outline

☐ All employees—pre-employment medical screening, release to participate in program.

☐ Signed waiver for usage of fitness center.

☐ Computerized HRA (health risk appraisals), nutritional questionnaire.

☐ Blood cholesterol, triglycerides, glucose, hemoglobin, and blood pressure.

☐ Key employee physical complete with 12-led EKG, MAX stress test.

☐ Fitness assessment: aerobic (YMCA sub-max bicycle), strength, flexibility, muscle endurance, and body composition. Goal-setting qualifies for cash incentives from wellplan.

☐ Programs:
1) Fitness
    a) Weight training, CWT
    b) Aerobics, low and high impact
    c) Stationary aerobic equipment
    d) Walk/jog/run
    e) Ski conditioning circuit
    f) Weekend bike tours

2) Health
    a) Smoking cessation
    b) Weight control
    c) Low back care
    d) Various lunch seminars with guest speakers: stress, AIDS, food facts and fallacies

3) Recreation
    a) Racquetball ladder
    b) Wallyball ladder
    c) Basketball
    d) Volleyball
    e) Battle of Departments
    f) Fall Fitness Festival
    g) Tae Kwon Do
    h) Corporate Cup
    i) Company picnic
    j) Golf league

☐ Program participation tracked by filling out exercise log cards

☐ Employee Development Board

☐ Needs and values assessment survey (every two years).

☐ Free juice, fruit, and raw vegetables (yogurt for a small price).

☐ Field Program: Cholesterol screening one time a year; small fitness center in one gas plant; air-dynes on platforms; pay employees' health club fees (must use nine times a month).

☐ No smoking policy in corporate headquarters.

(continued)

(Figure 6-7 continued)

Wellplan Statistics and
Estimated Potential Savings (EPS)

I. Employees who exercise thirteen times or more per month

    A. 1984—30%
       1985—30%
       1986—35%
       1987—35%

    B. Breakdown for 1987

       Amarillo/Fain—155 employees or 42%
       Division   — 54 employees or 24%
       All Spouses — 43   or ?%

Comments: 1987 leveling off may be due to several reasons:

    1. Incorporation of more blue collar workers into program.

    2. Since log cards are not utilized by everyone, some people may be exercising but are not counted.

    3. Stricter guidelines for Wellplan participation may have caused less participation.

II. Utilization of fitness center during January 1988 (Amarillo/Fain)

		Male	Female
60% of employees	1 time or more a week	76%	51%
56% of employees	2 times or more a week	70%	47%
41% of employees	3 times or more a week	53%	32%
9.5% of employees	5 times or more a week	15%	4%

Eight of twenty employees at Fain exercise regularly (three times or more a week) at the fitness center (40%)

January average daily attendance was 140 employees.

February average daily attendance was 120 employees.

Comments: The 1984 national average showed that only 19% of adult Americans participated in fitness-related activities more than sixty days a year (one time a week average). The National Health Council "hopes" that by 1990, 10% of Americans will be exercising three times or more a week. Lately they have been very pessimistic about reaching this goal. Mesa's attendance places it in the top level of corporate wellness employer participation. This level of commitment reflects better medical cost containment and lowers our absenteeism levels as exemplified by the following descriptive data.

III. Medical claims

    A. Lifestyle-related claims

       The following is a review of 1987 medical claims (claims that have a strong correlation to lifestyle health care habits). The subjects used were randomly selected according to exercise log cards. This is only a sample number from Amarillo/Fain employees.

Two categories:

1. Physically active—exercise records show this group to average three times a week or more of exercise.

2. Physically inactive—exercise records showed this group to average less than three times a week or no exercise in a week.

	Active	Inactive
Number of medical claims:	57	57
Total cost	$6,286	$12,082
Average/employee	$ 110	$215

Difference—$105
EPS—159.5 × $105 = $16,747.50

B. Mesa vs. national average

When Mesa is compared to the national average for annual health care claims, we do extremely well.

Mesa average	$ 616 annually/worker
National average (1986)	1,857
Difference	$ 1,241
EPS annually	$750,000

Comments: Personnel will work with manager of fitness center on an assessment of medical claims of nonexercisers vs. exercisers, maintaining confidentiality of individual claims.

IV. Absenteeism

The national average is 3.1 for males and 4.1 for females. The following are Mesa descriptive statistics for 1987.

Group 1: Individuals who exercised less than nine months and/or less than three times per week.

Group 2: Individuals who exercised three times or more a week for nine months or more in 1987.

	Combined	Male	Female	Mesa Average
Group 1	4.4 days	3.3	7.9	
Group 2	1.6 days	1.0	3.5	
Difference	2.8 days	2.3	4.4	3.46

Comments: Several reasons may explain the high absenteeism.

1. There was a great deal of maternity leave.

2. One injury is still on payroll.

3. Stress is high in the oil and gas business in general and Mesa is exposed to this stress. Some studies claim 50% of absenteeism is directly related to stress.

(continued)

(Figure 6-7 continued)

V. Cost benefits

The following is a researched and published equation used to estimate potential saving (EPS) from lowered absenteeism.

$$\begin{array}{ccccc} A & B & C & D & E \\ 1.75 \times & 2.8/220 \times & 2.75/100 \times & \$35{,}000 = & \$214.40 \end{array}$$

A. Multiplier for replacement costs
B. Difference between Groups 1 and 2 divided by number of work days.
C. Percentage of employees in Amarillo who exercise regularly.
D. Average salary at Mesa.
E. EPS per worker.

$$\begin{array}{ccc} F & G & H \\ \$214.40 \times & 209 = & \$44{,}809.60 \end{array}$$

F. EPS
G. Actual number of exercisers.
H. Annual savings.

Mesa vs. national average

Mesa   3.46
National   3.5
            _____
            .14   EPS = $20,382

Mesa average for nonexercisers is 4.4 days and if absenteeism was related to exercise, the fitness center helps attract healthier workers and individuals who deal with stress through exercise. Theoretically, the fitness center keeps absenteeism lower on the average.

Cost if the fitness center didn't exist and Mesa's average was 4.4 days:

EPS = $41,342.40

The employees ask for stress management classes but attendance is low because they feel they would be looked upon as weak if they admitted to being under stress at work.

VI. Summary of EPS vs operating cost in 1987

EPS medical claims	$ 16,747
EPS medical vs. national average	750,000
EPS absenteeism	44,810
EPS absenteeism vs. national average	20,382
Total	$831,939
1987 operating cost	$256,097
1987 Wellplan cash distribution	146,000
	$402,097
EPS 1987	$429,842

Comments: Not included in these figures are individual lifestyle changes. The following is the estimated potential costs (EPC) of five health risk appraisals (HRA) factors (per employee).

Smoking	$400
Alcoholism	$1,200
Nonexercise	$240
Cholesterol (above 200)	$208
Hypertension	$600

their most valuable possession—their health. The *Planning Model* for this program appears in Figure 6-8.

The *cost of the business problem* for the year prior to implementing the wellness program is $2.65 million. This amount includes the measures that will be used to evaluate the effectiveness of the program, such as absenteeism caused by sickness, health insurance claims costs for this self-insured company, the possible costs associated with employees' unhealthy lifestyle factors (such as lack of exercise or smoking, as well as weight, nutrition, and alcohol problems), and disability costs. If those costs continue at the same rate, then the company can project costs due to the problem at $10.6 million over the next four years.

Given this situation, the company may well consider a comprehensive wellness program as a *solution* to this costly business problem. This program might include examination of the company's records pertaining to absenteeism plus health insurance and disability costs. Also, the company needs to ascertain the sorts of unhealthy lifestyle factors engaged in by its employees so that the company can work on reducing these factors.

The company could contract with a local hospital to conduct health and lifestyle evaluations using questionnaires and various medical tests. Nurses from the hospital would give each employee feedback on his or her health assessment, along with recommendations for improving health and reducing health risk factors in the employee's life. The company would offer classes on many health-related topics, such as weight control, smoking cessation, nutrition, hypertension, and stress. Finally, the company might build and operate a fitness center—or subsidize the use of off-site exercise facilities—for its employees' use. All these services bring the *cost of the solution* to around $750 per employee per year. For a 1,000-employee company, that amounts to $750,000 per year, or $3 million over a four-year period.

Let's say that the wellness program has worked over a period of time. Similar to J&J's findings, the program has taken about three years to break even. After that, it started reducing company expenses below the cost of running the wellness program. Given this situation, instead

Figure 6-8. Planning Model for corporate wellness program.

BUSINESS PROBLEM

Current and potential employee health problems that will cost the company large amounts of money

COST OF BUSINESS PROBLEM

$2,650,000/year
or
$10,600,000 projected over 4 years

Costs included:

    A. Absenteeism caused by sickness
    B. Health insurance claims cost
    C. Unhealthy lifestyle costs
    D. Disability costs

A. Absenteeism
    = Number of employees × Average absenteeism rate per year × Daily average salary and benefits
    = 1,000 employees × 7 absence days/year × $100/day
    = $700,000/year
B. Health insurance costs
    = Number of employees × Average health insurance claims costs per employee per year
    = 1,000 employees × $1,250/employee/year
    = $1,250,000/year
C. Unhealthy lifestyle costs
    = Number of employees × Average cost for unhealthy lifestyle behaviors
    = 1,000 employees × $200/year
    = $200,000/year
D. Disability costs = $500,000/year

SOLUTION TO BUSINESS PROBLEM

Comprehensive wellness program

COST OF SOLUTION

$750,000/year
or
$3,000,000 for 4 years

Cost of solution
  = Number of employees × Average wellness expense per employee per year
  = 1,000 employees × $750/year
  = $750,000/year

$ IMPROVEMENT BENEFIT

Improvement benefit
  = Projected 4-year cost of business problem before wellness program − Cost of
    business problem after wellness program implementation
Cost before wellness program
  = $10,600,000 projected for 4 years.
Cost after wellness program implementation decreased 33% below projection.
Thus, after 4 years, the problem cost $10,600,000 × .67
  = $7,102,000 for four years
Projected 4 year cost − Actual 4 year cost
  = $10,600,000 − $7,102,000
  = $3,498,000

COST-BENEFIT RATIO

1.17:1

$3,498,000:$3,000,000

---

of the $10.6 million projected cost of the business problem over four years, the problem cost the company 33 percent less, for a total of $7.102 million—$3.498 million less than the company expected to pay out for the problem over the four-year period.

Since the four years of the wellness program cost $3 million, the *cost-benefit ratio* after four years showed a slight payback to the company of 1.17:1. After this time, the wellness program can be expected to yield even higher cost-benefit ratios. Perhaps most important, however, the company has learned that improving its employees' health is a long-term proposition, as is the commitment needed to make a wellness program a financial success for the company and a personal success for the employees who participate.

■ EMPLOYEE ASSISTANCE PROGRAM

Business Problems Addressed

Productivity
Turnover, Absenteeism, and Tardiness
Insurance Costs
Accidents
Benefits Costs

Overview of Solution

A company's employee assistance program (EAP) helps employees deal with such problems as alcoholism, drug abuse, and emotional, marital, and financial worries that could affect the employees' work effectiveness. Some EAPs even offer these services to members of the employees' families. These programs initially started out as extensions of Alcoholics Anonymous in the 1930s. This was followed by workplace alcoholism programs from the 1940s through the 1960s. After that, employers realized that EAPs could help employees with many nonalcoholism problems, too. As a result, EAPs were expanded to include the current broadbrush approach of helping employees overcome an array of personal problems.

Employees who face personal problems each day have a great need for such services. These services also affect the profitability of companies who shoulder the burden of these problems as they occur in the workplace. For instance, the U.S. Department of Health and Human Services estimates that the economic impact of alcoholism was $117 billion in 1987[7], a figure that is expected to increase to $150 billion by 1995. About 79 percent of this amount "represents products, goods and services never produced, never delivered" because of alcohol abuse problems, according to Thomas R. Burke, the Department's chief of staff. The National Council on Alcoholism calculates that alcohol use plays a key role in 98,000 deaths annually.[8] Drug use and personal problems also cause a great many workplace accidents. These figures do not even touch on the probably huge costs in terms of morale, organizational commitment, supervisory time, and a host of other costs that go hand in hand with workplace disruptions caused by employees' alcoholism, drug abuse, and personal problems.

Fortunately, EAPs represent an attack on these staggering costs. Some organizations' calculations of the annual cost savings reaped by their EAPs are shown in Table 6-3.[9]

Still other companies evaluate the effectiveness of their EAPs in terms of measurable factors, such as:

☐ Sickness disability cases
☐ Off-duty accidents
☐ On-the-job accidents
☐ Medical expenses
☐ Instances of lost work time
☐ Lost days
☐ Health insurance claims
☐ Job-related accidents

A well-planned EAP usually starts out with a needs assessment of what sort of problems the organization's employees tend to exhibit. These data can be collected through examining company records (such as accident, health benefit usage, and absence records), as well as interviewing or surveying employees and community agencies. Figure 6-9 shows components of a needs assessment for an EAP.[10]

After the EAP is established, it provides a place for troubled employees to go for help. Some EAPs are staffed by company employees who are substance abuse or mental health professionals. Other EAPs are operated by such professionals in their private offices. Many EAPs offer employees the opportunity to phone the EAP to discuss their

Table 6-3. Cost savings from employee assistance programs.

Company	Number of Employees	Number Using EAP	Rehabili-tation Rate (in %)	Annual Cost Savings
University of Missouri	7,000	1,002	80%	$ 67,996[a]
Scovill Manufacturing	6,500	180	78	186,550
Illinois Bell Telephone	38,490	1,154	80	254,448[b]
(family)		100		
U.S. Postal Service	83,000	?	75	2,221,362
Kennecott Copper	7,000	1,200/yr.	NA	448,400[c]
(with dependents)	28,000			
New York Transit	13,000	?	75	2,000,000
E. I. DuPont (with spouses)	16,000	176/yr.	70	419,200[d]
New York Telephone	80,000	300/yr.	85	1,565,000

(a) Plus a 40% decrease in use of health benefits.
(b) 31,806 disability days were saved and off-duty accidents decreased 42.2% and on-duty accidents decreased 61.4%. There were also savings in health insurance utilization and job inefficiency.
(c) The total included absenteeism, sickness and accident disability, and health insurance use. Absenteeism decreased 53%, weekly indemnity costs (sick accident) 75%, and medical costs 55%. The rehabilitation rate was not calculated. A conservative calculation found a $5.78 return for each $1.00 invested in the program.
(d) Alcohol program only.

Source: Berry, C. A. Good Health for Employers and Reduced Health Care Costs for Industry *(Washington, D.C.: Health Insurance Association of America, 1981), p. 28.*

Figure 6-9. Components of a needs assessment.

Who Should Be Involved?	How Should Information Be Collected?	What Kinds of Information?
Company Sources	*Direct Sources*	*Employee Concerns*
1. Employees	1. Surveys	1. Mental health
2. First-line supervisors	2. Personal interviews	2. Drug and alcohol
3. Union representatives	3. Group interviews	dependence
4. Management		3. Financial problems
5. Personnel counselors	*Indirect Sources*	4. Legal problems
6. Medical personnel	1. Personnel records (such	5. Personal problems
	as attendance records	
Community Sources	and disciplinary reports)	*Company Concerns*
1. Mental health	2. Organizational records	1. Job satisfaction
counselors	(such as medical claims	2. Job performance
2. Financial counselors	and accident reports)	3. Workforce characteristics
3. Legal counselors		
4. Drug rehabilitation		
counselors		

(From Balzer, W. K., and K. I. Pargament, "The Key to Designing a Successful Employee Assistance Program," Personnel, *July 1987, p. 52.)*

problems. Such hotline service makes the EAP readily accessible to practically any employee. It also ensures the anonymity of the caller.

EAPs seldom provide complete counseling themselves. Instead, the EAP counselor typically does a brief assessment of exactly what troubles the employee who seeks the EAP's help. Then, the counselor refers the employee to local professionals who provide the type of service that the employee needs. For instance, an alcoholic employee might receive referrals to alcoholism treatment centers. An emotionally distraught worker might receive a referral to a clinical psychologist or a local mental health clinic. In most instances, the company's health insurance pays for all or part of the treatment that the employee receives.

EAPs also play key roles in training supervisors to spot a personal problem that results in an employee's deteriorating job performance. The supervisors are not taught to treat these problems. Instead, they are instructed on how to refer employees for EAP counseling in a sensitive manner. In this training, the supervisors might be given a checklist of possible employee behaviors to observe carefully. If an employee exhibits these behaviors, then that might indicate that the employee's performance is affected by alcohol, drug, or emotional problems. An example of one such checklist appears as Figure 6-10.

Figure 6-10. Checklist of patterns of job performance deterioration.

Code: O = Observed, D = Documented, and R = Reported.

Personality Changes

_____ Edgy and/or irritable	_____ Nervousness and/or jitteriness
_____ More intolerant of fellow workers	_____ More resentful of fellow workers
_____ Boredom and apathy	_____ More suspicious of fellow workers
_____ Disenchantment and cynicism	_____ Mood changes after absence from work area
	_____ Attitude change

Work Behavior Changes

_____ Putting things off	_____ Spasmodic work pace
_____ Avoiding boss or associates	_____ Neglecting of details
_____ Lower quantity of work	_____ Mistakes or errors in judgment
_____ Decrease in the quality of work	

Concentration and Memory Changes

_____ Work requires greater effort	_____ Job takes more time
_____ There may be a hand tremor when concentrating	_____ Difficulty in recalling instructions, details, etc.
_____ Difficulty in recalling own mistakes	_____ Rigidity and impaired judgments

Employee Relations on the Job

_____ Over-reacts to real or imagined criticism

_____ Borrows money from co-workers

_____ Begins to avoid associates

_____ Steals from co-workers

_____ Wide swings in morale

_____ Complaints from co-workers

_____ Unreasonable resentments

_____ Decreased social involvement

Physical Changes

_____ Red or blurry eyes

_____ Weight fluctuations

_____ Accumulated stress

_____ Unsteady gait

_____ Body marks

_____ Flushed face, complexion changes at times

_____ Reporting to work sick from the after-effects of yesterday's drinking episode

_____ Hand tremors

_____ Physical fatigue

_____ Extreme nervousness

_____ Slurred speech

_____ Unusual scratches, cuts, bruises on arms

_____ Dilated or contracted pupils

Drinking

_____ Drinking during work hours

_____ Regular or periodic drinking at lunch

_____ Drinking before reporting to work

_____ Using breath purifiers to cover the odor of alcohol

Drugs

_____ Continued use of medication prescribed by physician

_____ Reports of use of over-the-counter drugs

_____ Continued use of over-the-counter drugs

_____ The odor or scent of marijuana

Changes in Job Efficiency

_____ Misses deadlines

_____ Complaints from customers

_____ Makes mistakes due to inattention or poor judgment

_____ Tenacity to job—doesn't change easily

_____ Waste more material

_____ Spasmodic work patterns

_____ Improbable excuses for poor job performance

_____ Mid-workday changes in job performance

Absenteeism

_____ Unauthorized leave

_____ Excessive tardiness

_____ Pattern of Monday and/or Friday absences

_____ Patterns of absences of 5–10 days

_____ Higher absenteeism rate than other employees for colds, flu, etc.

_____ Excessive sick leave

_____ Leaving work early

_____ Patterns of absences of 2–4 days

_____ Patterns of absences of 1–2 days

_____ Peculiar and improbable excuses for absences

_____ Frequent unscheduled short term absences

(continued)

(Figure 6-10 continued)

On-the-Job Absenteeism

_____ Long coffee breaks

_____ Physical illness on job

_____ Frequent trips to water fountain, bathroom

High Accident Rate

_____ Accidents on the job

_____ Frequent trips to nurses' office

_____ Accidents off the job

(Prepared by Joseph E. Troiani, M.A., M.H.A., C.A.C., EAP specialist, Chicago, Ill.)

How to Implement Solution

1. *Conduct needs assessment.* The needs assessment uncovers what problems an organization's employees face. It provides indications about what EAP services, if any, might help the company. The needs assessment's findings also should form the basis for the evaluation of the EAP. For example, if workplace accidents seem rather high in an organization and it is thought that these accidents may be related to employee substance abuse, then part of the company's EAP evaluation should include measures of reductions of workplace accidents.

2. *Set up EAP.* For this step, the company needs to decide whether to operate an in-house EAP or contract with an outside group of professionals to operate the EAP counseling and referral services.

3. *Train supervisors.* In many ways, supervisors make or break an EAP. They usually are the first ones to spot performance problems that may be caused by employees' personal problems. Also, many troubled employees feel hesitant to admit their problems. For this reason, supervisors may need to refer employees to EAP services in instances in which the employees would not have gone on their own accord.

4. *Evaluate EAP effectiveness.* EAP staff should be *required* to *measure* the effectiveness of the EAP. It may not be enough for them just to provide humanistic, appreciated services. Instead, a dollars-and-cents evaluation of EAP effectiveness proves exceedingly helpful. Such evaluations point out how an EAP is achieving, or not achieving, the ultimate financial goals it can help a company reach.

Deadline for Implementing Solution

A well-thought-out EAP takes 6 to 12 months to set up. This includes conducting the initial needs assessment, garnering needed organizational support and commitment, hiring or contracting EAP staff, and training supervisors.

Deadline for Measuring Profit Improvement

Within a year, an EAP should show some cost benefits on workplace problems it aims to help reduce.

EMPLOYEE-ASSISTANCE PROGRAM
REDUCES COMPANY COSTS

A 1,500-employee manufacturing company in the telecommunications industry became quite concerned about the toll alcoholism, drug abuse, and emotional problems took on its profitability. The company saw these personal problems as the cause of a rather expensive *business problem,* as outlined in the *Planning Model* seen in Figure 6-11.

Figure 6-11. Planning Model for employee assistance program.

BUSINESS PROBLEM

Employees' alcohol, drug abuse, and emotional problems cost the company money in terms of absenteeism, accidents, medical claims, and probably other expenses.

COST OF BUSINESS PROBLEM

$415,000 for year prior to EAP

Costs included:

    A. Absenteeism
    B. Accidents
    C. Health Insurance Claims

This evaluation focused on the first 100 troubled employees who used the EAP's services. The EAP examined the absenteeism, accidents, and health insurance claims of these 100 employees for a year.

A. Absenteeism
    = Number of troubled employees using EAP × Their average number of days absent during the year prior to the EAP × Their average salary and benefits per day
    = 100 employees × 10 days/year × $85/day
    = $85,000/year

B. Accidents = $70,000/year

C. Health Insurance Claims
    = Number of troubled employees using EAP × Their average claims per year
    = 100 employees × $2,600/year = $260,000/year

Cost of problem
    = $85,000/year + $70,000/year + $260,000/year
    = $415,000/year

SOLUTION TO BUSINESS PROBLEM

Employee assistance program

(continued)

(Figure 6-11 continued)

COST OF SOLUTION

$48,000

An outside independent EAP consultant charged $2/month for each of the company's 1,500 employees.

The first 100 troubled employees to use the EAP were seen during the EAP's first 16 months of existence, so the cost of the solution was

1,500 × $2/month × 16 months = $48,000

$ IMPROVEMENT BENEFIT

$174,000/year

Improvement benefit
> = Costs for the 100 troubled employees for the year before the EAP started − Cost for these employees for a year after the EAP helped them

Cost before EAP = $415,000

Cost after EAP helped the 100 employees included these employees':

A. Absenteeism
B. Accidents
C. Health insurance claims

A. Absenteeism
> = Number of troubled employees using EAP × Their average number of days absent during the year after they started using EAP × Their daily average salary and benefits per day
> = 100 employees × 6 days/year × $85/day
> = $51,000/year

B. Accidents = $40,000/year

C. Health insurance claims
> = Number of troubled employees using EAP × Their average claims per year
> = 100 employees × $1,500/year
> = $150,000/year

Cost after one year for these 100 troubled employees
> = $51,000/year + $40,000/year + $150,000/year
> = $241,000/year

Improvement benefit
> = $415,000/year − $241,000/year
> = $174,000/year

COST-BENEFIT RATIO

3.6:1

$174,000/year: $48,000/year

Since the company's needs assessment focused on absenteeism, accidents, and health insurance claims, these three expenses became the measure for evaluating the effectiveness of the EAP. If the EAP could help decrease these expenses caused by employees seen in the program, then the EAP would be perceived as effective from a bottom-line standpoint.

The first 100 employees seen in the EAP were used as the experimental group. That is, costs associated with their absenteeism, accidents, and health insurance claims were followed for one year after they were seen in the EAP. For the year before they used the EAP, the *cost of the business problem* caused by these 100 employees was $415,000.

The EAP *solution* was operated by an outside firm of clinical psychologists. For a fee of two dollars per month for each of the company's 1,500 employees, the EAP provided good-quality training of supervisors, plus counseling and referrals by the EAP staff. Since the EAP saw its first 100 troubled employees over a 16-month period, the *cost of the solution* for the evaluation period was $48,000.

The fine EAP services produced a $174,000 *improvement benefit.* This consisted of the reduction in absenteeism, accidents, and health insurance claims by the EAP's first 100 cases during the first year they used the EAP. By comparing this improvement benefit to the cost of the EAP, the *cost-benefit ratio* came out to 3.6:1. The EAP most certainly more than paid for itself. If other factors such as productivity and overtime expenses were taken into account, then the cost-benefit ratio would have proved even more impressive. In any case, the EAP definitely proved a fine investment for employee welfare, as well as for corporate profits.

■ ACCIDENT-REDUCTION PROGRAM

Business Problems Addressed

Absenteeism
Work-Group Effectiveness
Insurance Costs
Accidents
Benefits Costs

Overview of Solution

Any workplace accident can cost an organization quite a bit of money. The National Safety Council estimates that workplace accidents cost $34.8 billion in 1986.[11] These accidents affected 108,900 workers, resulting in 1.8 million disabling injuries[12] and 75 million lost workdays.[13] Expenses associated with workplace accidents include administrative expenses, medical care costs and disability payments, and loss of productivity. Other difficult-to-measure expenses also hit the employer who has workplace accidents. These costs include the work slowdown that inevitably occurs after an accident—employees would rather mill around discussing the accident than get back to work. Also, organizations with many accidents pay a price in terms of morale and organizational commitment, since accidents can affect employees' desire to work hard to help the organization achieve its goals.

All too often, safety-conscious employers decide that a training program might help reduce workplace accidents. Unfortunately, that may not hold true in reality. Employees certainly would learn about the causes and prevention of accidents. However, such knowledge does not necessarily go hand in hand with the trained employees *actually* carrying out accident-prevention measures on the job. For example, many companies train employees in the correct way to lift heavy objects (bend knees, not back, when lifting). Then, as soon as employees return to their workstations, they almost immediately resume their old habit of lifting objects in the wrong way—the way they are used to lifting, which causes back pain and accidents.

Fortunately, a rather straightforward option is available. Specifically, employers can put positive reinforcement to work to make accident-prevention programs yield measurable decreases in absenteeism. In general, positive reinforcement in the workplace occurs when an organization rewards employees for doing something good, such as using safety precautions to avoid accidents.

Two types of reinforcement are available to a company:

1. Formal reinforcement
2. Informal reinforcement

Formal reinforcement consists of providing awards or incentives for individuals or groups that do not have accidents. These awards can be money, merchandise, free meals, or safety patches. Informal reinforcement for accident prevention focuses on intangible yet noticeable awards. Thes incentives might include peer pressure, praise, and recognition aimed at promoting workplace safety.

A well-rounded accident-prevention program uses both formal and informal reinforcements to accomplish its goals. For example, such a program might zero in on rewarding intact work groups or teams for on-the-job safety. The program may offer formal, tangible awards to every member of a work group *only if* no employee in the work group has an accident for a month. If even one employee has an accident, then *no one* in the work group receives an award. That is the formal reinforcement aspect.

By setting up the formal reinforcement portion of the program this way, the work group members are bound to develop *peer pressure* that greatly encourages each employee to avoid accidents. Instead of having supervisors police the safety consciousness of employees in their work groups, the employees themselves will make sure that their fellow workers avoid accidents. If the tangible award proves desirable to the employees, then peer pressure will occur. If the award is not enticing to them, then no peer pressure will develop.

How To Implement Solution

1. *Analyze accident records.* Find out what sort of accidents tend to occur. Also, do the accidents tend to occur in certain work groups or departments, on specific shifts, or at

a particular time of day? Answering such questions can help pinpoint the type of accident prevention program that employees need.

2. *Determine what awards employees would find desirable.* It would not do an organization any good whatsoever to offer safety inducements that the employees are not enthusiastic about having. Thus, it is necessary to get the information from "the horse's mouth." To gather this information, a survey works very well. First, it allows employees to participate actively in determining the awards that may influence them to act in a safety-conscious way. Second, the very fact that they are asked about *safety and accident prevention* makes them realize that their employer considers such concerns important.

3. *Train employees.* Based on the accident records examination, training needs can be pinpointed. For example, if many accidents involve back injuries, then training in how to avoid such accidents is on the mark. Perhaps many accidents take place on a certain shift. Then, more training seems warranted for employees on that shift. If a large percentage of accidents happens around particular machines, then instruction on how to safely use those machines is in order. In summary, the training should fit the needs of the employees who may cause, or suffer from, workplace accidents.

4. *Award accident-free behavior.* For instance, the accident-prevention program may award work groups each month they are accident-free. The award must be something that the work group members would enjoy or value. The awards could be money, a free meal, merchandise, or whatever else they would enjoy that is within the company's award budget. Take note, however, whether employees stop valuing certain awards after earning them awhile. If that happens, try to change awards *before* they lose their desirability to the employees who could earn them.

Deadline for Implementing Solution

An accident-reduction program can be set in motion within just a few months. This time can be used to examine accident records, determine what awards employees would like, and start the training.

Deadline for Measuring Profit Improvement

Within a year after the program's implementation the company should realize benefits above the costs of the program.

ACCIDENT-REDUCTION PROGRAM

The plant manager of a manufacturing facility became quite concerned with the number and frequency of accidents in his plant that were posing a growing *business problem.* He knew something needed to be done to stem the outflow of money and decreasing employee morale caused by the accidents. The plant manager, along with his human resources manager, plant engineer, and plant nurse, developed a *Planning Model* (see Figure 6-12) for dealing with this problem.

The *cost of the business problem* was $309,810, the average expense of $6,735 per accident for each of the 46 accidents suffered in the plant during the year prior to starting the accident-reduction

Figure 6-12. Planning Model for accident reduction program.

BUSINESS PROBLEM

In a manufacturing plant, accidents among the 500 production employees were becoming an increasingly costly problem.

COST OF BUSINESS PROBLEM

$309,810/year

Cost
= Number of accidents/year × Average cost per accident
= 46 accidents/year × $6,735/accident
= $309,810/year

Note: Accident costs included management and administrative costs, medical care costs, and disability payments

SOLUTION TO BUSINESS PROBLEM

Accident reduction program

COST OF SOLUTION

$43,850

Costs included:

    A. Analyzing accident records
    B. Surveying employees to determine what awards they would find desirable
    C. Training costs
    D. Award costs

A. Analyzing accident records = $500
B. Survey
    = Number of employees × Survey cost per employee
    = 500 employees × $1.50/employee
    = $750
C. Training costs
    = Number of employees trained × Hours of training per employee × Average hourly wages and benefits per employee
    = 500 employees × 2 hours/employee × $14/hour
    = $14,000
D. Award Costs
    = Number of monthly awards given to accident-free work groups during the program's first year × Cost of each award per month
    = 286 monthly awards were earned by work groups × $100/award
    = $28,600

Cost of solution
    = $500 + $750 + $14,000 + $28,600
    = $43,850

$ IMPROVEMENT BENEFIT

$206,070/year

Improvement benefit
    = Annual cost before accident reduction program − Annual cost after start of accident
        reduction program
Annual cost before program = $309,810/year
Cost after program started
    = Number of accidents per year × Average cost per accident
    = 14 accidents/year × $7,410/accident
    = $103,740/year
Improvement benefit
    = $309,810/year − $103,740/year
    = $206,070/year

COST-BENEFIT RATIO

4.7:1

$206,070:$43,850

program. These costs, as calculated by the plant nurse, included management and administrative costs, medical care costs, and disability payments. It did not include the human pain, morale problems, or lowered productivity resulting from the accidents.

Given this rather costly problem, the *solution to the business problem* took the form of an accident-reduction program. The *cost of the solution* was $43,850 during its first year. This cost included analyzing the accident records to spot trends and training needs, surveying production employees to find out what sort of awards they might value, safety training on the problems noted in the accident records examination, and the cost of the awards.

As for the awards, the plant manager decided that each group that went a month without an accident would receive an award worth around five dollars per employee. Since most of the plant's 25 work groups had about 20 employees, the award averaged out to about $100 per work group for each accident-free month. Work groups had a total of 286 months without accidents (25 work groups × 12 months per year = 300 possible award months; deducting the 14 accidents for which work groups received no award = 300 months − 14 months = 286 months).

The awards work groups chose varied. One popular award was for a work group to go out for pizza after work, with the company chipping in five dollars per employee toward the pizza. Other popular awards included vouchers for free food in the plant cafeteria and reductions in the price employees had to pay for the company's products in the plant's retail outlet. One work group even donated its allotted funds one month toward a present for a well-liked employee on her 25th anniversary of working for the company. Importantly, since the employees tended to value the monthly awards they could earn, they acted increasingly vigilant about helping their colleagues prevent accidents. This sort of peer pressure certainly added to the effectiveness of the positive award approach to accident reduction.

And, apparently, the program paid off. Accidents decreased from 46 during the year prior to the accident-reduction program to 14 for the first year the program was in place. Even though the average cost per accident rose (from $6,735 per accident to $7,410 per accident), the total *improvement benefit* wound up at $206,070 per year. This improvement benefit, when compared to the cost of the accident-reduction program offered the company a 4.7:1 *cost-benefit radio,* a handsome payback. In addition to the financial enhancement was the improvement in the employees' quality of work life as a result of the accident-reduction program.

Chapter 7
Measures to Improve Employee
Attitudes and Job Satisfaction

An employee's attitude is an intangible entity that tangibly affects profits. Employees with good attitudes toward work and their organization are more profitable than employees who hold negative attitudes about their endeavors and their employer. Organizations can assess certain employee attitudes and then take action to improve the work environment. In doing so, the organization also can favorably affect both their workers' attitudes and *measurable factors*, such as:

☐ Turnover
☐ Absenteeism
☐ Productivity
☐ Management time spent on attitudinal problems
☐ Inferior workmanship and waste

Four human resources management techniques that can improve employee satisfaction and, at the same time, upgrade the bottom line are the following:

1. Attitude surveys
2. Exit interviews
3. Realistic job previews
4. Reducing employee grievances

This chapter discusses these four techniques.

HOW TO MEASURE TURNOVER

Turnover is a typical and costly result of poor attitudes among employees. That is, employees who hold negative opinions about their work or their employer are more apt to resign or act in such a manner that they get fired than employees who feel more pleased with their work situation. As with any work behavior that is costed out, turnover can be measured in dollars and cents, too. Doing this requires listing the many and varied costs associated with turnover. Three of the human resources management techniques covered in this chapter focus on reducing turnover expenses. These techniques are attitude surveys, exit interviews, and realistic job previews.

Instead of going through the rather lengthy, laborious formula to calculate turnover in each example for these three techniques, the expenses an organization might consider when costing out turnover could be found in *Costing Human Resources* by Wayne Cascio.[1] Some of the main expenses are:

1. Separation costs
   a. Exit interviews
   b. Administrative and record-keeping actions
   c. Separation pay and expenses
2. Replacement costs
   a. Communicating job opening
   b. Preemployment administrative and record-keeping actions
   c. Selection interviews
   d. Tests, psychological assessments of management candidates, or assessment center
   e. Meetings to discuss candidates
3. Training costs
   a. Booklets, manuals, and reports the new employee must become familiar with
   b. Education in workshops, seminars, or courses
   c. One-to-one coaching by an expert while working on the job
   d. Time to get up to par in suitably carrying out job duties

■ ATTITUDE SURVEYS

Business Problems Addressed

Productivity
Turnover, Absenteeism, and Tardiness
Work-Group Effectiveness
Merger, Acquisition, or Reorganization
Labor Relations

Overview of Solution

An attitude survey is a structured method to assess the opinions of employees on matters that affect their job satisfaction and productivity. Most organizations conduct an attitude survey (sometimes called a climate survey or opinion survey) when they sense that problems are brewing. They want to pinpoint the problems and nip them in the bud. Still other companies regularly conduct attitude surveys so that they can keep a finger on the pulse of their employees' opinions. For example, since 1958, International Business

Machines (IBM) has surveyed each of its employees about once every 18 months.[2] By doing so, IBM measures its employees' changing concerns.

Regardless of how often an organization conducts such surveys, the purposes generally center on finding out the following:

☐ Problems employees feel exist
☐ If the organization does well in terms of creating a suitable environment so it can continue what works well
☐ Changes that could make the organization an even better and more productive place to work

Surveys should *only* be conducted if top management is thoroughly committed to (1) informing employees of the results of the survey and (2) actually implementing changes indicated by the survey results. If these two actions do not occur, then employees are apt to perceive the survey as a waste of time. Even worse, if a survey results in no improvements being implemented, then employees are bound to feel somewhat betrayed and even less trusting of the organization's management than they were before the survey.

The survey itself usually consists of two main parts:

1. Questionnaire
2. Individual interviews or group discussion sessions

The questionnaire used generally consists of 50 to 100 items. Items are written so that all employees can read and understand them easily. These items assess how employees feel about factors that affect their job satisfaction and productivity. Some of the factors that a survey might focus on are shown in Figure 7-1. Examples of a factor and the questions that might pertain to that factor appear in Figure 7-2.

Figure 7-1. Factors frequently considered in an attitude survey.

Job satisfaction
Satisfaction with organization
Compensation
Benefits
Career growth and opportunities
Supervision
Collaboration with others
Desire to quit (Turnover)
Quality of work expected
Quantity of work expected
Attitudes of top management
Personnel policies and procedures

Figure 7-2. A factor assessed in an attitude survey along with sample survey items concerning that factor.

Factor: Supervision

Survey Number and Item	1	2	3	4	5
8. My manager helps me when I need help					
14. It's easy to talk with my manager					
26. My manager gives me feedback on how well I'm doing often enough					
34. I receive excellent supervision					
57. It's easy to find my manager when I need to talk with him/her					

Ratings: 1 = Strongly agree
2 = Agree
3 = Neutral/Neither agree nor disagree
4 = Disagree
5 = Strongly disagree

How to Implement Solution

1. *Design survey questionnaire.* Before developing the questionnaire items, it often proves helpful to interview a number of employees at all levels of the organization. Also, employees at all organizational levels must be asked if they can understand and read each item. If the wording is complex or hard to follow, then not all employees will be able to use it to express their opinions. The questionnaire definitely should contain space for employees to write their comments on any matter whatsoever. These written comments sometimes provide more useful information and ideas than the statistical data.

2. *Administer questionnaire.* All employees must be guaranteed confidentiality. Usually, surveys are completed during set times for each department or work group. A common survey will take from 20 to 60 minutes to fill out.

3. *Analyze questionnaire data.* After all survey questionnaires are completed, the statistical data are tabulated, and some preliminary findings could be inferred.

4. *Conduct individual or group interviews.* During these interviews, employees are asked to give specific examples and ideas on factors covered by the questionnaire. If the questionnaire generally provides the bare bones of employees' opinions, the interviews, in effect, put meat on the bones. If individual interviews are conducted, a good rule of thumb is to conduct one-hour interviews with a random sample of about 20 percent of all employees. When group interviews are conducted, about 5 to 10 employees might be in each group. Group interviews generally last from 60 to 90 minutes.

5. *Analyze feedback and plan action.* After all questionnaire data are analyzed and the interviews are completed, the people conducting the attitude survey meet with decision-makers in management. During these meetings, the survey results are presented

and discussed. Then, action plans are devised to (1) overcome at least some of the problems pinpointed by the attitude survey and (2) continue doing whatever the survey indicates works well in the organization.

6. *Follow up actions*. Action planning is not enough. Whatever actions are planned must be turned into reality. Also, all employees in the organization need to be told about the survey's results and the actions that will be taken as a result of the survey findings.

Deadline for Implementing Solution

In a small organization, the attitude survey process (other than carrying out the follow-up actions) can be carried out in a month or less. For larger companies, the process may well take from three to six months.

Deadline for Measuring Profit Improvement

The time frame for measuring profit improvement depends on what problems the survey's follow-up actions address. For example, if the organization wants to reduce turnover, then it may be reasonable to get a good measure of turnover reduction a year after the survey's completion. Some measurable improvements could take less than a year, others could take more.

REDUCING TURNOVER USING AN ATTITUDE SURVEY

The vice-president in charge of an 800-employee data-processing (DP) division at a large corporation faced a *business problem* in one of his key data departments: very high turnover. In fact, this 72-employee department's turnover stood at 43 percent annually, quite a bit more than the 12 percent annual turnover experienced by the rest of this large DP division. As shown in the *Planning Model* in Figure 7-3, the *cost of this problem* stood at nearly half a million dollars a year, because each of the 31 employees who left per year cost the company $15,240.

The *solution* chosen to tackle this business problem was an attitude survey, with follow-up actions taken based on the survey's results. The *cost of the solution* was $8,280. This included costs for the question-naire's development, administration, and data analysis; interviewing 20 percent of the employees in the department; and feedback and action planning.

The survey uncovered a number of problems, one of which included major difficulties with the two supervisors in the department. One of the supervisors proved superb at technical matters but left much to be desired with her interpersonal skills. The other supervisor was practically the opposite: He exhibited great interpersonal skills, but fell behind in his knowledge of the ever-changing technology in his department's aspect of the DP field. Also, the department's manager and supervisors focused so exclusively on the work that needed to be done that they ignored the training needs of the department's many

Figure 7-3. Planning Model for attitude survey to reduce turnover.

BUSINESS PROBLEM

A 72-employee data processing department has 43 percent turnover per year, quite a lot higher than the 12 percent turnover in the remainder of the company's large, 800-employee data processing division.

COST OF BUSINESS PROBLEM

$472,440/year

Cost
= Number of turnovers per year × Cost per turnover
= 31 turnovers/year × $15,240/turnover
= $472,440/year

SOLUTION TO BUSINESS PROBLEM

Attitude survey with follow-up actions

COST OF SOLUTION

$8,280

Costs included:

    A. Questionnaire costs
    B. Interviewing costs
    C. Feedback and action planning costs

A. Questionnaire costs
    = Creating questionnaire + Administering questionnaire + Statistical analysis of questionnaire data
    = $1,000 + (72 employees × 1 hour × $30/hour) + $1,000
    = $1,000 + $2,160 + $1,000
    = $4,160
B. Interviewing costs to interview 20% of employees (16 employees interviewed)
    = Salary and benefits of employees during interview + Consultant's fees while interviewing employees + Salary and benefits of typist who transcribed interview results
    = (16 employees interviewed × 1 hour/interview × $30/hour) + (1 consultant-interviewer × 16 hours of interviews × $90/hour) + (1 typist × 4 hours of typing × $10/hour)
    = $480 + $1,440 + $40
    = $1,960
C. Feedback and action planning costs
    = Average salary and benefits of managers during feedback and action planning + Cost of consultant during feedback and action planning

= (4 managers × 8 hours × $45/hour) + (1 consultant × 8 hours × $90/hour)
= $1,440 + $720
= $2,160

Cost of solution
= $4,160 + $1,960 + $2,160
= $8,280

$ IMPROVEMENT BENEFIT

Improvement benefit
= Cost of problem for the year before attitude survey − Cost of problem a year after attitude survey
Cost before attitude survey = $472,440/year
Cost after attitude survey
= Number of turnovers/year × Cost per turnover
= 10 turnovers/year × $15,240/turnover
= $152,400/year
Improvement benefit
= $472,440 − $152,400
= $320,040

COST-BENEFIT RATIO

38.6:1

$320,040:$8,280

---

programmers and systems analysts. This, too, caused much consternation among the department's staff. Finally, the programmers and systems analysts bristled at working in a crowded atmosphere that lacked any privacy. They wanted their own individual offices or at least high partitions around each desk. They claimed that such physical changes would give them a sense of privacy and professionalism.

The action planning resulted in shake-ups in the department's management. The two supervisors were replaced by senior-level systems analysts. The manager exchanged jobs with another in the DP department. The new manager made sure that the staff received its much needed and wanted training. Also, partitions were placed around each programmer's and systems analyst's desk.

The actions stemming from the attitude survey unquestionably worked. Turnover fell from its previous 43 percent to only 14 percent. This 14 percent turnover rate was very much in line with the 12 percent turnover rate experienced by the rest of the data-processing division. Given this greatly reduced turnover rate, the *improvement benefit* stood at $320,040 annually. That means that the attitude survey and resulting follow-up actions produced a 38.6:1 *cost-benefit ratio.*

■ EXIT INTERVIEWS

Business Problems Addressed

Turnover
Manager and Executive Effectiveness

Overview of Solution

An exit interview is a variation of an attitude survey: It assesses employees' attitudes after they have decided to leave the company. In contrast, a typical attitude survey explores employees' attitudes while they still work for the organization. Exit interviews usually prove most helpful when they uncover causes for turnover. These causes can be many and varied. After employees decide to leave an organization, they often become more open about the concerns that led them to resign.

In general, an exit interview follows a fairly set format, often consisting of the following:

☐ Return of company property by the employee
☐ Explanation of the wages and benefits that the company will pay to the employee after departure
☐ Examination of the reasons the employee is leaving. This part of the interview may vary, depending on whether the separation is a result of resignation, firing, or layoff.

Figure 7-4 shows the exit interview checklist used by Unisys Corporation.

How to Implement Solution

1. *Develop exit interview form.* The form should be short and easy to use. As much as possible, it should elicit quantifiable information.

2. *Conduct exit interviews.* Each exit interview should take from 30 to 60 minutes. In particularly emotionally charged situations, an exit interview can take even longer. The interview should allow the person leaving time to make his or her feelings and reasons for leaving known. If the interview is too structured, then the person leaving may not have freedom to express opinions that could help the organization reduce costly, and perhaps unnecessary, turnover.

3. *Analyze exit interview data and plan follow-up actions.* Here is where the exit interview can help an organization improve. When a complaint is heard repeatedly from departing employees, then the company may want to make some changes. For example, if a large percentage of departing employees cite compensation, career growth, or management practices as their reasons for departing, then the organization may take actions to overcome problems in those areas. On the other hand, it may turn out that employee

Figure 7-4. Exit interview checklist used at Unisys Corporation.

UNISYS CORPORATION
World Headquarters
EXIT INTERVIEW CHECKLIST

EFFECTIVE DATE CURRENT POSITION		CORPORATE UNIT/DEPARTMENT	
FIRST NAME MIDDLE INITIAL LAST NAME	EMPLOYMENT DATE		COST CENTER
CLASSIFICATION TITLE	STATUS: EXEMPT ☐ NON-EXEMPT ☐ HOURLY ☐		

TYPE OF ACTION (SHOULD BE SAME AS CHECKED ON PERSONNEL ACTION NOTICE):

VOLUNTARY QUIT ☐ (COMPLETE ALL REMAINING SECTIONS OF FORM)

RELEASE ☐   DISCHARGE   ☐   RETIREMENT ☐

LAYOFF ☐   LEAVE OF ABSENCE ☐   OTHER (EXPLAIN IN REMARKS SECTION)

☐ **A.   BENEFITS DISCUSSED**
   ● MEDICAL, DENTAL EXTENSIONS—GROUP
   ● LIMITED COVERAGE—INDIVIDUAL

☐ **B.   ELIGIBILITY/ENROLLMENT FORM PRESENTED**
   ● INSTRUCTIONS
   ● EXPLANATORY LETTER
   ● PRICE SHEETS

☐ **C.   BEST FINAL DISTRIBUTION FORM SIGNED**

☐ **D.   CONFIDENTIAL INFORMATION FORM SIGNED**

☐ **E.   PACKAGE INSPECTION INFORMATION DISTRIBUTED**

☐ **F.   RETURN OF COMPANY PROPERTY**
   ● ID CARD
   ● HEALTH ID CARD
   ● AMERICAN EXPRESS CARD/
     BALANCE OUTSTANDING
   ● TELEPHONE CREDIT CARD
   ● KEYS
   ● MANUALS/DOCUMENTS
   ● OFFICE EQUIPMENT: B20, OFISWRITER,
     TYPEWRITTER, ETC.

☐ **G.   UNUSED VACATION DAYS**

☐ **H.   PERSONAL PROFILE RETRIEVED**

☐ **I.   FORWARDING ADDRESS AND PHONE NO.**
   _____
   _____
   _____

INTERVIEWER'S COMMENTS AND EVALUATION OF REASONS FOR TERMINATION:
_____
_____
_____
_____
_____
_____
_____
_____
_____
_____

INTERVIEWER'S NAME/POSITION   DATE OF INTERVIEW

complaints are caused by factors beyond the organization's control, such as prevailing market conditions or economic cycles. In that case, the organization may decide to live with a certain turnover level, since there is no way to change those conditions that foster turnover.

4. *Carry-out action plans.* Implementing action plans affords the organization the opportunity to improve itself and lower its turnover rate.

Deadline for Implementing Solution

An organization can design an exit interview and begin using it within a month.

Deadline for Measuring Profit Improvement

In a year or less after the action plans are put into effect, based on exit interview data, the organization should begin to notice profit improvements. For example, turnover might be pinpointed as a costly problem in the organization. If the exit interviews expose the reasons for turnover, then the company knows what actions are indicated to reduce the unwanted turnover. After beginning these actions, the company can start measuring their effectiveness. Within a year, the cost of the exit interview effort should be more than paid for by the decrease in expensive and bothersome turnover.

EXIT INTERVIEWS IN ACTION

A nationwide engineering firm felt severe financial and business repercussions from the recent 55 percent turnover by its branch office managers. This firm, with its 55 branch offices each headed by a senior engineer, relied heavily on these branch managers to operate a complete profit-and-loss center in their respective cities. The disruptions, lower productivity, and lost billings following each resignation posed a serious *business problem* for the engineering firm. It also proved to be a very costly problem that threatened to shake the foundations of the firm. The *cost of the business problem* was $4.5 million per year. That amount, as shown in the *Planning Model* in Figure 7-5, resulted from the firm's calculations of the cost of each branch office manager turnover and decreased productivity and billing following each resignation.

Figure 7-5. Planning Model for exit interviews used to reduce turnover.

BUSINESS PROBLEM

Sudden 55% turnover by branch office managers of a 55-office engineering firm.

COST OF BUSINESS PROBLEM

$4,500,000

Costs included:

  A. Turnover of branch managers
  B. Lost Productivity and Billings

A. Turnover
    = Number of branch manager resignations × Cost per resignation
    = 30 resignations × $50,000/resignation
    = $1,500,000
B. Lost productivity and billings
    = Number of resignations × Average amount of lower branch office productivity and billings/resignation
    = 30 resignations × $100,000/resignation = $3,000,000

Cost of problem
    = $1,500,000 + $3,000,000
    = $4,500,000

SOLUTION

Conduct exit interviews with former branch managers plus follow-up actions. Uncover the causes of turnover and then reduce those causes, thereby helping to lower turnover.

COST OF SOLUTION

$1,112,200

Costs included:

    A. Developing exit interview
    B. Conducting exit interviews
    C. Analyzing exit interview data and planning follow-up actions
    D. Carrying out action plans

A. Developing exit interviews = $500
B. Conducting exit interviews
    = Number of exit interviews × Cost per exit interview
    = 30 exit interviews with former branch managers × $250/exit interview
    = $7,500
C. Analyzing data and planning follow-up actions
    = Cost of systematizing and analyzing date + One day meeting of one consultant and four company executives
    = $1,000 + ($1,000 + (4 executives × $550/day in salary and benefits))
    = $1,000 + $1,000 + $2,200
    = $4,200
D. Carrying out action plans
    = Total number of branch managers × Extra money used for bonuses for branch managers/year
    = 55 branch managers × $20,000/year
    = $1,100,000/year

(continued)

(Figure 7-5 continued)

Cost of solution
    = \$500 + \$7,500 + \$4,200 + \$1,100,000
    = \$1,112,200

\$ IMPROVEMENT BENEFIT

\$3,750,000

Improvement benefit
    = Cost of problem before exit interviews − Cost of problem a year after exit interviews
Cost of problem before exit interviews = \$4,500,000
Costs of problem after exit interviews included:

A. Turnover
B. Lost productivity & billings

A. Turnover
    = Number of branch manager resignations × Cost/resignation
    = 5 resignations × \$50,000/resignation
    = \$250,000
B. Lost productivity and billings
    = Number of resignations × Average amount of lower branch office productivity and billings/resignation
    = 5 resignations × \$100,000/resignation
    = \$500,000

Costs after exit interviews
    = \$250,000 + \$500,000
    = \$750,000
Improvement benefit
    = \$4,500,000 − \$750,000
    = \$3,750,000

COST-BENEFIT RATIO

3.8:1

\$3,750,000:\$1,112,200

For help, the firm called in a consultant who had expertise in reducing turnover. The consultant determined that an innovative and on-target *solution to the business problem* was to do a variation of the typical exit interview. Usually exit interviews are conducted at the time employees leave an organization. Since the former branch managers had already left the company, the consultant conducted exit interviews of the departed branch managers. He called all 30 former branch managers and interviewed them at length about the reasons they resigned. The consultant also met with the four top executives of the engineering firm to discuss the findings of the exit interviews and plan actions to stem the outflow of valuable and expensive management talent.

All in all, the *cost of the solution* turned out to be $1,112,200. Most of this amount came from the $1.1 million bonus pool the firm needed to set up. The reason: One of the main problems uncovered in the exit interviews was that the former branch managers felt exasperated by the firm's bonus system when they compared it to that of competitors and even to the opportunity of opening up their own firms. Although a $1.1 million dollar bonus pool initially looked like a huge expense, the firm's top executives determined that it was worth the stability that it could bring to the branch manager ranks. Also, it was a lot less than the $4.5 million the firm lost because of the sudden and sizeable turnover. A number of other changes also were made. For instance, one disliked regional manager who proved vastly better at arguing than collaborating was replaced by a calmer and more people-oriented regional manager.

The firm's top executives found that the solutions worked quite well. Over the year after the solutions were in place, turnovers among the branch managers decreased to nine percent, from its previous 55 percent rate. As a result, the total *improvement benefit* amounted to $3.75 million. This improvement resulted in a 3.8:1 *cost-benefit ratio.* In addition to that return on investment, the engineering firm realized a stability in its management ranks that added to its ease of operation and credibility among its corporate customers.

■ REALISTIC JOB PREVIEWS

Business Problem Addressed

Turnover

Overview of Solution

A basic principle of social psychology is that the more a person knows what to expect *before* entering a situation—such as a new job, school, residence, or relationship—the more likely the person will be satisfied after he or she learns the realities of the situation from actual firsthand experience. This principle underlies the proven effectiveness of realistic job previews (RJP). An RJP is given to a potential new employee *before* the person is hired by an organization. The RJP generally gives the applicant a good sense of what to expect on the job.

An RJP involves telling the potential employee about three main work ingredients:

1. *Tasks the person would perform*. The person needs to be told exactly what sort of work the job entails.

2. *Organizational behavior norms*. Here, the applicant finds out what sort of behavior is expected. Some basic behaviors include the pace of work (fast-paced, slow-paced), creativity expected, decision-making procedures, numbers and types of co-workers, and work environment.

3. *Company policies and procedures*. These include compensation and benefits, work hours, and the necessity for overtime and weekend work.

The techniques used can include written descriptions, tours of plants or office facilities, videotape or slide presentations, and question-and-answer sessions.

A good deal of research confirms the effectiveness of RJPs.[3,4] In general, applicants going through an RJP tend to accept the job offered less often than candidates without an RJP. Productivity of employees selected with and without an RJP are virtually the same. However, turnover is lower for employees with the RJP experience, and their job satisfaction is higher. RJPs hold promise for helping to reduce costly and disruptive turnover and improving employee morale.

How to Implement Solution

1. *Interview current and previous employees*. This step focuses on what new employees should know *prior to* beginning to work for the organization. Both current and past employees can give valuable insight into this. They should be asked, "What do you know now about working here that you wish you knew *before* you began working here?"

2. *Analyze interview data*. All the information gathered during the interviews needs to be examined. What ideas were repeated? Which information should potential new employees be told so they find out what it might be like to work in a particular job in this company?

3. *Design RJP*. The RJP should be based on the data gathered during the interviews.

4. *Carry out RJP*. Put the best job candidates through the RJP. Let them find out what it would be like to work in the organization.

Deadline for Implementing Solution

An organization can complete the interviews, data analysis and RJP design in just one to three months. Then, it can begin using the RJP with applicants it seriously considers hiring.

Deadline for Measuring Profit Improvement

Turnover reduction will be a major beneficiary of RJPs. Depending on how many people go through the RJP, the organization can begin measuring turnover reduction six to 12 months after RJP use begins.

USING AN RJP TO REDUCE EXPENSIVE TURNOVER

A restaurant chain suffered from high turnover among its restaurant managers. Specifically, in the past year, 35 of its 85 managers quit.

This high turnover represented a costly *business problem* for this popular chain. In fact, it was costly to the tune of $2,450,000 for the previous year. This *cost of the business problem* included expenses related to turnover and the lowered restaurant profitability that followed each manager's resignation, as profiled in the *Planning Model* in Figure 7-6.

To overcome this costly problem, the company decided on the *solution* of giving RJPs to candidates who survived the chain's typical interviewing and testing process and seemed to possess the potential to do well in the restaurant manager position. The RJP consisted of the company's recruitment director (herself a former restaurant manager) getting together for an entire afternoon and evening with each promising candidate and the candidate's spouse. The spouse was included because the interviews of current and former managers uncovered that a major reason for resignations was the problems created by managers' spouses. So, it was thought that if the spouse went through the RJP, then *both* the candidate and the spouse jointly could decide if the candidate should take the position.

The RJP included a description of the tasks, organizational behavior norms, and the company policies that every restaurant manager needed to follow. The tasks included all the usual duties of a restaurant manager, including the fact that each manager would have to be ready at all times to "roll up his or her shirt sleeves" and do any job in the restaurant. The company policies included discussion of the base salary, bonus program tied to restaurant profitability, insurance, and vacation.

Probably most important, based on comments made during the interviews, was the discussion of the organizational behavior norms. This restaurant *demanded* extreme commitment from all of its managers. For instance, managers were expected to move to a different town at least once every 3 years. These relocations generally needed to be completed on short notice.

Candidates also found out that the work environment could best be described as "workaholic." Sixty-hour work weeks were commonplace for managers. Eighty-hour weeks certainly were not unheard of. Also, since the restaurants' atmosphere was rather upbeat and youthful, the spouse needed to know that the waiters and waitresses tended to be attractive, young, and playful. The spouses of successful candidates needed to accept this fact, since a good number of resignations occurred, in part, due to spouses feeling threatened by the possibility or reality of affairs occurring between the restaurant manager and the waiters or waitresses.

After all this information was told to the candidate and spouse, the couple went with the recruiting director and some other corporate managers (all of them former restaurant managers) to one of the company's local restaurants for dining and socializing. Then, the candidate and spouse were told that they must take seven days to decide

Figure 7-6. Planning Model for using realistic job previews to reduce restaurant manager turnover.

BUSINESS PROBLEM

High turnover by restaurant managers of an 85-restaurant chain

COST OF BUSINESS PROBLEM

$2,450,000/year

Costs included:

  A. Turnover
  B. Lowered profitability per restaurant following each turnover

A. Turnover
    = Number of turnovers/year × Cost per turnover
    = 35 turnovers/year × $40,000/turnover
    = $1,400,000/year
B. Lowered profitability
    = Number of turnovers/year × Average lowered profitability following each turnover
    = 35 turnovers/year × $30,000/turnover
    = $1,050,000/year

Cost of problem
    = $1,400,000/year + $1,050,000/year
    = $2,450,000/year

SOLUTION TO BUSINESS PROBLEM

Giving realistic job previews to promising candidates for the restaurant manager position

COST OF SOLUTION

$91,500

Costs included:

  A. Interviewing current and previous restaurant managers
  B. Analyzing interview data
  C. Designing realistic job preview
  D. Carrying out realistic job previews with promising candidates

A. Interviewing
    = Number of interviews conducted X Cost per interview
    = 100 interviews × $100/interview
    = $10,000

B. Analyzing interview data = $1,000
C. Designing RJP = $2,500
D. Carrying out RJP
    = Number of promising candidates given the RJP × (Interviewers' time + Travel expenses for candidates and spouses)
    = 65 candidates × ($400 + $800)
    = 65 × $1,200
    = $78,000

Cost of solution
    = $10,000 + $1,000 + $2,500 + $78,000
    = $91,500

$ IMPROVEMENT BENEFIT

$1,540,000/year

Improvement benefit
    = Cost of problem before RJP − Cost of problem after implementing RJP
Cost of problem before RJP
    = $2,450,000/year

Costs after implementing RJP included:

A. Turnover
B. Lowered profitability per restaurant following each turnover

A. Turnover
    = Number of turnovers/year × Cost per turnover
    = 13 turnovers/year × $40,000
    = $520,000/year
B. Lowered profitability
    = Number of turnovers/year × Average lowered profitability following each turnover
    = 13 turnovers/year × $30,000/turnover
    = $390,000/year

Cost of problem after implementing RJP
    = $520,000 year + $390,000/year
    = $910,000/year
Improvement benefit
    = $2,450,000/year − $910,000/year
    = $1,540,000/year

COST-BENEFIT RATIO

16.8:1

$1,540,000:$91,500

whether to take the position. This cooling-off period gave the candidate and spouse time to really ponder whether to accept the job offer. Without this time, some candidates grabbed the job too readily, without thoroughly discussing its pros and cons with their spouses. The entire *cost of the solution* for the first 65 candidates going through the RJP was $91,500. These candidates were the pool from which the chain filled restaurant manager positions.

The solution helped the company reduce its costly turnover of restaurant managers. The *improvement benefit* amounted to $1,540,000 per year and a 16.8:1 *cost-benefit ratio*.

■ REDUCING EMPLOYEE GRIEVANCES

Business Problem Addressed

Labor Relations

Overview of Solution

Grievances by employees easily become quite expensive. The time involved adds up very quickly, which costs money in the form of the salaries, benefits, and productivity lost during the grievance process. For example, researchers investigated the amount of time grievances took for members of a union local for one year.[5] They discovered that the union's members went through 500 grievances during the year. These 500 grievances consumed 4,580 hours.

Let us assume that in addition to the 4,580 hours the union members spent on these grievances, union representatives and members of company management also spent similar amounts of time. In total, then, these 500 grievances consumed 13,740 hours of time. Organizations paid the salary and benefits of those involved. The companies against whom the grievances were filed paid the grieving employees and managers for 9,160 hours (4,580 hours for the grieving employees + 4,580 hours for members of company management who responded to the grievances = 9,160 hours). If the salaries and benefits of the employees and managers total around $40 per hour, then these 500 grievances could have cost a company $183,200 in just one year in salaries and benefits. It does not even take into account the productivity lost during the grievance processes.

No company wants to spend money unnecessarily. So, any time grievances can be reduced, the company saves money. Reducing grievances also makes intangible, yet quite real, sense from a labor relations perspective. Specifically, the number of grievances a company has against it is to some degree a gauge of its labor relations atmosphere. Companies with better labor relations climates tend to have less grievances initiated by irritated employees.

In general, reducing grievances requires an analysis of the reasons for grievances. Then, management can decide how to decrease the causes that erupt into grievances. This takes a good deal of commitment on the part of managers and the company, since reducing the cause of certain grievances may require changing the way managers are used to managing. However, the benefits may well outweigh the costs.

How to Implement Solution

1. *Analyze grievance records.* This step entails examining the causes for each grievance. Some common causes revolve around

- □ *Supervisors' behavior.* An old labor relations phrase says: "First-line supervisors are the first line of defense against having problems with employees." This holds true in terms of the causes of grievances. It is not uncommon for employees to file a grievance because of how their supervisors treat them.
- □ *Pay and benefits.* Employees' ire is easily aroused when they suspect they are not receiving 100 percent of the wages and benefits the organization is supposed to provide to them. Such suspicions readily transform into a grievance.
- □ *Following written policies and procedures.* When employees feel that formal policies and procedures have not been followed, they may well resort to filing a grievance to rectify what they perceive as an injustice. Some of the policies and procedures that come under examination include suspensions, discipline, time off, and transfers.

Since the causes of grievances are not the same for each firm, a detailed categorization of grievances is necessary. Also, it helps to see *where* the grieving employees work. For example, do a large percentage of them work in a certain plant department or location? If so, then the solution may lie in improving that area, not the entire company.

2. *Plan action.* After analyzing the grievance records, managers can determine what actions may decrease the causes of the grievances. For example, if grievances occur because supervisors perform work that only production employees should do, then one action planned can be to make sure that supervisors know the boundaries between their work and the work of their subordinates.

3. *Put plans into action.* The company needs a concerted effort to reduce the causes of grievances. Each manager should be involved in reducing grievances in his or her department or work group. While human resources professionals can oversee and advise the grievance reduction actions, it is up to each line manager to make sure the actions actually are carried out. The human resources professionals involved in these endeavors need to provide frequent feedback to managers on how well they do in reducing grievances.

Deadline for Implementing Solution

The analysis of grievance records, action planning, and follow-up actions take three to six months to implement.

Deadline for Measuring Profit Improvement

Measurable improvements should be noticeable within a year or less. It may prove useful to give each manager quantitative feedback on how well his or her department has done at decreasing grievances, as well as how that translates into dollars and cents. Managers who do not measurably decrease grievances among their employees should have their managerial talents deeply scrutinized, especially if the cost involved is substantial and avoidable.

DECREASING GRIEVANCES BY EMPLOYEES

Given the huge costs that employee grievances can cost a company, a hypothetical example sheds light on the costs and benefits of decreasing grievances. To use the information mentioned earlier, let's say that a company decides that its large number of grievances is a *business problem* it cannot afford to ignore. The *cost of the business problem,* as shown in the *Planning Model* in Figure 7-7, stands at $412,200. That takes into account the salaries and benefits of the employees and supervisors involved in the grievances. It also adds in the idea that the value of the employees and supervisors to the company is 125 percent of their salaries and benefits.

Figure 7-7. Planning Model for decreasing employee grievances.

BUSINESS PROBLEM

A company's management sees that the grievances filed by employees costs the company a lot in financial terms, as well as in terms of the firm's labor relations climate.

COST OF BUSINESS PROBLEM

$412,200/year

Costs included:

    A. Time of grieving employees
    B. Time of supervisors handling grievances
    C. Lost productivity due to time spent on grievances

A. Employees' time
    = Number of hours employees spent in grievance procedures in a year $\times$ Average wages and benefits of employees during grievance procedures
    = $4,580 hours/year $\times$ $15/hour
    = $68,700/year
B. Supervisors' time
    = Number of hours supervisors spent in grievance procedures in a year $\times$ Average salaries and benefits of supervisors during grievance procedures
    = 4,580 hours/year $\times$ $25/hour
    = $114,500/year
C. Lost productivity
    = 125% of value of employees' time + supervisors' time
    = 1.25 $\times$ ($68,700/year + $114,500/year)
    = 1.25 $\times$ $183,200/year
    = $229,000/year

Cost of problem
   = $68,700/year + $114,500/year + $229,000/year
   = $412,200/year

SOLUTION TO BUSINESS PROBLEM

Planned grievance reduction procedure

COST OF SOLUTION

$58,000 for first year

Costs included:

   A. Analyzing grievance records
   B. Action planning how to reduce grievances
   C. Carrying out action plans

A. Analyzing grievance records
   = Number of human resources professionals examining grievance records × Number
     of hours spent × Hourly salary and benefits of the professionals
   = 1 professional × 40 hours × $25/hour
   = $1,000
B. Action planning
   = Number of managers involved in action planning for grievance reduction × Hours
     spent by each manager in planning meetings × Average salary and benefits per
     hour
   = 25 managers × 4 hours/manager × $30/hour
   = $3,000
C. Carrying out action plans
     Number of grievance reduction meetings held in one year × Number of management
       personnel in meetings × Average length of each meeting × Average salary and
       benefits of management personnel in meetings
   = 12 meetings/year × 100 management personnel × 1.5 hours/meeting × $30/hour
   = $54,000/year

Cost of solution
   = $1,000 + $3,000 + $54,000
   = $58,000 for one year

$ IMPROVEMENT BENEFIT

$206,100/year

Improvement benefit
   = Cost of problem for the year before grievance reduction efforts − Cost of problem
     after one year of grievance reduction efforts

(continued)

(Figure 7-7 continued)

Cost of problem before efforts
 = $412,200/year
Costs of problem after a year of grievance reduction efforts included:

A. Employees' time
B. Supervisors' time
C. Lost productivity

A 50% reduction in each of these costs means that the grievance reduction efforts brought
 the expense of the problem down to $206,100/year
Improvement benefit
 = $412,200/year − $206,100/year
 = $206,100/year

COST-BENEFIT RATIO

3.6:1

$206,100:$58,000

The company decides that the needed *solution to the business problem* is a well-planned grievance-reduction effort. Taking into account the time and money spent (1) analyzing grievance records, (2) planning how to lessen the number and cost of grievances, and (3) carrying out the action plans, the *cost of the solution* turns out to be $58,000 for the first year. The company might decide that a good action plan includes monthly meetings for 100 of its management personnel to review the causes and cures of grievances against the company. Also, specific grievances brought against the company could be discussed in an effort to make all the management personnel realize that they are in this effort together.

Let's say that the endeavor pays off by reducing the cost of grievances by 50 percent over the next year. That means that the cost of the problem drops by half. The *improvement benefit* is $206,100 annually. Since the cost of the solution for that year is $58,000 and the improvement benefit is $206,100 in fewer grievance costs, the company could enjoy a 3.6:1 *cost-benefit ratio* for its grievance-reduction efforts. While that is a respectable return on investment, the company also gains in at least one other big way. By reducing the number of grievances, the organization also probably improves the company's employee relations environment. That could catalyze more job satisfaction and commitment by employees and an easier-to-manage workplace for the company.

Chapter 8
Work-Group Effectiveness Techniques

A lot of money can be made—or lost—in work-group effectiveness. Here, the term "work group" refers to any group of employees who need to collaborate to complete work. A work group could be a production team, the executive officers of an organization, or people who work in the same department. Since most work is accomplished through a number of people cooperating, improving work-group productivity readily adds directly to the bottom line. Human resources professionals have at their fingertips a number of ways to improve work-group effectiveness. These methods include:

☐ Teambuilding
☐ Quality circles and productivity improvement groups

These techniques are discussed in this chapter, along with case examples of implementing the *Planning Model* to strengthen organizational profitability. The cost of the problem section of the *Planning Model* is different for teambuilding, quality circles, and productivity improvement groups than for most other techniques. Specifically, the cost of the problem usually ends up being not applicable (N/A), because such work-group effectiveness techniques tend to take advantage of potential opportunities to enhance work-group effectiveness, and thus the bottom line, rather than targeting specific problems whose costs are readily calculated.

■ TEAMBUILDING

Business Problems Addressed

Productivity
Work-Group Effectiveness

Interdepartmental Collaboration
Manager and Executive Effectiveness
Merger, Acquisition, or Reorganization

Overview of Solution

Teambuilding sessions prove useful when people who need to collaborate are not doing so as well as they could.[1] Such less-than-optimal teamwork thwarts accomplishing work in the most economical and efficient manner. Why does this occur? Because group difficulties and interpersonal problems stand in the way of the work-group's effectiveness.

For this reason, a valuable teambuilding session must delve into both group problems and interpersonal problems existing in the work group. The teambuilding session usually lasts one full day. Sometimes half-day followup sessions are needed. Participants should include all the people who need to collaborate but are not doing that as well as possible. The session generally accomplishes the most when it is held off site, away from the organization. Good locations include meeting rooms at local hotels or conference centers. Participants should be encouraged to dress informally to break down some of the power barriers associated with work attire.

Teambuilding sessions work best when they are conducted by an outside teambuilding expert, because the teambuilding session explores a lot of interaction and interpersonal behavior of the participants. If a member of the work group leads the session, then many of these behaviors may not be noticed, brought up, or openly discussed. Teambuilding is *not* group psychotherapy. However, it *does* confront personal and interpersonal concerns that are best facilitated by an *expert* in such matters rather than just a well-meaning trainer or manager who is not highly skilled at running intense teambuilding sessions.

Here is an outline for a well-run teambuilding session:

Step 1: The group identifies its top four *group problems* that, if overcome, would enable the group to collaborate more productively. (*Note:* The group delineates these problems during this step. It does not solve them until Step 3.)

Step 2: The group then confronts overcoming the *interpersonal problems* that hamper its effectiveness. This *must* be done in a very nonthreatening way. One method to do this is to have each participant give every other participant two types of feedback using this sort of phrasing: "When I deal with you, I like that you [fill-in compliment or positive feedback]" and "When I deal with you, I wish that you would [fill-in helpful suggestion]."

For example, one participant may say to another participant, "When I deal with you, I like that you are so organized and respect my time. When I deal with you, I wish that you would talk in a softer voice and compliment my performance more often."

It is important to note that the second feedback comment was stated in a positive, suggestion-oriented way, rather than as a criticism. Between the lines, the person might have been saying, "You scream like a maniac, and all you ever do is criticize. Why don't you act pleasant and say something nice for a change?" However, if the participant would have stated his or her between-the-lines thoughts, the person receiving the feedback just would have felt attacked and defensive. That is why *insisting* that participants use nonthreatening feedback language proves so very crucial.

Step 3: The team solves its four biggest *group problems* that it delineated during Step 1. This problem solving is done as a group so that the participants experience working as a *team* that collaborates. The problem solving needs to entail developing action plans, including timetables to complete each action step.

How to Implement Solution

1. *Hold teambuilding session.* As mentioned in the Overview of Solution, the session should last one full day, usually from 9 A.M. until 5 P.M. It should be held off site.

2. *Carry out action plans during teambuilding session.* These collaboratively developed action plans will lead to the work group overcoming the problems it had as a group that kept it from operating well.

Deadline for Implementing Solution

Usually a teambuilding session can be scheduled and conducted within one month.

Deadline for Measuring Profit Improvement

This timeframe depends on what sort of action plans the teambuilding participants develop. If the action plans do not include any activities that would result in profit improvement, then no such measures can be taken. However, if the action plans include items that could result in profit improvement, then such bottom line increases can be measured after those actions are carried out. For instance, a group of managers might come up with a way to train employees better so they can perform more productively. *After* the training and the improved performance get put into action, then productivity improvement measurements can be taken. Then the group can convert these improvements into dollars and cents.

Or, if the team decides to reorganize how it completes its work, then profit improvement measurements are appropriate *after* the work group implements such actions. In both instances, the profit improvement measurement depends on the actions taken by the group, since teambuilding sessions are a technique that results in action planning. However, teambuilding is not solely a profit improvement activity in and of itself.

PROFIT IMPROVEMENT THROUGH TEAMBUILDING

A major *business problem* confronted a $10 million printing company. Specifically, for a number of years, the company enjoyed a profitable market niche doing a particular type of specialty printing. Then, other printing companies caught onto this great moneymaking specialty and began encroaching on the company's market. Within five years, the company's profit margins had shrunk tremendously.

Because of these factors, the company confronted the need to increase profits in an increasingly competitive market niche. Equipment was not the problem, since the company's production lines used the latest models of efficient, high-speed printing and binding equipment. Office and administrative work was computerized. Workforce quality also was not the problem. Indeed, most employees were highly experienced in their jobs and had worked for the company for over 10 years.

Furthermore, the way to increased profits was not in improving workers' motivation, since the workforce exhibited good morale and an admirable work ethic. In fact, the employees never felt a need for a union, although most competing firms in their region were unionized.

Since the company's goal was to improve profits, there was no actual *cost of the problem,* as indicated in the *Planning Model* exhibited in Figure 8-1. The firm's president and its human resources director discussed the business problem and possible human resources-oriented solutions. They decided to try a one-day teambuilding session as the *solution to the problem,* because the two of them wondered whether the department heads could collaborate better or differently in order to improve company profits.

Figure 8-1. Planning Model for using teambuilding to improve profits.

BUSINESS PROBLEM

A printing company wants to produce more profits in its increasingly competitive market

COST OF THE PROBLEM

?

No specific cost, since the company's goal is to improve profitability and not to overcome a specific problem in the usual sense.

SOLUTION TO BUSINESS PROBLEM

1-day teambuilding session

Participants included the company president and all 10 department heads. An outside teambuilding expert conducted the session.

COST OF SOLUTION

$4,650

Costs included:

  A. Participants' daily salary and benefits
  B. Teambuilding consultant's daily fee
  C. Hotel, meals and refreshments costs during teambuilding session

A. Participants' daily salary and benefits
   = Number of participants × Average daily salaries and benefits
   = 11 participants × $300/day
   = $3,300

B. Consultant's fee = $1,000
C. Hotel, meals and refreshments
   = $350

Cost of solution
   = $3,300 + $1,000 + $350
   = $4,650

$ IMPROVEMENT BENEFIT

$520,000/year in increased sales
or
$130,000/year in increased profits

Improvement in sales
   = Amount of increased sales per week × Number of weeks per year
   = $10,000/week × 52 weeks/year
   = $520,000/year in increased sales
Improvement in profits
   = Amount of improvement in sales per year × Percentage of sales that is profit
   = $520,000/year × 25% = $520,000/year × .25
   = $130,000/year in increased profits

COST-BENEFIT RATIO

112:1 for increased sales
$520,000: $4,650 for increased sales
or
28:1 for increased profits
$130,000: $4,650 for increased profits

The teambuilding session was conducted by a management psychologist with expertise in teambuilding. The day-long session was held in a meeting room at a local hotel. Participants included the company president, along with all 10 department heads.

The president kicked off the session by saying that its purpose was for the assembled company managers to figure out ways to work better together in such a way that the company could *measurably* better its profit picture. After this introduction, the consultant led the group through three main steps:

1. Identifying the group's four primary problems as a group that, if surmounted, would help the group perform better
2. Letting each participant give feedback and suggestions to each

other participant on their positive points and their interpersonal areas needing improvement

3. Planning how to overcome each of the top four group problems the team identified in the beginning of the session

The *cost of the solution* was $4,650 for the one-day teambuilding session. This cost included the salaries and benefits of the company president along with the 10 department heads, the management psychologists' fee, plus the cost of the meeting facilities, meals, and refreshments.

A fascinating—and ultimately quite profitable—phenomenon occurred during the second step of the session. It ended up that the sales director and production director typically did not communicate very well. The sales director thought the production director acted annoyingly detail-oriented and took too long to get needed answers. The production director felt the sales director was too pushy and loud. Because of these *interpersonal* problems, the two of them conversed as little as possible at the company.

While discussing this interaction difficulty and its effect on their work, the sales director suddenly gasped, "Oh, my goodness!! I had no idea that the equipment could print materials two inches longer and bind printing three inches wider than we normally do now. We've been turning down at least $10,000 a week in orders for exactly that kind of extra-long and extra-wide printing!"

The company could take in orders for at least $520,000 per year if it just produced this very long and wide printing. That was the *improvement benefit* in terms of sales. Since so few other printing companies printed such specifications, the profit margin on that sort of printing was 25 percent or more. So, the over half million dollars in increased sales translated into a least $130,000 per year in added profits for the company.

Indeed, the first action this group decided to take after the teambuilding session was to begin accepting orders immediately for the extra-long and extra-wide printing. An interesting sidelight to this situation is that this same 11-person group met each and every Friday morning for a weekly management meeting. During all of these meetings, this problem had never come up. Without the teambuilding session, it may never have arisen. If that had happened, then the firm never would have been able to take profitable action in overcoming this readily solvable buisness problem.

In terms of the *cost-benefit ratio,* this teambuilding session turned out to be a huge success. The $4,650 investment made to conduct the session annually produced $520,000 in new sales plus $130,000 in new profits. These financial improvements could be repeated year after year. The $4,650 investment could pay for itself 112:1 for increased sales or 28:1 for increased profits during just the first year after the teambuilding session. Given that these improvements would be repeated for a number of years, the cost-benefit ratio over a longer period of time would be even more extraordinary.

■ QUALITY CIRCLES

Business Problems Addressed

Productivity
Work-Group Effectiveness

Overview of Solution

A quality circle (QC) is a group of 5 to 10 employees who meet weekly to pinpoint, investigate, and solve quality and productivity problems encountered in their work.[2,3] QCs also are referred to as productivity improvement groups because of their keen focus on enhancing productivity. Members of each quality circle generally come from the same work group or department. The leader is the work-group's supervisor or a senior-level employee who is just a step below being a supervisor. A QC facilitator customarily heads up all of an organization's QC undertaking. This person often comes from the human resources department, although sometimes the facilitator works in the production or quality assurance departments. The facilitator spends part of his or her work hours on QC matters, in addition to the facilitator's regular job duties. In organizations with a great many QCs, the facilitator's job can be a full-time position.

The overseer of an organization's QC efforts is its steering committee, a sort of board of directors of the QCs. The steering committee is composed of executives or department heads in the organization who meet once every two months to listen to each QC leader deliver a presentation on what his or her QC accomplished and how their projects are progressing. Since steering committee members hold high posts in the organization, they tend to have a vested interest in making sure that quality circles in their departments succeed. So, they often help reduce red tape that may stand in the way of implementing solutions that the QCs devised. Figure 8-2 diagrams a typical QC organization.

To ensure that QCs focus on profit improvement, they must be directed to do precisely that. Without such direction, QCs almost invariably tend to meander off into tackling unmeasurable projects, such as "communications problems," rather than profitability enhancement projects. During their weekly, hour-long meetings, QCs typically should follow a rather structured set of steps, shown in Figure 8-3. This may sound rather rigid. However, when a QC ignores these structured steps, it tends to get sidetracked, wasting valuable time and effort.

The leader of each QC plays a crucial role. The leader does *not* tell QC members what to do or what solution the QC should follow. Instead, the leader expedites and promotes open discussion and creative, analytical thinking. While doing so, the leader acts more like a discussion leader than a boss. Important groundrules for a QC leader's behavior appear in Figure 8-4.

How to Implement Solution

1. *Obtain top management commitment.* QC efforts inevitably fail when they do not first have the blessing of top management.

Figure 8-2. Typical quality circle organization.

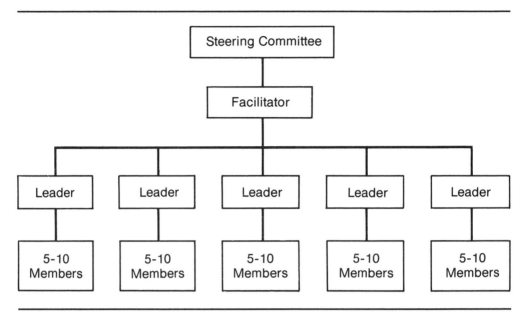

2. *Form steering committee.* This committee contains members of top management. All committee members should have one or more QCs in their department or division, so they feel *personally responsible* for making sure that their QCs succeed in a big way.

3. *Choose facilitator to train and guide QCs.* The facilitator needs a tremendous amount of skill in both training and persuading. This person must train the QC leaders. Also, since QCs do not possess any formal organizational authority, the facilitator must be a master at diplomatically influencing people over whom he or she has no control to support and help the QC efforts. Because most QC facilitators spend only part of their work time on QC activities, the person must do well at time management so that all their QC and other duties can be accomplished.

4. *Train QC leaders.* In general, steering committee members should choose many or most of the QC leaders. The facilitator trains each leader in the principles and methods used by successful QCs.

5. *Hold QC meetings.* Each QC needs to meet once per week, usually for *exactly* one hour. The meetings occur during the participants' normal work hours. They are paid their usual wages while attending QC meetings.

6. *Hold steering committee meetings.* The steering committee needs to meet about every two months. At every meeting, all QC leaders report on the projects their QCs completed and have in-progress. The cost-benefits of each project must be presented, so the steering committee knows the sort of profit improvements produced by their organization's QC endeavors. Any QC that does not manifest profit improvements for the organization probably should be disbanded by the steering committee.

Figure 8-3. Structured steps used by successful quality circles.

Steps Followed by Successful QC	Tactics Used
1. Orient QC members to QC history and purpose	Lecture Discussion Questions and answers
2. Choose QC's broad objective	Brainstorming
3. Generate list of problems related to broad objective	Brainstorming
4. Choose 2–6 problems to solve	Determine best possible cost-benefits and time involved to solve problems
5. Analyze each problem	Determine problem's exact costs Cause-and-effect analysis
6. Create solutions to problems	Brainstorming
7. Choose solutions to use	Review alternatives generated during previous step Determine cost-benefits
8. Obtain approvals needed to implement chosen solutions	Talk with affected staff Use steering committee members' influence
9. Implement solutions	Assign solution implementation to QC member
10. Evaluate implemented solutions' cost-benefits	Assign data gathering to QC member Calculate actual cost-benefits

Figure 8-4. Guidelines followed by successful quality circle leaders.

The effective QC leader:

- Acts enthusiastic—a work-focused cheerleader
- Leads group problem-solving discussions, but does not himself/herself solve problems nor tell the QC what to do
- Follows an agenda—*always*
- Goes by the book at all times, that is, follows each step used by successful QCs—does not skip steps or take shortcuts in problem pinpointing, investigating, and solving; implementing solutions; and evaluating
- Starts and ends every meeting on time

Deadline for Implementing Solution

It takes three to six months to acquire top management support, form a dedicated steering committee, choose a facilitator and leaders, train the leaders, and enroll QC members.

Deadline for Measuring Profit Improvement

QCs should begin producing profit improvements within six months after they start operating. Before that, QCs often need to spend time learning how to function smoothly. Also, new QCs sometimes go on one or two wild goose chases in terms of projects they tackle. It takes awhile for QCs to learn which projects will deliver profit improvements and which will prove too time-consuming to complete or too hard to measure in dollars and cents.

QUALITY CIRCLES ENHANCE CORPORATE PROFITABILITY

The data processing division of a Fortune 100 company decided that it wanted to improve its productivity and encourage creative problem solving. The main *business problem* addressed by this organization focused on how to increase white-collar productivity, specifically the productivity of its computer programmers and systems analysts. Since this business problem zeroed in on potential profit improvement, rather than an ongoing costly problem, no dollars can be attributed to the *cost of the problem*. Figure 8-5 shows the *Planning Model* used to handle this situation.

Figure 8-5. Planning Model for quality circles to improve productivity.

BUSINESS PROBLEM

The data processing division of a major corporation wanted to improve productivity among its professional staff.

COST OF BUSINESS PROBLEM

N/A

Since this problem actually grasped an opportunity, rather than solved a exact problem, a precise cost for the business problem cannot be given.

SOLUTION TO BUSINESS PROBLEM

Set up quality circles in a number of computer programming departments

COST OF SOLUTION

$48,724 for first year of QCs

Costs included:

    A. Training quality circle leaders
    B. Salaries and benefits of quality circle members' participation in quality circles
    C. Salary and benefits of facilitator
    D. Salary and benefits of executives involved in steering committee meetings

A. Training
    = (Number of QC leaders trained × Average hourly salaries and benefits of QC leaders × Number of hours of training) + (Number of QC facilitators providing training × Average hourly salaries and benefits of QC facilitators × Number of hours of training)
    = (5 QC leaders × $25/hour × 14 hours) + (1 QC facilitator × $30/hour × 14 hours)
    = $1,750 + $420 = $2,170
B. Member costs
    = Average number of members on each QC × Average hourly salaries and benefits of members × Number of 1-hour QC meetings per year × Number of QCs
    = 7 employees/QC × $25/employee × 45 QC meetings/year × 5 QCs − $39,375/year
C. Facilitator costs
    = Number of QC facilitators × Average number of hours spent on QC activities per week × Average salaries and benefits × Number of weeks worked per year
    = 1 facilitator × 2.5 hours/week × $30/hour × 50 weeks/year
    = $3,750/year
D. Steering committee costs
    = ([Number of members on steering committee × Average hourly salaries and benefits of members] + [Number of QC leaders attending each steering committee meeting × Average hourly salaries and benefits of QC leaders] + [Number of QC facilitators attending each steering committee meeting × Average hourly salaries and benefits of QC facilitator]) × Number of steering committee meetings per year × Hours of each steering committee meeting
    = ([6 members × $56/hour] + [5 leaders × $25/hour] + [1 facilitator × $30/hour]) × 6 steering committee meetings/year × 1.5 hours/meeting
    = ($336 + $125 + $30) × 6 meetings/year × 1.5 hours/meeting
    = $491 × 6 meetings/year × 1.5 hours/meeting
    = $4,419/year

Cost of solution
    = $2,170 + $39,375 + $3,750 + $4,419
    = $49,714 for first year of QCs

$ IMPROVEMENT BENEFIT

$326,000 for first year

(continued)

(Figure 8-5 continued)

COST-BENEFIT RATIO

6.6:1

$326,000:$49,714

The chosen *solution to the business problem* was to set up five quality circles. The steering committee consisted of the directors of each of the six large departments within the division. The division's training manager acted as the facilitator. He was a member of the human resources department staff. Leaders either were supervisors or employees whom steering committee members considered promotable to supervisory positions within the next year.

The facilitator trained the leaders. Then, each leader solicited employees within his or her department to volunteer to participate on the department's quality circle. Each leader received requests to join from two to three times the number of people who could belong to each QC, so they could pick and choose QC members. Each circle met one hour per week during 45 weeks over the next year.

The *cost of the solution* was $49,714 for the first year that the QCs operated in the organization. This figure consisted mainly of the salaries and benefits of employees involved in the QC endeavors as QC leaders, QC members, steering committee members, and the facilitator.

The QCs were told that they *absolutely* needed to focus on cost-benefits. They also received word that any QC that did not more than pay for itself after six months would be disbanded. These directives painted a clear, profit improvement-oriented picture for the QCs. They responded well. Each QC began showing favorable cost-benefits within three to six months after it started operating. The projects they undertook included helping staff produce more in less time; decreasing the amount of printing expenses incurred in the data processing division; enhancing machine speed; devising a new, billable computer service; and even decreasing furniture and maintenance costs.

All of this creative thinking and group problem solving paid off. It produced a $326,000 *improvement benefit* in savings and profit enhancements during the first year of the QCs, amounting to a 6.6:1 *cost-benefit ratio*. However, the payback was not the only benefit that the organization gained from its QCs. A few other benefits included:

☐ QC leader positions turned out to be superb experience for moving into supervisory positions. A number of QC leaders received such promotions, largely as a result of their QC leadership roles.
☐ Members learned to start and end meetings on time, even when

attending non-QC meetings. This noticeably improved the quality and efficiency of meetings held in the division.

☐ Participants learned pragmatic teamwork and group problem-solving techniques that they continued to use on the job when they were away from their QCs.

☐ QC members and leaders learned the importance of keeping their eyes clearly focused on corporate profit improvement. This was in sharp contrast to their usual focus on providing professional services without noticing their impact on the bottom line.

Chapter 9
Strategies for Human Resources Planning, Layoffs, and Outplacement

One of the most difficult human resources specialties to link directly to corporate profit improvement is human resources planning (HRP). It is much easier to manage compensation and group effectiveness to wind up with measurable profit improvement. Nevertheless, HRP plays an important role in carrying out an organization's business plans. After all, people have to implement business plans. So, having the right people with the right skills in the right positions definitely helps accomplish the business' short-term and long-term goals. Most companies spend little effort deciding whether HRP endeavors actually add to the bottom line. Three ways, discussed in this chapter, in which HRP can add to profitability are:

1. Improving management succession
2. Effecting layoffs and reducing management positions
3. Starting in-house outplacement services

■ IMPROVING MANAGEMENT SUCCESSION

Business Problems Addressed

Turnover
Manager and Executive Effectiveness

Overview of Solution

Most organizations need more top caliber managers and executives. A major step toward achieving this goal is management succession planning. On-target succession plans help a company pinpoint and develop management talent from within its own ranks.[1]

Without such planning, changes in management positions easily can disrupt an organization with lower productivity, turnover, and shattered morale, resulting in lower profitability.

Management succession planning generally entails meetings of the company's senior management, as well as managers one to three levels below the top executives. Each of these executives needs to carefully examine the organization's annual and long-term business goals. Given these goals, each manager must decide what positions or jobs are needed to accomplish the organizations business goals. Then, after drawing up their organizational charts for the upcoming one to three years, the managers decide:

- ☐ Which management positions are needed to accomplish the business goals
- ☐ Who is best qualified to serve in each position
- ☐ Which employees could be replacements for each manager, over the next year, as well as up to three years in the future
- ☐ What sort of on-the-job development and formal training does each manager and potential replacement need in order to do a good job now and in the future
- ☐ Who are high potential employees who possess the capability to move into senior management posts

Figure 9-1 portrays the management succession planning process (called Management Continuity Review) at Rexnord, Inc.

After detailing the plan, each manager must take personal responsibility for putting these plans into action. While human resources professionals should play key roles in organizing and helping with succession planning, such planning is *not* and cannot purely be a human resources department program. Instead, managers in every department in the company must create and follow through on their succession plans. To make sure this happens, top management is wise to insist that each manager have his or her performance appraisal partly based on how well the manager created and implemented management succession plans. By doing so, all managers realize that attaining their succession plans bears a direct relationship to their stature and future compensation in the organization. When managers consistently focus on putting their plans into action, then the organization benefits by having smooth and orderly transitions in its management ranks. It also helps ensure that employees with high potential receive the developmental experiences they need to put their management potential to the test.

How to Implement Solution

1. *Obtain top management commitment*. Unless senior level managers accept the entire succession planning process, it is not worth even trying to start. After all, succession planning is a management technique for *all* managers, not just human resources managers. The top executives need to use succession planning devoutly. By doing so, they set the tone for how important such planning is, both to the organization and each manager's career.

2. *Devise management succession planning procedures*. This responsibility usually falls into the human resources department's realm. Larger organizations often have one or more human resources professionals who specialize in management planning and devel-

Figure 9-1. Diagram of Rexnord's Management Continuity Review Program.

People are the key to any successful organization and, it is sound management practice to anticipate and plan for organizational changes. Planning for other management activities is accepted practice; acquisitions, financial forecasts, profit planning, introducing new products, and the like. The same rationale and planning should apply to the management of human resources, hence, the importance of succession planning. The practical advantages of a meaningful succession plan are obvious: growth, continuity, productivity, and profits. Rexnord's ability to maintain continuity of excellent management is an essential determinant of future success.

Introduction

The Management Continuity Review (MCR) program is an important management planning tool for supporting the strategic and operating objectives of the business. It is a process designed to protect and feed the "Management Resource Health" of Rexnord. It reflects the status of our management "bench," and it provides a medium for describing the quality and performance of managers, designating high-potential individuals, and establishing management development plans and priorities. Ultimately, the purpose of the system is to assure the optimal utilization of management resources so that Rexnord has the right numbers and kinds of managers/professionals, possessing the right level of skills, in the right positions, at the right times.

Purpose

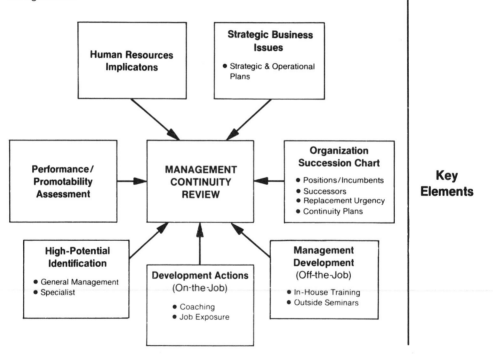

Key Elements

opment. Organizations without such a staff member frequently use the training manager or the human resources director to devise the succession planning process.

3. *Carry out the succession planning process.* This usually involves four steps:

☐ Distributing the succession planning procedures to each manager who needs to devise such plans

☐ Training and consulting with each manager who might need help to carry out the plans

☐ Having top management for the company and each division review each managers' succession plans, and either approve or alter the plans

☐ Using the succession plans in each department, division, and corporate headquarters

Deadline for Implementing Solution

It takes about three to six months to receive top management approval, generate succession planning guidelines, and have managers create succession plans that link up with business goals. After that, it is important to monitor the use of these plans to make sure managers carry them out. Such monitoring is an ongoing process.

Deadline for Measuring Profit Improvement

How long it takes to measure profit improvement depends on what *measurable* problems the succession plans address. If one intent is to reduce turnover among newly promoted managers or decrease the profitability lost caused by promoting mediocre managers, then such profit improvement measures can be taken about a year after the management succession plans are implemented.

IMPROVING MANAGEMENT SUCCESSION'S IMPACT ON THE BOTTOM LINE

A 20,000-employee corporation, a leader in the transportation industry, never used to pay more than lip service to management succession planning. Each year, the company's executives laid out the basic scenarios they would use to make sure that the company's management succession proceeded calmly. However, shortly after this exercise, the executives promptly would toss their so-called succession plans into a file folder or the round file, never to be seen again.

After a while, this sort of succession planning affected the company's bottom line. It accounted, in part, for the ouster of the firm's chairman and president, along with some other key executives. The new regime included a much more planning-oriented chief executive, along with a progressive new vice president of human resources. The human resources executive surveyed the personnel aspects of the company's problems. He uncovered the fact that the company's lackadaisical management succession planning process actually had harmed the company quite a bit over the past year.

He noted that *business problems* erupted because quite a few promotions were given to mediocre managers and a good number of the promoted managers used their promotions as stepping stones to executive positions in other companies. He calculated that the poor performance and turnover expenses, as displayed in the *Planning Model,* Figure 9-2, resulted in the company absorbing $16,375,000 for the previous year as the *cost of the business problem.*

Figure 9-2. Planning Model to improve management succession planning.

BUSINESS PROBLEM

A company's lackadaisical management succession planning produces too many replacements for management positions who prove (1) less-than-satisfactory in their managerial roles or (2) leave the company within one year of being promoted.

COST OF BUSINESS PROBLEM

$16,375,000/year

Costs included:

    A. Estimated lower profits due to mediocre performance by inexperienced managers
    B. Turnover expenses

A. Lower profits
    = Number of mediocre, inexperienced managers × Estimated average annual amount their departments' profits are less (and/or costs are higher) than under their predecessors
    = 85 managers × $175,000/year
    = $14,875,000/year
B. Turnover expenses
    = Number of managers who resigned less than one year after being promoted × Average turnover cost per manager
    = 30 managers/year × $50,000/manager
    = $1,500,000/year

Cost of problem
    = $14,875,000/year + $1,500,000/year
    = $16,375,000/year

SOLUTION TO BUSINESS PROBLEM

Improving the management succession planning process by making it an integral part of the annual and long-term business planning procedures

COST OF SOLUTION

$640,000/year

Costs included:

    A. Management succession planning meetings
    B. Management planning specialist

A. Meetings
    = Number of managers involved in management succession planning meetings ×

Average number of days each manager spent in such meetings × Average daily salaries and benefits of these managers
= 350 managers × 4 days/year × $400/day
= $560,000/year

B. Specialist
= Specialist's annual salary and benefits
= $80,000/year

Cost of solution
= $560,000/year + $80,000/year
= $640,000/year

$ IMPROVEMENT BENEFIT

$7,775,000/year

Improvement benefit
= Cost of problem before solution was implemented − Cost of problem after solution was implemented
Cost before implementing solution = $16,375,000/year
Costs after implementing solution included:

A. Estimated lower profits due to less-than-satisfactory performance by newly promoted managers
B. Turnover expenses

A. Lower profits
= Number of less-than-satisfactory, newly promoted managers × Estimated average annual amount their departments' profits are less (and/or costs are higher) than under their predecessors
= 35 managers × $195,000/year
= $6,825,000/year
B. Turnover expenses
= Number of managers who resigned less than one year after being promoted × Average turnover cost per manager
= 19 managers/year × $50,000/manager
= $950,000/year

Cost after implementing solution
= $6,825,000/year + $950,000/year
= $7,775,000/year
Improvement benefit
= $16,375,000/year − $7,775,000/year
= $8,600,000/year

COST-BENEFIT RATIO

13.4:1

$8,600,000:$640,000

The human resources executive determined that a better, more business-focused management succession planning process would prove worthwhile to the company both in terms of day-to-day management, as well as by cutting down some of the expensive problems catalyzed by poor management succession. To coordinate the succession efforts, he hired a management planning specialist, an industrial psychologist with expertise in such planning, as well as in managerial assessment, training, and development.

The *cost of the solution* was $640,000 a year. This cost included the four days of succession planning meetings participated in by the organization's top 350 executives. It also incorporated the salary and benefits of the management planning specialist. The new chairman of the board and president heavily stressed the necessity of conscientious succession planning. Without such active, top-level encouragement, the new succession planning process could have gone down the tubes, just as it did under the company's previous top brass.

To measure the effectiveness of the new, more intense succession planning process, the financial impact of turnover and lower profits in departments headed by mediocre or inexperienced managers were calculated a year into the new process. The outcome documented the crucial role that succession planning can play in a company's financial picture. Both measures decreased to a total of $7,775,000 per year. That means that the *improvement benefit* was $8,600,000 per year. These two improvements alone accounted for a 13.4:1 *cost-benefit ratio.* That payback does not even take into account other, unmeasured benefits gained by the company including the value of having a better management staff and the many advantages that painstaking succession planning produces for an organization.

■ LAYOFFS AND REDUCING MANAGEMENT POSITIONS

Business Problem Addressed

Merger, Acquisition, or Reorganization

Overview of Solution

For most organizations, the cost of employees is the greatest single overhead expense. Employees, obviously, are crucial to carrying out the company's tasks. However, more and more organizations realize that laying off employees is sometimes a necessary and relatively quick way to reduce expenses and thus increase the bottom line. Sometimes the layoffs come as part of a merger or acquisition. In such instances, the overlapping, redundant, or excessive staff can be de-employed. Doing so often enhances efficiency and speeds up paying off the debt incurred in financing the merger or acquisition. Reorganizations are somewhat of a different story. In such circumstances, the company generally wants to refocus its business efforts, so it needs to restructure the way in which it operates.

Or, companies seek to become lean and mean. They achieve that by laying off layers of management or other levels of employees so that those who remain need to work harder *and* smarter to carry out their endeavors.

In mergers, acquisitions, or reorganizations, layoffs help decrease certain costs. The main cost saving comes from the organization not paying the salaries and benefits of people they let go. The organization also does not pay for the same amount of facilities (such as offices and phones) or support staff (such as secretaries and assistants). These changes create additional savings.

Although budget-conscious managers have an eye toward savings, there are obvious negative side effects to layoffs. For one, morale of remaining employees may plummet, which could result in decreased productivity. Also, some benefits managers assert that costs for psychosomatic and emotional claims rise following layoffs. Expenses stemming from layoffs include the following:[2]

☐ Severance pay
☐ Unused vacation pay
☐ Unemployment, pension, and other benefits costs
☐ Administrative expenditures to handle the layoff paperwork

Regardless of these potential pitfalls, organizations continue to use layoffs as a viable option for reducing expenses and streamlining operations.

How to Implement Solution

1. *Determine goals of layoffs.* These objectives might include the need to reduce expenses by doing away with unnecessary layers of bureaucracy or by changing business conditions. Whatever the reasons, the organization must possess a clear picture of exactly what benefits it aims to gain from layoffs *before* it plans how to implement the layoffs.

2. *Plan layoff method.* A number of methods exist for planning which employees to layoff.

These methods include:

☐ *Management decision.* Here, select executives decide who, when, where and how layoffs will be made
☐ *Consensus.* Managers at various levels of the organization decide which positions are necessary and which can be scrapped
☐ *LIFO method.* LIFO is an accounting term meaning last in, first out. In many instances, the LIFO method is an easy and seemingly fair way to lay off employees, since it places value on an objective measure, namely, seniority. However, the organization then loses control over who leaves. Events could transpire to create a situation in which employees with high potential who are fairly new to the organization are de-employed, while less productive employees with seniority remain. When this occurs, organizations often wonder if the money they saved from the layoffs is more than offset by current and future lost productivity.

During mergers or acquisitions, a number of specific layoff methods, described in Figure 9-3, might be put into action.[3]

Figure 9-3. Methods to make personnel reductions during a merger or acquisition.

Employees can best swallow the invariable layoffs if they know the logic behind the layoffs. A hidden or vague layoff method only fuels more crisis and panic than a clearly explained approach.

Typical layoff techniques include the following:

☐ Acquiring company employees stay while employees of the acquired company get laid off.

☐ "Trickle down," that is, executives are appointed at the top. These executives choose the next layer of management below them, and lay off people who are not chosen. This top-down process is repeated downward throughout the organization.

☐ Assessments of managers, using business-oriented psychological and ability tests plus in-depth, two- to four-interviews, conducted with the goal of keeping the best and laying off the rest.

☐ "Sandwich": Alternate layers of employees between the two companies. For instance, the top layer probably is drawn from the acquiring company, the next layer down is from the acquired company, and the layers continue to alternate down the organization.

☐ Seniority.

(From Mercer, M. W. "Making Mergers Work: Successfully Managing the People and Organizational Problems," Directors and Boards, Spring 1988. Copyright © 1988 by Michael W. Mercer.)

3. *Carry out layoff procedure.* Layoffs are always traumatic—for the employees being laid off, the managers who must tell employees that they no longer have a job, and the remaining employees. For these reasons, it is best to get it over with as quickly as possible. Doing so reduces the tension, lets remaining employees mourn the losses of their former colleagues, and starts the organization on the road to recovery from the shock.

Deadline for Implementing Solution

Most layoffs are done fairly quickly after the decision is made to use this human resources management technique. Although layoff purposes and methods require careful planning, they often end up being decided under short deadlines. For this reason, human resources managers must keep in mind the options available to them, so they can initiate action on short notice.

Deadline for Measuring Profit Improvement

Since there are some expenses incurred in laying off employees, cost reductions—and, thus, profit improvements—may not be noticeable for two to six months.

REDUCING MANAGEMENT LAYERS TO PARE EXPENSES

A 10,000-employee equipment manufacturing company found it increasingly difficult to beat its domestic and foreign competition on price. The company worked hard to upgrade the technology and procedures it used but, it still continually experienced problems in the marketplace because it was not competitive. After reviewing the situation, top management decided that perhaps the company had grown complacent with its eight layers of management, consisting of about 400 management employees. This sort of bureaucracy, they reasoned, created a *business problem* that cost a lot and may also have slowed down the speed with which the company could respond to market pressures and innovative ideas. The company determined that the *cost of the business problem* stood at $10 million per year. That represented all the salaries and benefits paid to the company's 400 employees who held management positions, as shown in Figure 9-4.

Figure 9-4. Planning Model for reducing management layers to pare expenses

BUSINESS PROBLEM

A company has increasing difficulty competing on price with its competitors. The company determines that a major cause of this business problem is its costly, probably excessive layers of management that developed over the years.

COST OF BUSINESS PROBLEM

$10,000,000/year

Main cost is the salaries and benefits paid to the company's management staff
= Number of managers × Average weighted salary and benefits of each manager
= 400 managers × $25,000/year
= $10,000,000/year

SOLUTION TO BUSINESS PROBLEM

Reduce the number of management layers from 8 layers down to seven layers. In terms of numbers of managers, the company aimed to decrease management positions from 400 managers down to 340, especially by doing away with certain middle management positions.

COST OF SOLUTION

$324,000

Costs included:

A. Meetings of plan layoffs
B. Layoff expenses, such as severance, outplacement, and other costs

(continued)

(Figure 9-4 continued)

A. Meetings
= Number of managers participating in layoff planning meetings × Number of days of meetings × Participants' average daily salary and benefits
= 30 managers × 2 days × $400/day
= $24,000
B. Layoff expenses
= Number of laid off managers × Average layoff expense per manager = 60 laid off managers × $5,000/manager
= $300,000

Cost of solution
= $24,000 + $300,000
= $324,000

$ IMPROVEMENT BENEFIT

$2,520,000/year

Improvement benefit
= Cost of problem before layoffs − Cost of problem a year after layoffs
Cost of problem before layoffs = $10,000,000/year
Cost of problem after layoffs
= Number of managers in company × Average weighted annual salary and benefits of each manager
= 340 managers × $22,000/year
= $7,480,000/year
Improvement benefit
= $10,000,000/year − $7,480,000/year
= $2,520,000/year

COST-BENEFIT RATIO

7.8:1

$2,520,000:$324,000

The *solution to the business problem* was to decrease its number of management personnel from 400 to 340. To accomplish this feat, 30 executives and other managers held a series of meetings to discuss how to restructure the management ranks. The expenses from these meetings, along with the cost of the layoffs, added up to $324,000 as the *cost of the solution.*

By reducing its management staff by 15 percent, from 400 to 340, the company realized an *improvement benefit* of around $2.5 million. This improvement stemmed from the cutback in the amount of the organization spent on management salaries and benefits. Most important, this improvement went straight to the bottom line, and it would be repeated each year if the company stayed at its new management staffing level. Given these savings, the solution generated a 7.8:1 *cost-benefit ratio* for the first year the layoffs were in effect.

■ IN-HOUSE OUTPLACEMENT SERVICES

Business Problems Addressed

Turnover
Merger, Acquisition, or Reorganization

Overview of Solution

Outplacement consulting services provide advice to companies on how best to implement terminations and professional job search counseling to terminated employees.

Figure 9-5 delineates the benefits that outplacement services provide both to organizations and to terminated employees.

Figure 9-5. Benefits of outplacement service.

Companies gain through:

- Professional advice on pretermination planning
- Speed in releasing employees who no longer fulfill the organization's needs
- Increased savings through
  —Reduced severance packages
  —Skill in quickly acting on terminations, thus saving continued salaries and benefits to affected employees
  —Potentially lower unemployment compensation payments, since terminated employees immediately begin quality job searches that could speed up job finding
- Decreased possibility of expensive and annoying lawsuits or EEO complaints
- Faster staffing changes due to performance problems, mergers, acquisitions, reorganizations, or relocations
- Helping other employees continue their work by quickly and sensitively concluding an unpleasant situation

Terminated employees benefit by:

- Releasing emotions and openly talking about their predicament
- Gaining understanding of what went wrong
- Regaining self-confidence and a sense of purpose
- Determining career goals and strategies to achieve those goals
- Receiving professional advice on job hunting
- Decreasing the potential time it might take to land a new job

(Adapted from materials supplied by the Association of Outplacement Consulting Firms, Inc., Parsippany, New Jersey.)

While such services are quite commendable, they can cost a company tremendously. For instance, it is common practice for an outplacement consulting firm to receive 15 percent of the final compensation earned by a terminated employee. Each $50,000 per year manager who is outplaced can cost his or her former employer $7,500 in outplacement fees. A $100,000 executive requires a $15,000 fee for outplacement. If a number of people are being outplaced, then it is easy to see how quickly these expenses can mount.

Even group outplacement costs a good deal of money. A common group outplacement technique consists of offering a job hunting seminar to a cluster of terminated employees. Then, these employees receive some one-on-one coaching on certain matters, especially on preparing a good resume. Even this group outplacement approach is expensive, often $1,500 or more per job hunting workshop, plus $100 or more for each person the outplacement professionals meet with individually.

To counter these big bucks going to outplacement consulting firms, some companies hire their own outplacement professionals to do this work. Or, they assign some of their current human resources professionals do the job. Employees involved in training or employee relations often assume such roles. The in-house outplacement services easily can cost far less than using outside outplacement firms. For example, an outplacement consulting firm could charge a company $45,000 just to outplace a half dozen $50,000 per year managers (6 outplaced managers X $7,500 in outplacement fees per manager = $45,000). For that same $45,000, a company easily could pay its full-time, in-house outplacement specialist $30,000 per year or more plus benefits. Even if the company rented office space for the terminated employees to use while job hunting, the fees still probably would end up lower for in-house consulting services compared to using outside outplacement consulting services. Given these figures, it is simple to see the cost-effectiveness of in-house outplacement services.

How to Implement Solution

1. *Forecast outplacement volume.* For this step, a company must determine how many people it may outplace within the next year or so. Using in-house services quickly becomes more cost-effective as the number of potentially outplaced employees increases.

2. *Decide who should provide in-house outplacement services.* Two main types of people seem most suited to furnish these services:

☐ Training or employee relations staff who currently work for the company
☐ Specialists the company can hire just to provide outplacement

3. *Provide off-site offices and secretarial support.* Companies invariably do not want terminated employees hanging around the facilities where they used to work. To handle this situation, many companies rent office space away from the company's own offices. This space can be used for outplacement workshops, one-on-one job hunting coaching sessions, and perhaps even as a place for select terminated employees to use phones and photocopy machines while they search for new jobs. Note, however, not all companies feel obligated to provide such facilities for their ex-employees. Also, some companies will let only certain employees use these office facilities for their job hunting endeavors.

Deadline for Implementing Solution

If the company uses current human resources staff members, then in-house outplacement services can be activated quite quickly, usually within two to four weeks. However, if the organization decides to hire outplacement specialists to do the job, then the time to implement the solution depends on how long it takes to recruit the right people and get them started providing services.

Deadline for Measuring Profit Improvement

In-house outplacement services decrease the costs of outplacement compared to using more expensive outside consulting firms. For instance, a company going through transitions and many terminations might spend $100,000 or more a year on outplacement consulting services. The company could provide the same level of outplacement services for quite a bit less just by using one or more of its employees to handle the outplacement chores. So, if the company forecasts continued need for outplacement services, setting up in-house assistance is a monetarily wise decision.

IN-HOUSE OUTPLACEMENT SERVICES CUTS OUTPLACEMENT COSTS

A large distribution company experienced two huge changes. First, its major market underwent rapid and profound changes. Second, it acquired another company whose business was overlapping and complementary. As a result, the new, combined company had a large number of employees who either were redundant or who worked in areas of the business that were shrinking. As a humanistic gesture and also to try to avoid possible lawsuits from disgruntled employees, the company provided outplacement assistance to the employees it terminated.

During the first year of downsizing, the company realized that its outplacement expenses mounted rather quickly. Given the company's business changes, it decided that the outplacement costs were a *business problem* that needed substantial reduction. The *cost of the business problem* was the $600,000 spent on outplacement during the first year of the company's major layoffs, as set forth in Figure 9-6.

The company studied several options. It could stop providing any outplacement assistance. Although the company considered that option financially desirable, it also seemed unpalatable from an employee relations viewpoint. Another option was to reduce the amount of outplacement services it provided to former employees. However, that would leave some of its ex-employees out in the cold in their job hunting, and the company felt a commitment to continue serving the affected employees.

The *solution to the business problem* that the company finally decided to use was to provide in-house outplacement services. These services were provided by three human resources professionals who

Figure 9-6. Planning Model for using in-house outplacement services.

BUSINESS PROBLEM

During a long downsizing period, a company decides it spent too much on outplacement consulting services. However, the company still wanted to aid its laid off employees with help in job hunting and getting their lives in order.

COST OF BUSINESS PROBLEM

$600,000/year in outplacement consulting fees

SOLUTION TO BUSINESS PROBLEM

Company provided in-house outplacement
consulting services

COST OF SOLUTION

$160,000/year

Costs included:

- A. Employees providing in-house outplacement services
- B. Off-site office space and secretarial services for outplacement

A. Employees
= Number of outplacement specialists × Average annual salary and benefits per specialist
= 3 specialists × $40,000/year
= $120,000/year
B. Office space and secretarial services = $40,000/year

Cost of solution
= $120,000/year + $40,000/year
= $160,000/year

$ IMPROVEMENT BENEFIT

$440,000/year

Improvement benefit
= Costs before in-house outplacement services − Costs after implementing in-house outplacement services
Costs before in-house outplacement services = $600,000/year
Costs after implementing in-house outplacement services = $160,000/year

Improvement benefit
  = $600,000/year − $160,000/year
  = $440,000/year

<u>COST-BENEFIT RATIO</u>

3:1

$480,000/year:$160,000/year

---

already worked for the company. They earned an average of $40,000 per year, including benefits. The company also arranged for office space and secretarial services. Managers who had held positions over a certain level were allowed to use the office space for their job hunting.

The outplacement specialists also conducted job hunting workshops and coaching sessions in the offices. The secretary answered the phone with the name of the company to give the impression that the job seekers actually still worked for their previous employer. She also typed resumes and certain other job hunting materials for the terminated employees. The *cost of the solution* amounted to $160,000 for its first year of operation.

The cost of the solution was considerably less than the $600,000 per year that the company had previously paid for outside outplacement consulting services. In fact, the *improvement benefit* was $440,000 per year in lower outplacement expenses. This reduction in expenses resulted in a 3:1 *cost benefit ratio* for this solution. Financially, the solution certainly seemed worthwhile. Also, the company determined that the quality of outplacement assistance remained high. And, perhaps most important, the company was not sued by disgruntled ex-employees. Without the outplacement assistance, the company reasoned that some terminated employees may have tried to retaliate by initiating lawsuits against the heartless company. Although it cannot be measured, the company's general counsel and vice president of human resources considered the in-house outplacement services to be an important deterrent to lawsuits from the ex-employees.

Chapter 10
Recruitment and Selection

Two of the major duties carried out by human resources managers are finding job candidates and then helping to choose the *best* job candidates. After all, employees are the driving force in most organizations. For that reason, human resources professionals involved in recruiting and selection play a make-it-or-break-it role in the success of practically any business enterprise.

Fortunately for these professionals, techniques exist to improve how often they help their organizations hire the best possible job candidates. And these techniques can be measured in dollars-and-cents terms that non-human-resources executives appreciate. Toward this end, this chapter discusses three cost-beneficial approaches for selection and recruitment:

- ☐ Employment tests, psychological assessments of management candidates, and assessment centers
- ☐ Intensive prehiring reference checks
- ☐ Reducing recruitment costs

Each of these techniques will be discussed, along with a case example using the six-step *Planning Model*. It should be noted that academic, nevertheless relevant, statistical formulas have been developed especially to determine the economic usefulness of various selection and training programs. This approach often is called utility analysis. It consists of formidable equations that require a high level of statistical knowledge, along with some rather complex calculations.

Unfortunately, these calculations and components of the equation prove rather difficult even for academic researchers who possess a great deal of statistical prowess. The utility equations devised thus far seem keenly more attuned to the needs of academic researchers than to the practical needs of managers and professionals in the business world. However, suggested reading is provided for those of you who desire to pursue the subject in greater depth.[1, 2, 3]

■ EMPLOYMENT TESTS, PSYCHOLOGICAL ASSESSMENTS OF MANAGEMENT CANDIDATES, AND ASSESSMENT CENTERS

Business Problems Addressed

Productivity
Turnover, Absenteeism, and Tardiness
Sales Force Performance
Manager and Executive Effectiveness
Recruitment and Hiring

Overview of Solution

The reason to use employment tests, psychological assessments, and assessment centers is to have valid and reliable methods to choose job candidates who are likely to perform well on the job.

By choosing such candidates, productivity improves. In fact, a survey of research studies on the use of aptitude and ability tests showed that using such tests resulted in productivity increases of 2.6 percent to 43.5 percent, with the median improvement being 10.4 percent.[4] In practically every circumstance, the gain in productivity outweighs the cost of the tests, psychological assessments of management candidates, or assessment centers, meaning that use of such selection devices is cost beneficial.

Developing a useful selection device usually requires the skill of a professional with expertise in employment test development and related statistical procedures, typically an industrial psychologist who specializes in enabling organizations to improve their effectiveness through applying behavioral science techniques, such as developing valid and reliable tests and assessments.

In developing the selection device, three concepts are particularly crucial:[5]

1. Validity
2. Reliability
3. Nondiscriminatory results

Volumes have been written on these concepts. In brief, validity refers to how accurately (validly) a selection device predicts which candidates would perform well on the job. Reliability generally alludes to whether the results are reproducible. For instance, if two people each score the same test, will they both come up with the same score? If so, the test is reliable in a key sense. If not, then the test is not reliable. An unreliable test is of minimal value. Finally, the issue of equal employment opportunity (EEO) guidelines comes into play. To use a selection device, an organization should make sure that the device does not discriminate. If the test discriminates, then two problems may arise. First, the company could end up losing costly and bothersome legal disputes. Secondly, the company might miss the opportunity to hire potentially excellent candidates. Skilled industrial psychologists are aware of these concerns and build selection devices that are valid, reliable, and nondiscriminatory.

To build a selection device, the industrial psychologist must carry out a number of steps:

1. Analyze job to determine what knowledge, skills, and abilities (KSAs) someone needs on the job.

2. Develop test using questions or exercises that indicate how well a candidate has the KSAs needed to perform the job successfully.

3. Determine how well the test is valid, reliable, and nondiscriminatory.

Three useful selection devices are:

☐   Employment tests
☐   Psychological assessments of management candidates
☐   Assessment centers

Employment tests generally are questionnaires taken by job candidates. They ask questions that pinpoint how well the candidate possesses the KSAs needed. These tests are available in two ways: They can be ordered from test publishers' catalogs or from psychologists who can either create custom-made tests or statistically validate existing tests to meet a company's specific needs.

Caveat emptor. Simply purchasing tests from a catalog easily proves "penny wise and pound foolish," because an ability test must validly or accurately determine if a job candidate possesses a high likelihood of doing well in a specific job in a specific organization. A company gains nothing by buying tests from a catalog, since such a test almost invariably will *not* pinpoint if a candidate is likely to do well in a specific job in that particular company.

To overcome this potential problem, an industrial psychologist can conduct a validity study. Such a study statistically pinpoints test cut-off scores and norms a company should use to hire top-notch candidates for specific jobs. Such validity studies should be used by companies to make sure their employment tests validly indicate which job candidates actually can perform well on the job.

After a valid, reliable, and defensible test is developed, it might be scored either by hand or by computer. Apparently, organizations use many types of tests on a wide basis. From 25 to 33 percent of the companies surveyed by the American Society of Personnel Administrators use mental ability, psychological, and personality tests; approximately 10 percent give honesty tests; and over 80 percent make use of secretarial tests.[6]

Psychological assessments of candidates for management positions usually require less scientific and more intuitive skills on the part of the industrial psychologist who conducts them, because it is practically impossible to quantify exactly what a manager does.

In general, a psychological assessment of a management candidate profiles how well a candidate may perform in a specific position in a particular company. Without an assessment, a company may have the manager on its payroll for 6 to 12 months before the company can observe how well the candidate actually performs. Since taking so long to find out how a candidate actually performs is quite expensive (in terms of salary and benefits, as well as in possible lost profitability that a better candidate would have brought to the company), psychological assessments provide cost-effective, quick ways to help make important hiring decisions.

An assessment of a candidate usually consists of three major parts:

1. Recommendations to management
2. Background of candidate
3. Evaluation of candidate
   a. Motivations
   b. Problem-Solving Approach
   c. Communications Skills
   d. Management Style
   e. Interpersonal Skills
   f. Personality and Temperament

Before an assessment is done, the industrial psychologist conducting the assessment discusses the position with the executive doing the hiring. This discussion focuses on characteristics needed to perform well in the job, as well as on the organizational climate in which the position exists. The assessment itself consists of the industrial psychologist:

1. Administering tests to the candidate, and
2. Conducting a two- to four-hour in-depth interview

The psychologist then writes a report based on the test results and interview. The report predicts how the candidate would perform in the job for which he or she is being considered. A sample of such an assessment report appears in Figure 10-1. Finally, the person doing the hiring and the industrial psychologist discuss each candidate who had been assessed. They compare the candidates' crucial strengths and weaknesses to determine which candidate seems best to hire.

Another selection device is an assessment center. Based on the job analysis, tests, job simulations, and exercises can be created that indicate how well candidates might perform in key KSAs required in the job. The tests usually can be scored by hand or by computer. However, the simulations and exercises invariably need to be scored by raters or judges who are trained to observe and evaluate candidates' actions on these procedures.

Some of the types of exercises used to tap candidates' potential are[7]:

☐ *Business games* in which candidates demonstrate key job skills, such as knowledge of finance and planning procedures, group problem solving, decision making, and other business skills
☐ *Leaderless group discussions* to see how each candidate acts in group situations. For example, does a candidate take an active or passive role, a diplomatic or aggressive manner, or a leader or a follower role? Leaderless group discussions allow raters to observe such important tendencies
☐ *In-basket exercises* in which each candidate must demonstrate how and why they organize their time and their subordinates' time
☐ *Job simulations* which show how a candidate might perform in specific job situations

Figure 10-1. Psychological assessment of a management candidate.

CANDIDATE: G

POSITION: Vice-President of
Finance and Administration

_____ Company

RECOMMENDATIONS TO MANAGEMENT

Mr. G_____ is an above-average candidate for the position of vice-president of finance and administration. In general, his assets center on his strong technical, work-oriented skills and superior motivations. His shortcomings revolve around interpersonal and communications matters.

On the plus side, Mr. G_____ is a very motivated, bright, hard-working individual. He is quite results-focused. However, he does need a degree of attention and recognition on a fairly consistent basis. But he dislikes being watched over. Give him a basic direction, let him have a relatively free reign, and he will get the job done.

He shows both analytical and creative abilities. As a clear-headed thinker, he will jump into a pile of details and figure out how to make sense of it all. After careful, thorough analysis, Mr. G_____ has come up with some rather creative approaches to systematize operations and enhance the bottom-line. He also expresses his ideas clearly, although he tends to convey many details that his audience may not want or need to hear.

Mr. G_____ appears to have applicable background in areas that would benefit the company. Some of these areas include cost accounting, creating systems to improve profitability, computerizing functions, and MRP.

On the liability side, Mr. G_____ manages with more concern for projects than for the people who must carry out his orders or live with the results of his projects. Although Mr. G_____ enjoys working in a well-functioning, collaborative team, he sometimes fails to notice his work's impact on people.

Mr. G_____ is incredibly detail-focused. This is a mixed blessing. On the one hand, the vice-president of finance and administration position calls for a strong detail-orientation. However, from a communications point-of-view, Mr. G_____ tends to get too detailed. He tells people more details than they may well need to know or wish to spend the time to hear.

He could also be warmer and friendlier. He is too wrapped up in his work, sometimes failing to form and maintain friendly working relationships.

His writing needs a good deal of improvement. At the present time, it does not convey the professionalism that ought to be a part of an executive's writing skills.

If Mr. G_____ is positively considered by management for this position, then the following developmental recommendations would enhance Mr. G_____'s performance:

1. Encourage him to express himself more concisely. Let him know when he gets bogged down in excessive and unnecessary details.

2. Give him feedback on his demeanor. More sociability and a bit more smiling could work wonders in getting people to cooperate with him.

3. Survey his staff periodically about how he deals with them. He sometimes overlooks the people in his drive to finish projects. The level of changes he will need to implement for the company will require a staff that works "with" him rather than just "for" him. If some rocky times occur, then a formal intensive teambuilding session would prove useful.

4. Provide Mr. G＿＿＿＿＿ with training for both his writing skills and his group presentation skills. Both need upgrading for Mr. G＿＿＿＿＿ to appear more professional and authoritative.

5. Advise him on how to influence and persuade people more effectively. The power of his logic and detailed analyses will not carry adequate weight to sway some people, especially those affected by proposed changes or "old timers" who feel protected by the status quo. The company has too much at stake in its vice-president of finance and administration position to risk having excellent, innovative plans short-circuited by ineffective persuasion techniques. A negotiating seminar could help him.

These RECOMMENDATIONS TO MANAGEMENT were prepared by
MICHAEL W. MERCER, PH.D.
Industrial Psychologist

CANDIDATE: G   POSITION: Vice-President of
                                                          Finance and Administration

BACKGROUND

Mr. G＿＿＿＿＿ received a B.A. in ＿＿＿＿＿ from the University of ＿＿＿＿＿ in 1969. From January 1970–November 1971, he served in the U.S. Armed Forces. He was discharged early because of an injury. In 1974, he earned his M.B.A. from ＿＿＿＿＿ University.

He began his career with ＿＿＿＿＿. From April 1974–June 1976, he worked for ＿＿＿＿＿ in Chicago, first as a senior financial analyst and then as a plant controller. Then, from June 1976–September 1978, he served as operations controller for ＿＿＿＿＿ in Mexico.

From September 1978–July 1985, Mr. G＿＿＿＿＿ was controller for ＿＿＿＿＿. During the July 1985–January 1987 timeframe, Mr. G＿＿＿＿＿ acted as group controller for five companies of ＿＿＿＿＿ Corporation.

(continued)

(Figure 10-1 continued)

EVALUATION OF CANDIDATE

MOTIVATIONS

Mr. G_____ shows a strong level of motivation. As a very results-focused individual, he craves to see the tangible outcomes of his efforts. He values measuring how he improves the bottom-line.

He enjoys analytical problems. He relishes diving into a swamp of problems and figuring out what to do. As an innately detail-focused person, Mr. G_____ takes tremendous pleasure in such activities.

This fellow works long and hard. He plugs away in a dogged, determined, and resolute manner. He is also a competitive person in a certain sense. He does not play competitive games to hurt his colleagues; instead, he shows a great drive to prove to the world that he can do better than his predecessors in any organization he is with.

Mr. G_____ prides himself in his innovative abilities. He likes to create new ways to make things work better. To do so, he has a strong need to be in charge.

He would become demotivated if he had only routine or administrative matters to handle. He is an executive-caliber individual who fairly readily shifts his focus from the "big picture" of his organization to analyzing the myriad small details that result in successful strategy completion.

PROBLEM-SOLVING APPROACH

Mr. G_____ is extremely detail-focused. He gets quite wrapped up in noticing every tiny detail and determining its usefulness. He spends a good deal of time concentrating on details and making sure everything fits perfectly in place. In this sense, Mr. G_____ is a perfectionist in his thinking, planning, and actions.

Although such a profound detail-orientation can prove quite positive, especially for someone in a financial management role, Mr. G_____ can at times overdo it. Such a concern for detail can drag a project on for more time than it should. Also, along the same lines, Mr. G_____ sometimes does not take into account how much time he makes other people spend in their involvement with his work.

Nevertheless, he certainly is an analytical thinker. He dives into the guts of a problem, looks into each nook and cranny, and unfailingly comes up with workable solutions.

COMMUNICATIONS SKILLS

This person explains his ideas in a clear manner. As mentioned earlier, he is very detail-focused. Due to this focus, he sometimes strays into excessive and unnecessary detail. He tells his audience more than it needs to know. People get quite an earful from Mr. G_____ —often more than they bargained for.

His presentations to groups would definitely be thorough in their preparation of facts and figures and plans. However, his delivery style would probably be uninspiring to his audience.

Mr. G_____'s listening skills are mostly on-target. He pays close attention to what people say to him. He responds accurately to questions they ask of him. Mr. G_____ seldom goes off on tangents.

A major deficit in Mr. G_____'s skills is his writing ability. His writing is not as polished as an executive's should be. He does convey his essential ideas to his readers. However, Mr. G_____ makes noticeable spelling, grammar, and punctuation errors.

MANAGEMENT STYLE

Mr. G_____ focuses a lot on systems that he helps develop and put into action. He thinks through the details with great depth and breadth. He analyzes alternatives. However, as someone who is not too people-oriented, Mr. G_____ tends to skim over how people will accept and implement the systems. In this sense, he sometimes overlooks the people issues that his work creates.

In contrast, Mr. G_____ does a fine job of dealing with the structural problems various departments face as he develops and implements systems. He understands and conveys how each department or function fits into the programs he creates, even if he does not focus quite enough on how the people in these departments will react.

INTERPERSONAL SKILLS

This fellow is a serious, straight-forward person. He appears somewhat stiff. Mr. G_____ does not smile readily. He presents a professional, though somewhat distant, impression to others.

As such, it takes Mr. G_____ awhile to warm up to people he has just met. Fortunately, he becomes more animated, lively, and warm after he gets to know someone.

PERSONALITY & TEMPERAMENT

Mr. G_____ shows a moderate level of energy. While he may feel enthused about a project, he certainly does not show it too overtly. He is more of a thinker than someone who wears his feelings and reactions for others to see.

He needs attention from others in fairly regular doses. He longs for praise, attention, and recognition. Mr. G_____ begins to wonder about his skills and abilities when such attention is not forthcoming from management.

As a very detail-focused individual, Mr. G_____ is also fairly cautious. In fact, he sometimes focuses more than necessary on potential problems or drawbacks. While such caution often proves necessary, it also could keep him from spotting opportunities.

This EVALUATION OF MANAGEMENT CANDIDATE was prepared by
MICHAEL W. MERCER, PH.D.
Industrial Psychologist

Assessment centers do a good job at evaluating candidates' abilities in a number of areas, including:[8]

☐ Communications skills—both verbal and written
☐ Motivations
☐ Leadership
☐ Organizing and planning
☐ Analytical thinking
☐ Management techniques

One difficulty with assessment centers is the magnitude of the work necessary to set them up. Then, raters must be trained and that takes more time and expense. When the assessment center is in operation, the raters (usually company employees) must be away from their normal jobs to carry out their rater responsibilities. All in all, while assessment centers can provide a lot of useful information on job candidates, their comparatively high expense and complicated operations make them less than fully desirable by many organizations. In contrast, tests and psychological assessments take much less time and cost a good deal less than assessment centers.

How to Implement Solution

The best way to proceed is to contact an industrial psychologist. This professional can conduct the job analysis and create valid, reliable, and nondiscriminatory selection devices. As in most professions, not every person in a profession is equally adept at each technique. Comparatively few psychologists specialize in working with businesses and organizations. Most psychologists are clinical psychologists who focus on mental health-oriented treatment and do not possess special training or expertise for working with organizations. However, some psychologists specialize in helping organizations improve their effectiveness, especially in terms of selection and productivity concerns. Just as different surgeons specialize in different types of surgery, industrial psychologists also often specialize in developing particular types of selection devices. For example, such a psychologist often possesses great expertise in employment tests, psychological assessments of candidates for management positions, or assessment center development. Few industrial psychologists possess equal skill in all three of these quite technical and complex selection devices.

Here are guidelines for an organization to find an industrial psychologist to help with its selection device development:

1. Obtain names of management psychologists from other companies that have used them.

2. When interviewing psychologists, obtain work samples of employment tests, psychological assessments of management candidates, or assessment centers that they developed, along with references from companies they worked for or consulted.

3. Determine how smoothly the management psychologist would collaborate with key members of the organization. After all, a sense of interpersonal comfort plays a crucial role in most organizations' use of consultants, including industrial psychologists.

Most important, the organization must make a commitment to evaluating the effectiveness of the selection device it eventually uses. As the upcoming case example shows, when possible, evaluate the selection device in dollars-and-cents terms or on some other *measurable* performance dimensions.

Deadline for Implementing Solution

1. *Tests*. Developing most tests takes anywhere from a couple of months to a year. The more research done on the test's validity, reliability and nondiscriminatory nature, the longer the test takes to develop. In practice, many companies that use tests "want them yesterday," meaning that the companies do not want to wait for lengthy research. While such speed may be desirable, it also could cost the company in two main ways in the future. First, the company may not have a test developed to the point that it can choose the absolute best candidates possible. Secondly, the company may not have the data it would need if it went into court on a possible discrimination charge stemming from the use of the test as a selection device.

2. *Psychological assessments of management candidates*. This selection device is the quickest of the three. Most industrial psychologists can conduct an entire assessment and discuss it with the executive doing the hiring during a four to eight hour time period. Usually the written report can be written, typed, and in the hands of the hiring executive very shortly after that.

3. *Assessment centers*. This selection device takes a few months to a full year to get up and running.

Deadline for Measuring Profit Improvement

As soon as an organization can, it should measure the difference in productivity between candidates hired using the old method and candidates hired using tests, psychological assessments, or assessment centers. In general, within a year, a company should have a pretty good idea of how much more productive and profitable the employees are who were chosen using the more scientific selection devices.

USING TESTS TO CHOOSE SALESPEOPLE WHO SELL MORE

A service company wanted more sales, thus higher profits, from its sales force. Each salesperson sold an average of $170,000 per year. Yet, this company did not consider that enough. The *business problem* it perceived was that its sales force performance could stand some improvement. Since the company wanted to improve sales force performance, there was no *cost of the business problem* in the usual sense of the term, as indicated the *Planning Model* shown in Figure 10-2.

The company decided that a *solution to the business problem* would be to create and use an employment test to choose better salespeople. It contracted with an industrial psychologist to conduct the job analysis, devise the test, and evaluate how well the test was valid, reliable, and nondiscriminatory. The psychologist took two months to

Figure 10-2. Planning Model for better sales force selection

BUSINESS PROBLEM

A service company believed that its sales force's performance could improve.

COST OF BUSINESS PROBLEM

N/A

SOLUTION TO BUSINESS PROBLEM

Develop and use a valid, reliable, nondiscriminatory salesperson employment test

COST OF SOLUTION

$10,000

$ IMPROVEMENT BENEFIT

$500,000

Improvement benefit = Sales of salespeople hired using the new employment test −
    Sales of salespeople hired using previous selection method (interviews only)
Annual sales were calculated for the first 25 salespeople hired using the employment test,
    as well as for the last 25 salespeople hired using the previous interview-only selection
    method.
Sales = 25 salespeople × Average annual sales per salesperson
Sales of salespeople using new employment test
    = 25 salespeople × $190,000/year
    = $4,750,000/year
Sales of salespeople using previous interview-only selection method
    = 25 salespeople × $170,000/year
    = $4,250,000/year
Improvement benefit
    = $4,750,000/year − $4,250,000/year
    = $500,000/year

COST-BENEFIT RATIO

50:1 in terms of sales improvement
$500,000/year: $10,000
or
7.5:1 in terms of profit improvement
(15% profit margin)
$75,000/year:$10,000

complete this step. Then, the organization began using the tests to choose salespeople. The *cost of the solution* for validating and purchasing totaled around $10,000.

To evaluate the effectiveness of using the test, the enterprise compared the annual sales of the last 25 salespeople hired under its preceding selection method, which consisted only of interviews, to annual sales of the first 25 salespeople hired using the new selection method (interviews and the test). The company used the same training and compensation methods for both groups, so those factors probably would not account for differences in their sales performance. This evaluation uncovered that the salespeople hired using the new employment test sold an average of $190,000 per year. That is 12 percent more than the average of $170,000 per year sold by salespeople hired using interviews only. This sales improvement yielded a half million dollar *improvement benefit* for the organization.

Using these figures, the company calculated the *cost-benefit ratio* based on (1) sales increase and (2) profit improvement. The $500,000 annual sales improvement yielded a 50:1 cost-benefit ratio. Given the company's 15 percent profit margin, the sales increase amounted to $75,000 per year more profit for the company produced by the first 25 salespeople chosen with the new employment test. That profit enhancement resulted in a 7.5:1 cost-benefit ratio for the company in terms of the profit that its $10,000 investment in a new test produced.

Significantly, this splendid cost-beneficial employment test would continue to reap benefits for quite a few years, because the better salespeople, chosen with the new employment test, may continue to outproduce their counterparts each year. The company's profitability would increase. Also, since the salespeople earned a good portion of their take-home pay from commissions, the salespeople picked using the employment test would reap greater financial rewards at the same time by being chosen for a job in which they excel.

■ INTENSIVE PREHIRING REFERENCE CHECKS

Business Problems Addressed

Productivity
Insurance Costs
Accidents
Employment
Benefits Costs

Overview of Solution

Intensive prehiring reference checks increasingly are becoming a business necessity for a number of reasons. First, employers can be held liable for the actions of their employees. For example, if an employee has an accident or commits illegal acts during his or her work time, then the employer can be held legally and financially accountable for such difficulties.

Second, intensive prehiring reference checks prove useful in reducing insurance and worker's compensation costs. For instance, the Life Insurance Marketing and Research Association in Farmington, Connecticut, says that falsified employee records cost life insurance companies $30 million per year. Also, some employees may go from employer to employer, getting jobs and then claiming the same on-the-job injury.[9] The result is that the employer pays workers' compensation expenses as a result of not checking the workers' compensation history of the employee. That can add up to a lot of money.

Third, intensive prehiring reference checks help a company know whether it is about to hire the person they think they are about to hire. About a third of all resumes contain false information.[10] Reference-checking experts say that lying about education is the most common fraudulent data job candidates use. This fact is important for employers to realize. For instance, if a company wants to hire an engineer, the company should find out if the person being considered *really* did complete the engineering degree indicated on his or her resume or job application, and is legally licensed to practice engineering.

Finally, in-depth reference checking lets an employer know if a person might act untrustworthy in certain occupations. For instance, a person with a very bad credit rating who owes a lot of money might be more likely to steal than an employee who did not have such difficulties. While a bad credit rating does not necessarily mean that a person will steal, it might give the person's potential employer cause to wonder if this person should be allowed to work in situations where theft easily could solve the person's money woes.

How to Implement Solution

The four above-described reasons point to the usefulness of solid reference checking before an organization hires a job candidate. However, there can be a thin line between uncovering information on a potential employee and appearing to violate the job candidate's privacy. To help avoid these sorts of problems, or at least shift some of the potential liability, many companies use professional reference-checking firms to do this work. Nevertheless, some guidelines need to be followed, such as:

- ☐ Obtain *written* permission from the job candidate to do a reference check
- ☐ Verify only job-related background information
- ☐ Obtain public records that reflect job-related information, such as records on worker's compensation claims, court cases, and credit history

According to Gerry Belko, executive director of F.S.B. Associates, a reference-checking and human resources consulting firm in Winnetka, Illinois, checking into six main areas may prove most useful.[11] These areas include:

- ☐ Past employment
- ☐ Criminal record
- ☐ Credit history
- ☐ Motor vehicle report
- ☐ Academic background
- ☐ Worker's compensation claims

However, an organization should, as suggested above, only do background screenings on *job-related* areas. For instance, if a company is hiring drivers, then it makes sense to look into candidates' driving records, since such information is job-related. If a bank wants to hire tellers, then it probably would want to know if the applicants it is considering have criminal histories. Such data justifiably could be job-related.

Deadline for Implementing Solution

Most reference checks can be completed in 1 to 14 days. The amount of time required depends on the complexity and amount of information needed. For instance, checking academic credentials can be done fairly quickly by contacting schools that an applicant stated he or she attended. However, driving records or criminal records may need to be investigated in a number of states. That takes time. The amount of time and money spent on conducting intensive prehiring reference checks can easily be worth it even if only one or two potentially costly candidates are not hired as a result of such background probes.

Deadline for Measuring Profit Improvement

Within a year, an organization should be able to measure the difference in certain work-related measures of people hired with intensive reference checks compared to the organization's employees hired without such reference checks. For instance, a company might be concerned about the number of accidents its drivers have had while driving under the influence (DUI) of alcohol or drugs. So, after it institutes intensive prehiring reference checking, it could compare the number of DUI-related accidents its nonreference-checked drivers had compared to the ones committed by its reference-checked drivers. If the organization's reference-checked drivers committed less DUI-related accidents (or, hopefully, none at all), then that indicates that the closer screenings are worthwhile.

REDUCING COSTS THROUGH INTENSIVE PREHIRING REFERENCE CHECKING

Because of its drivers' actions, a package delivery company faced a costly *business problem.* Specifically, some of its drivers had accidents while driving under the influence of alcohol or drugs, stole goods they were supposed to deliver, and sometimes broke other laws while on duty. Figure 10-3 presents the *Planning Model* used to deal with this problem. Had the company investigated the pasts of the drivers causing the expensive problems, it would have found information that probably would have led the firm to avoid hiring them. For example, one driver with a rape conviction sexually assaulted a woman to whom he delivered a package. Other drivers who had DUI convictions on their driving records wound up in accidents when they drank alcohol or took drugs while on duty. Obviously, *thorough* reference checking *before* hiring these drivers would have helped the company avoid some of the expenses caused by these problem employees.

The organization decided that the *solution to its business problem*

Figure 10-3. Planning Model for reducing costs by using intensive prehiring reference checks.

BUSINESS PROBLEM

A package delivery company absorbed a great deal of expense as a result of its drivers' accidents, thefts, and illegal activities. The company did not know that a number of the drivers causing the trouble had backgrounds that may have indicated problems could erupt on the job.

COST OF BUSINESS PROBLEM

$160,000/year

Costs included expenses related to:

A. Drivers' accidents due to DUI
B. Drivers' stealing
C. Sexual molestation committed by an on-duty driver who had a rape conviction in his past

A. Accidents = $90,000/year
B. Stealing = $30,000/year
C. Sexual molestation = $40,000/year

Cost of problem
   = $90,000/year + $30,000/year + $40,000/year
   = $160,000/year

SOLUTION TO BUSINESS PROBLEM

Intensive prehiring reference checking by an outside reference checking firm

COST OF SOLUTION

$20,625

Cost
   = Number of candidates for driver position who had their references checked × Cost per reference check
   = 165 candidates had references checked × $125/reference check
   = $20,625

$ IMPROVEMENT BENEFIT

$157,000/year

Improvement benefit
  = Annual cost of problems by drivers who did not have their references checked −
     Annual cost of those same problems among drivers whose references were checked
  = $160,000/year − $3,000/year
  = $157,000/year

COST-BENEFIT RATIO

7.6:1

$157,000:$20,625

---

would be to have an outside agency conduct in-depth reference checks on all candidates the company considered for the driver position. To determine if the reference checks proved useful, the company compared the costs associated with its drivers' DUI-related accidents, stealing, and sexual assault problems for two groups: (1) the drivers previously hired without detailed reference checks and (2) drivers employed for whom the company commissioned intensive prehiring reference checks. The *cost of the business problem* by those drivers without fully checked references was $160,000 per year. During the same year, the drivers hired with careful background investigations produced only $3,000 in expenses for the company (that expense was for one accident). Comparing the two groups shows an *improvement benefit* of $157,000 per year. That is, the drivers hired with complete reference checks caused $157,000 per year less in avoidable expenses than their counterparts hired with minimal reference checks.

Thus, although the $20,625 *cost of the solution* seemed rather steep, it proved more than worthwhile, because the *cost-benefit ratio* from using this solution to a costly business problem turned out to be 7.6:1.

■ REDUCING RECRUITMENT COSTS

Business Problem Addressed

Employment

Overview of Solution

One controllable expense that rests mostly within the control of the human resources department is the cost of recruiting. If the human resources department handles recruitment, then it can take steps to decrease the cost of this activity. Obviously, an organization always wants high quality candidates for its available jobs. The lower the cost of filling these jobs, the higher the profitability.

Lessening recruitment expenses requires studying the costs involved in finding qualified candidates from each recruitment source. Then, the recruiting professionals must determine which sources are the most cost effective, that is, which sources offer the most quality candidates for the least money. Another way to reduce expenses is to take more recruiting functions in-house. To do so, for instance, executive searches that used to be handled by expensive headhunters (often taking one-third of the first year compensation of the position they fill) might be performed by recruiters already on the company's payroll. Also, when outside sources *must* be used, such as newspapers for ads or selected employment agencies, lower costs may be negotiated to decrease expenses.

How to Implement Solution

1. *Examine recruitment records.* This should be done with an eye toward pinpointing the best, most cost-effective recruiting sources. Also, it may become apparent that some recruitment expenses can be cut out altogether, since they do not produce enough quality candidates to justify their use. Still other sources may be used less if the human resources staff do some of the work previously done by the recruitment source. Some of the recruitment sources that can be affected included the following:

- ☐ Company recruiting staff
- ☐ Employment agencies and search firms
- ☐ Advertisements for job openings
- ☐ Job fairs
- ☐ In-house employee referral program

2. *Make cuts as appropriate.* This step puts the information gleaned in the previous step into action. For instance, a company may find that it gets many of its better employees through advertising in a certain newspaper, whereas it obtains few quality candidates from job fairs. So, the company could use the ads more and the job fairs less.

Deadline for Implementing Solution

This solution does not take long to implement. It usually can be done within one to three months.

Deadline for Measuring Profit Improvement

Lessened recruiting expenses should take hold within a few months. However, a company may want to wait longer before adding up the cost savings, because the company needs to ascertain if it still obtains enough quality candidates as it reduces its recruiting costs.

REDUCING A COMPANY'S RECRUITING COSTS

An electronics company suspected that it could trim its recruiting costs, which it felt were steeper than they needed to be. Furthermore, the organization thought its recruiting staff could tackle this *business problem* without sacrificing on the quality of candidates it brought into the enterprise. As shown in Figure 10-4, the annual *cost of this business problem* was $809,000, the cost for the previous year's recruitment efforts.

As a *solution to the business problem,* two members of the recruiting staff spent a few days examining records and action planning exactly how to cut expenses. They discovered that they got the most quality candidates for the money spent through two main sources: (1)

Figure 10-4. Planning Model for reducing recruitment expenses.

BUSINESS PROBLEM

A company believed that it could lower the amount of money it spent on recruiting with no negative effect on the caliber of people it employed.

COST OF BUSINESS PROBLEM

$809,000/year

Costs included:

A. Company recruiting staff
B. Employment agencies and search firms
C. Advertising job openings
D. Job fairs
E. In-house employee referral program

A. Company recruiting staff = $140,000/year
B. Agencies and search firms = $550,000/year
C. Advertising = $65,000/year
D. Job fairs = $8,000/year
E. Referral program = $46,000/year

Cost of problem
   = $140,000/year + $550,000/year + $65,000/year + $8,000/year + $46,000/year
   = $809,000/year

SOLUTION TO BUSINESS PROBLEM

Examine recruiting records to pinpoint most cost-effective recruiting sources. Use this data to reduce expenses

COST OF SOLUTION

$1,500

(continued)

(Figure 10-4 continued)

Cost
= Number of recruiting staff members examining recruiting records and planning cost reduction tactics × Number of days spent examining and planning × Average daily salaries and benefits per staff member
= 2 staff members × 3 days × $250/day
= $1,500

$ IMPROVEMENT BENEFIT

$171,000/year

Improvement benefit
  = Cost of previous year's recruiting methods − Cost of new, reduced cost recruiting methods
Cost of previous recruiting methods = $809,000/year
Cost of new, reduced cost recruiting methods included:

A. Company recruiting staff = $150,000/year
B. Agencies and search firms = $310,000/year
C. Advertising = $115,000/year
D. Job fairs = $0
E. Employee referral program = $73,000/year

Cost of new, reduced cost methods
    = $150,000/year + $310,000/year + $115,000/year + $73,000/year
    = $648,000/year
Improvement benefit
    = $809,000/year − $648,000/year
    = $161,000/year

COST-BENEFIT RATIO

107:1

$161,000:$1,500

---

advertising in selected trade and professional magazines and (2) the company's in-house employee referral program. For the referral program, the company paid a finder's fee to any employee who referred someone to the company that the company eventually hired. The recruiters also discovered the fact that job fairs proved practically worthless for the time and money involved. Also, these human resources professionals decided that they could step up their efforts in recruiting. By doing so, they figured that the firm could lower the amount of fees it paid to employment agencies and search firms. In all, the *cost of the solution* was only $1,500 for the time spent examining records and action planning.

This small investment unquestionably paid off handsomely. By reducing two recruiting sources and increasing the use of two others, the recruiters decreased costs to $648,000 per year. That produced a $171,000 per year *improvement benefit* over the previous year's recruiting expenses. That improvement occurred although the level of recruiting remained fairly comparable during both years. As a consequence, the *cost-benefit ratio* of this solution was 107:1. In the outcome, recruiting staff members needed to work harder to earn their pay, but the company saved a large amount of money. Since this amount was a reduction in expenses, it translated directly into bettering the bottom line.

Chapter 11
Training and Development

Billions upon billions of dollars are spent each year to train employees. Estimates vary, but they provide a sense of the incredible magnitude of the training enterprise in the United States. For example, the American Society of Training and Development estimates that companies annually spend $210 billion on both formal and informal training.[1]

Given this huge expense, human resources managers always must keep one key point in mind: Are the training dollars more than coming back to the organization in terms of increased profitability? Unfortunately, most human resources managers do not bother to evaluate the financial impact of training. Instead, they tend to evaluate other phenomenon, especially the reactions of the trainees. Training expert Donald Kirkpatrick delineates four ways to measure training effectiveness:[2]

1. *Reaction*. How did the participants like the training seminar?
2. *Learning*. Did the participants actually learn what the instructors taught them?
3. *Behavior*. Did participants improve their behavior on the job as a result of the training program's effectiveness?
4. *Results*. How did the training enable participants to improve organizational profitability or productivity in a measurable way?

Determining whether training helps participants produce better results is the true bottom line of whether the amount spent on training proves worth it. The way the personnel department at Combined Insurance Company of America's Chicago Service Center makes sure this occurs is embodied in its Training Objectives, displayed in Figure 11-1. This chapter discusses a number of types of training whose effectiveness can be measured in financial terms.

Figure 11-1. Training objectives followed at Combined Insurance Company of America's Chicago Service Center.

TRAINING OBJECTIVES

There are 10 justifications for the expenditure of training dollars and time once a need has been clearly established.

They are to:

1. Increase product knowledge
2. Increase productivity
3. Improve service through increased effectiveness and efficiency
4. Teach or increase skills
5. Increase sales
6. Increase profits
7. Teach people how to set and achieve goals
8. Increase wellness levels
9. Cross-train
10. Otherwise develop people to improve the company's ability to do well in our marketplace

In each training program and its component parts, we must utilize learning assumptions to attain one or more of the above objectives.

Also, a post-program evaluation report must be completed by each participant, outlining what principles, ideas, and techniques they were exposed to in the program and specifically indicate how they will use what they learned.

The report should be directed to their respective department heads with a copy to the personnel department within one month of completing the course.

This is a condition precedent to receiving credit for having successfully completed the program.

Human resources managers who are responsible for training must keep in mind that others in the organization often want to bask in the glory of a training program that results in bottom line improvements. This occurs because the effectiveness of training can become a variation of the chicken-or-the-egg question. For instance, a training department puts on a terrific seminar that aims to improve the bottom line. Sure enough, in a follow-up evaluation a few months later, the training department discovers the fact that indeed the skills taught in the program resulted in measurably increased productivity. So, the training department might want to take the credit.

But as soon as that occurs, the department managers whose employees attended the training program claim that they paid particular attention to reinforcing the skills taught in the training program over the last few months. The department managers say they deserve the credit for the profit improvement. Then, the engineering department could announce that it focused its endeavors on helping to improve the efficiency and effectiveness of the employees who attended this special training program. Finally, top management also claims credit. After all, senior managers might declare that it was their idea to hold the training program in the first place. Plus, they made sure that all company resources and in-company publicity zeroed in on helping employees become more productive in precisely the skills taught in the training program.

What should a training manager do in a situation like this? Simple. Realize that everyone wants a pat on the back. Also, acknowledge that the effectiveness of training almost invariably relies on interdepartmental efforts. No single department can take total credit—or blame—for a training program's effectiveness. However, such largess does not preclude the *importance* of *measuring* the bottom line effectiveness of a training endeavor. And such measurement very, very often falls in the hands of the human resources professionals charged with providing or overseeing the training conducted in the company.

With these considerations in mind, this chapter discusses four types of training that can produce measurable improvements for an organization, as follows:

1. Training to avoid expensive equal employment opportunity problems
2. Training nonsales support staff to sell
3. Technical skills training
4. Performance management training

■ TRAINING TO AVOID EXPENSIVE EQUAL EMPLOYMENT OPPORTUNITY PROBLEMS

Business Problem Addressed

Equal Employment Opportunity

Overview of Solution

Organizations probably spend billions of dollars each year as a result of Equal Employment Opportunity (EEO) problems. Any manager who ever experienced an EEO complaint process knows the wrenching emotions and the tremendous amount of time and effort that went into handling the charge. If the charge was thrown out during an EEO hearing, then the organization needlessly wasted time and money. However, if the charge resulted in a monetary settlement, then the organization rightly can feel cheated by the employees who discriminated and thus unnecessarily cost the company money.

It is precisely because EEO discrimination can be avoided that training becomes so important. Why? Because the two major ways to lower the number and intensity of EEO complaints are through company policies that prohibit any form of discrimination, and training employees to avoid committing EEO offenses.

Both solutions fall within the realm of the human resources department. Usually the human resources department takes responsibility for such employment-related policies. Also, it is in the human resources department's purview to train employees in what is acceptable and unacceptable EEO-related behavior.

How to Implement Solution

1. *Diagnose organization's EEO problems.* To do this analysis, examine company records. For instance, if the organization has spent money to settle sexual harassment charges, then its employees certainly need training on how to prevent such charges. However, a broadbrush EEO training program may prove best if the company has a record of committing an array of EEO offenses. The essence of this diagnosis is to make sure that the training does not, as the phrase goes, shoot a mouse with an elephant gun. Train people in what they need, rather than what they do not need.

2. *Provide relevant training.* Based on the diagnosis, offer training that addresses the avoidable problems that squander the company's money. The training requires some review of EEO laws and guidelines. It also benefits from a heavy dose of specific do's and don'ts that employees can keep in mind to guide their on-the-job behavior.

3. *Evaluate training effectiveness.* This step answers the question of whether the cost of EEO complaints decreases after the training. If it does, then the training helped get the point across. If not, then either the training proved ineffective or managers are not enforcing the company's EEO policies. For the former problem, the training program can be improved. To address the latter problem, better communication of policies, along with stricter disciplinary actions for infractions, needs to be implemented.

Deadline for Implementing Solution

The diagnosis step should take about a week, but the timeframe depends on how many EEO-related cases the company has had. After the diagnosis phase concludes, training can be designed and started within a month or two.

Deadline for Measuring Profit Improvement

In a company with few EEO complaints, it may take a year to measure the decrease in the dollars spent on EEO grievances. For companies with many EEO complaints, especially charges that result in the firm's paying settlement claims, the decrease in these disbursements should become measurable within half a year.

TRAINING TO PREVENT SEXUAL HARASSMENT

A division of a major oil company found itself bogged down in a costly, yet quite avoidable, *business problem* as a result of quite a few sexual harassment complaints by female employees. The company seldom doubted the accuracy of the claims, since so many employees openly made sexual remarks and advances to female employees and even to female visitors. Indeed, managers often referred to the company as a "boys' club," since almost all employees were male and it was in a macho sort of industry and environment.

During the previous year, the *cost of the problem* amounted to almost three-quarters of a million dollars, as detailed in Figure 11-2. This amount stemmed from two sorts of expenses. First, since the company realized that its environment bred harassment, the organiza-

Figure 11-2. Planning Model for training to prevent sexual harassment.

BUSINESS PROBLEM

A company spent a great deal of money due to sexual harassment charges against it. These charges were avoidable; therefore, the decreased profitability was unnecessary.

COST OF BUSINESS PROBLEM

$722,000/year

Costs included:

    A. Cost to settle sexual harassment complaints
    B. Turnover due to sexual harassment

A. Settlement costs
    = Annual number of sexual harassment complaints × Average cost to settle each sexual harassment complaint
    = 26 complaints/year × $21,000/complaint
    = $546,000/year
B. Turnover
    = Annual number of turnovers due to sexual harassment × Average cost per turnover
    = 22 turnovers/year × $8,000/turnover
    = $176,000/year

Cost of problem
    = $546,000/year + $176,000/year
    = $722,000/year

SOLUTION TO BUSINESS PROBLEM

Train all management staff in how to avoid sexual harassment charges

COST OF SOLUTION

$11,160

Cost
    = Number of managers attending sexual harassment workshop × Average hourly salary and benefits of attendees × Number of hours of workshop
    = 465 managers × $16/hour × 1.5 hours
    = $11,160

$ IMPROVEMENT BENEFIT

$674,000/year

Improvement benefit
    = Cost of problem before implementing solution − Cost of problem after implement-
       ing solution
Cost before implementing solution = $722,000/year
Costs after implementing solution included:

    A. Settlement costs
    B. Turnover

A. Settlement costs
    = Annual number of sexual harassment complaints × Average cost to settle each
       sexual harassment complaint
    = 1 complaint/year × $34,000
    = $34,000/year
B. Turnover
    = Annual number of turnovers due to sexual harassment × Average cost per turnover
    = 1 turnover/year × $14,000/turnover
    = $14,000/year

Cost after implementing solution
    = $34,000/year + $14,000/year
    = $48,000/year
Improvement benefit
    = $722,000/year − $48,000
    = $674,000/year

COST-BENEFIT RATIO

60:1

$674,000/year:$11,160

---

tion seldom bothered to fight the complaints. Instead, the company just paid off the complainants to settle the suit as quickly and as inexpensively as possible. These "pay offs" (the term the company used) rang up a $546,000 per year tab. Second, the sexual harassment caused turnover costing $176,000 for the year. Some of the females who filed complaints left the company rather than continue to work in that environment. Also, some of the male employees who sexually harassed females departed from the organization either because they were fired or too embarrassed to continue.

Such turnover expenses are not unusual in sexual harassment situations. For example, the U.S. Office of Management and Budget estimates that sexual harassment resulted in $189 million in turnover between May 1978 and December 1980.[3]

To stop this unnecessary outflow of funds and the morale problems the harassment engendered, the company embarked on a two-prong *solution.* First, it reissued its antisexual harassment policy and made sure it was posted on all bulletin boards. Second, the company instituted a *required* sexual harassment workshop for all managers, from first-line supervisors to the top executives. A total of 465 managers attended this one and one-half hour workshop.

The *cost of the solution* turned out to be a quite reasonable $11,160. In return, the *improvement benefit* was $674,000 per year in dramatically reduced sexual harassment expenses. This improvement showed a 60:1 *cost-benefit ratio* for the endeavor. As mentioned earlier, the fine results from training may have been due to a number of factors, including the training, top management's fervent concern about this problem, or other causes. Regardless, the training to prevent sexual harassment played a key role in increasing the company's profitability and not paying complainants or lawyers or overcoming turnover problems.

There is an interesting sidenote to the company's superb decrease in sexual harassment complaints. In the year following the training, the company needed to resolve only one sexual harassment complaint. It cost the company a pretty penny, though. The complaint and the departure of the secretary who complained cost the organization $48,000. The woman who complained did so because her boss inappropriately touched her on quite a few occasions. Amazingly, her boss was a manager in the human resources department!

■ TRAINING NONSALES SUPPORT STAFF TO SELL

Business Problem Addressed

Sales Force Performance

Overview of Solution

The following scenarios are becoming increasingly common:

- You order a hamburger at a fast food restaurant, and the cashier asks you, "Will you be drinking cola or coffee with your hamburger?"
- You deposit a check at your local bank, and the teller says to you, "I notice that you usually have extra money in your savings account. You'll get a much higher interest rate if you put some of that untouched money into one of our bank's certificates of deposit. Let me get a financial counselor to tell you how you can make this extra money so easily. OK?"
- You call the phone company to ask about your bill. After the customer service representative handles your question, she says to you, "You seem to use your phone a lot, don't you" After you say, "Yes, I sure do use it a lot," the customer service representative says, "You probably realize that when you're on the phone people who want to reach you

just get a busy signal, so they hang up. That means you're missing phone calls. So you won't ever again miss a phone call, we could hook up call waiting for you. Then, whenever someone tries to call you while you've got the phone line tied up, you'll hear a beep, and be able to easily find out who is calling you. Let me sign you up for this service. You'll find it really helpful, and you'll like how easy it is to use."

What do all these occurrences have in common? In each situation, a nonsales person discreetly tried to sell. This is a breakthrough in sales that more and more companies use. They are beginning to use their normally nonsales support staff—such as cashiers, tellers, and customer service representatives—to pitch their wares. After all, these employees already are on the payroll. Furthermore, they spend a good deal of time with customers. And finally, they often talk to the customer exactly when the customer may feel most inclined to buy.

Teaching nonsales support staff to sell or help sell is an area that is ripe for the picking. Smart companies realize that their "sales" staff can be increased many times over by using support staff as a type of salesperson. Since more companies do this, the results probably can be quite lucrative.

How to Implement Solution

1. *Determine which nonsales support staff to train*. This step entails realizing which cashiers, customer service representatives, or other employees normally speak with customers about financial or sales-oriented matters. These are the people who profitably can begin selling for the organization.

2. *Train them in add-on and referral selling*. Add-on and referral selling are two main ways that nonsales support staff can sell. Add-on selling occurs when a customer has already decided to buy something and the support staff member suggests a logical additional—or add-on—item to buy. For instance, the fast-food cashier might suggest a logical extension of a hamburger that a customer is buying, namely, something to drink while eating the hamburger or a bag of french fries.

Referral selling occurs when a sales support person uncovers a need of a customer and then *refers* the customer to a salesperson within the company. For example, a depositor may mention to a friendly bank teller that she is going out to look at new cars. The bank teller then may *refer* the depositor to the loan officer who handles car loans.

3. *Evaluate training effectiveness*. Organizations should try to measure the effectiveness of add-on and referral selling. Sometimes this proves rather difficult. For instance, would the fast-food chain customer have bought a beverage anyway, even without the cashier suggesting it? Would the depositor have come back to the bank later to inquire about a car loan? These questions are hard to answer. Nevertheless, some measures of effectiveness should be gathered. For instance, the company could measure how much more it sold of a particular item since the support staff started add-on and referral selling.

Deadline for Implementing Solution

The entire process of determining whom to train and training should be completed within a few months.

Deadline for Measuring Profit Improvement

Measures of profit improvement can be taken fairly shortly after the support staff completes the training. If this nonsales staff is not readily increasing sales, then the training may not have worked well or the company may not be suitably encouraging the sales efforts of its nonsales staff. Companies need to know this soon after the training, so that they can put into place the needed organizational or training enhancements. By doing so, the company can respond in a way that encourages its special sales efforts.

INCREASING REFERRAL AND ADD-ON SELLING IN A BANK

A bank saw a profit-making opportunity in a *business problem.* Since its founding, it had drawn clear lines of distinction among the job duties of its tellers, financial counselors, and branch managers. As the financial services industry evolved, the bank realized that it needed to make almost all of its employees who had customer contact into salespeople in one form or another. This need pointed to a *solution to the business problem:* teach its tellers, financial counselors, and branch managers how to do add-on and referral selling.

The *cost of the solution* came to $63,360, as delineated in the *Planning Model* in Figure 11-3. This sum included the cost of the sales training consultants who conducted the training needs analysis and the training. It also incorporated the salaries and benefits of the tellers, financial counselors, and branch managers who participated in the training.

The training and the bank's new sales-oriented (rather than just service-oriented) push worked magnificently. The *improvement benefit* from this new approach amounted to almost $50 million per year. Add-on sales increased with financial counselors more than doubling the number of bank products sold each time a customer visited them.

Figure 11-3. Planning Model for bank training to increase add-on and referral selling.

BUSINESS PROBLEM

A bank decided that its staff members could sell financial products and services even while they carried out their normal nonsales activities.

COST OF BUSINESS PROBLEM

N/A

SOLUTION TO BUSINESS PROBLEM

Train tellers, financial counselors, and branch managers in (1) referral selling and (2) add-on selling

COST OF SOLUTION

$63,360

Costs included:

A. Consultants doing training needs analysis, as well as designing and conducting training
B. Trainees' (tellers, financial counselors, and branch managers) salaries and benefits during training

A. Consultants = $30,000
B. Trainees' salaries and benefits
   = Number of trainees × Average salary and benefits per day × Number of days of training
   For tellers: 75 tellers × $72/day × 2 days
   = $10,800
   For financial counselors: 50 financial counselors × $104/day × 2 days
   = $10,400
   For branch managers: 20 branch managers × $152/day × 4 days
   = $12,160

Cost of solution
   = $30,000 + $10,800 + $10,400 + $12,160
   = $63,360

$ IMPROVEMENT BENEFIT

Over $49,200,000/year

Referral selling increased from $10.8 million/year to $60 million/year. So, improvement benefit in referral selling
   = $60,000,000/year − $10,800,000/year
   = $49,200,000/year.
Add-on selling increased from an average of 1.3 to 2.86 bank products sold each time a financial counselor was visited by a customer. However, the bank did not calculate a dollar value associated with the increased add-on selling.

COST-BENEFIT RATIO

776:1 for referral sales increases
$49,200,000/year:$63,360
77.6:1 in increased profits
if bank made 10% profit on these sales

These products included special accounts, investments, loans, safe deposit box rentals, and other products the bank offered. However, the bank did not calculate the value of this add-on selling that definitely contributed to the bank's bottom line.

A comparison of the amount of increased referral selling to the cost of the training bears a 776:1 *cost-benefit ratio.* If the bank made a 10 percent profit on these new sales, the cost-benefit ratio would be 77.6:1. Given the need for practically all organizations to increase sales, these figures show how very lucrative an investment in this sort of sales training can be.

■ TECHNICAL SKILLS TRAINING

Business Problems Addressed

Productivity
Work-Group Effectiveness

Overview of Solution

When employees do not know how to do the technical aspects of their work, then the organization suffers. It cannot produce its goods or services as efficiently or as effectively as possible. For this reason, technical skills training takes on a great deal of importance. Indeed, although some people may consider the enterprise's training budget as an expendable item, these same people rightfully could get upset if their employees did not know how to carry out their jobs in the quickest and most productive manner possible. Such reactions underscore the significance of training employees in needed technical skills.

This work may be carpentry or data processing, toiling on a production line or engineering new product designs. Regardless of the specifics of the skills needed, proper training plays an integral role in an organization's success. Some technical training occurs in on-the-job coaching or just through learning by watching others. However, some skills are best learned in a more formal, structured setting in a class or seminar. This section focuses on the sort of formal training that employes need to do their jobs well.

How to Implement Solution

1. *Conduct job analysis.* To do a useful job analysis, determine what specific knowledge, skills and abilities (KSAs) people need to complete their work successfully.

2. *Compare the job analysis with employees' current ability levels.* Using the job analysis as a guide, pinpoint how well job holders can carry out their duties. It is the discrepancy between their current job performance and the KSAs needed to carry out their jobs well that needs to be addressed.

3. *Provide needed technical skills training.* Figure out what KSAs employees could learn best through on-the-job coaching or mentoring. Also, employees can develop certain skills simply by reading manuals or books. However, employees learn some KSAs best by

attending courses and seminars. These classes may be offered at the company or at local colleges, universities, and vocational schools.

4. *Evaluate whether employees do their jobs better*. The basic and most important question is: After the training—through on-the-job experiences, readings, or formal coursework—does the employee perform better? Also, does this improvement show up as increased productivity or decreased expenses?

Deadline for Implementing Solution

A job analysis usually can be completed for most jobs in one-half to two days. After that, it requires fairly little time to decide what training an employee needs and then get that employee into the appropriate training.

Deadline for Measuring Profit Improvement

If better trained employees will result in less expenses (for example, decreased waste or overtime costs), then the decreases can be measured soon after the training. If training aims to increase productivity, then measures of such increases often can be made within a few months of employees having completed training.

REDUCING THE COST OF UNDERTRAINED DATA PROCESSING PROFESSIONALS

A division of a major food company experienced a very expensive *business problem* in its data processing (DP) department. As a result of sudden changes in the business's direction, and thus it DP needs, a key business unit had six DP professionals who were not functioning up to par because of their inadequate training. The new DP director determined that these employees caused two major problems. Specifically, they (1) cost the division a good deal of money to make up for the technical skills they lacked and (2) provided less than satisfactory service to the business unit that needed the expertise they were supposed to render.

The annual *cost of the business problem* was $326,880. As shown in Figure 11-4, this included money for outside contract programmers to do some of the work these six programmers were supposed to do. It also involved their manager's estimate that they were productive only one-half of the time and also that the manager spent more than the normal amount of time coaching them on how to do their work.

The *solution to the business problem* was twofold. The manager of these six professionals first did a thorough job analysis to determine exactly what technical skills these programmers needed. Then, given the job analysis information, a training program was found to equip the programmers with the technical skills they lacked. The *cost of this solution* amounted to $40,032. As expected, the solution worked well. The adequately trained programmers eliminated the need for the company to pay expensive outside contract programmers to make up

Figure 11-4. Planning Model for decreasing costs through proper technical training.

BUSINESS PROBLEM

Six improperly trained data processing professionals cost a company a lot of money to make up for their lack of certain skills. Also, a key business unit received inadequate help from these six DP professionals.

COST OF BUSINESS PROBLEM

$326,880/year

Costs included:

A. Contract programmers' costs
B. Cost of six employees being productive only one-half time
C. Cost of manager spending extra time with these inadequately trained employees

A. Contract programmer costs = $162,000/year
B. Cost for employees' nonproductive time
   = Number of inadequately trained employees × Average percentage of time they are less than fully productive × Average annual salary and benefits
   = 6 employees × .50 unproductive time × $48,000/year
   = $144,000/year
C. Cost of manager's extra time
   = Number of hours per month spent on extra coaching per employee × Hourly salary and benefits × Number of employees needing special coaching × 12 months/year
   = 10 hours/month × $29/hour × 6 employees × 12 months/year
   = $20,800/year

Cost of problem
   = $162,000/year + $144,000/year + $20,880/year
   = $326,880/year

SOLUTION TO BUSINESS PROBLEM

Conduct detailed job analysis to determine what skills the programmers need. Then, provide them with the needed technical training.

COST OF SOLUTION

$40,032

Costs included:

A. Job analysis
B. Training

A. Job analysis
   = Number of hours for managers to complete job analysis × Hourly salary and
     benefits of manager
   = 8 hours × $29/hour
   = $232
B. Training
   = (Number of employees receiving special technical training × Cost of training per
     employee) + (Number of employees receiving training × Salaries and benefits of
     employees during training)
   = (6 employees × $4,200/employee) + (6 employees × $2,600/employee)
   = $40,800

Cost of solution
   = $232 + $40,800
   = $41,032

$ IMPROVEMENT BENEFIT

$287,728/year

Improvement benefit
   = Cost before implementing solution − Cost after implementing solution
Cost before implementing solution = $326,880/year
Cost after implementing solution included:

   A. Contract programmers' costs
   B. Costs of 6 employees being productive less than full-time
   C. Cost of manager spending extra time with inadequately trained employees

A. Contract programmers' costs = $0
B. Cost of employees' nonproductive time
   = Number of inadequately trained employees × Average percentage of time they are
     less than fully productive × Average annual salary and benefits
   = 6 employees × .10 of the time × $48,000/year
   = $28,800/year
C. Cost of manager's extra time
   = Number of hours per month spent on extra coaching per employee × Hourly salary
     and benefits × Number of employees needing special coaching × 12 months/year
   = 4 hours/month × $29/hour × 6 employees × 12 months/year
   = $8,352/year

Cost after implementing solution
   = $28,800/year + $8,352/year
   = $37,152/year
Improvement benefit
   = $326,880/year − $37,152/year
   = $289,728/year

(continued)

(Figure 11-4 continued)

<u>COST-BENEFIT RATIO</u>

7.2:1

$289,728/year:$40,032

---

for their lack of expertise. Also, the six programmers were productive in their jobs almost all the time, as their manager estimated. Finally, they needed much less extra coaching from their manager. As a consequence of these factors, the *improvement-benefit ratio* totaled $289,728 per year. That produced a 7.2:1 *cost-benefit ratio* from furnishing the needed technical skills training. Also, although not quantified, the DP division could help a particular key business unit much better now that it possessed a properly trained staff.

■ PERFORMANCE MANAGEMENT TRAINING

Business Problems Addressed

Productivity
Work-Group Effectiveness
Manager and Executive Effectiveness

Overview of Solution

Question: What do companies as different CIGNA (a large insurance company) and Yellow Freight System (one of America's biggest trucking companies) have in common?

Answer: Both companies' training departments have provided performance management training that has resulted in *measurable corporate profit improvement*.[4,5,6] This is bottom line-oriented training at its finest.

In general, performance management programs prove much more extensive than the typical goal-setting and performance appraisal programs found in many organizations. Performance management programs also take more time and care to train managers to:

☐ Specify *measureable* productivity goals for both work groups and individuals they manage
☐ Provide objective feedback on how work-group and individual performance stacks up against the productivity goals
☐ Wield interpersonal skills to reward or reinforce productive on-the-job performance, while altering job performance that does not meet or exceed productivity goals

Actually, it is hard to imagine a well-run performance management program *not* adding to the bottom line, and research bears out this assertion. Scrutiny of 28 research reports on the effectiveness of providing objective feedback to employees on their productivity, an integral ingredient of performance management systems, found that productivity invariably increased. These productivity boosts ranged from 5 percent to 482 percent.[7]

Performance management undoubtedly offers human resources professionals a cost-effective way to play key roles in upgrading the bottom line. However, one key fact stands out: An effective performance management program requires intense involvement, encouragement, and enthusiasm from all levels of management, starting with the chairman of the board and proceeding all the way down to first-line supervisors. Without such commitment, a performance management program will flounder. Garnering such support falls on the shoulders of training staff within the human resources department.

Performance management programs do not start and stop in an organization's seminar rooms. Instead, each manager who attends performance management training *must* carry out *measurable* goal setting and objective feedback reporting on his or her job. Often these duties are reported both to the manager's own supervisor, as well as to the performance management trainer. A built-in part of the program consists of actually implementing the productivity improvement strategies and tactics presented in the performance management classroom.

Yellow Freight System, Inc., for example, illustrates what it considers the seven components of its performance management system, "Performance Management—The Yellow Freight Way," in the drawing. Figure 11-5 illustrates how employees and managers need to pull together on seven factors that promote top-notch performance.

Yellow Freight's program has featured management involvement at all levels, intensive training, videotapes, lots of job aids that participants can use in their daily activities, and job models that describe positions in very measurable terms. A job aid on solving employee performance problems is shown in Figure 11-6. A job model appears in Figure 11-7.

How to Implement Solution

1. *Analyze performance improvement needs.* This analysis entails interviewing managers at all levels of the organization to determine performance problems. Such problems are the main areas that might be addressed in the performance management program. For instance, Yellow Freight's performance management program initially focused on improving the profitability produced at its hundreds of terminals, since a big potential payback existed there.

2. *Advertise top management's support and involvement.* Without top management's enthusiastic role in the process, a performance management system is doomed to failure. Such support may be demonstrated in company newsletters, speeches by top management, and videotapes of top executives' reactions to the program, which can be shown during training sessions.

3. *Train all managers.* The first managers who need to go through the training are top executives. They must know exactly what all lower level managers will do as a result of the program. Hopefully, the top managers will immediately begin using performance management skills and *demand* that their subordinates do likewise.

4. *Evaluate in bottom-line terms.* A crucial portion of CIGNA Corporation's performance management program, called the Basic Management Skills training program, is participants' on-the-job measurement of how their skills result in productivity improve-

Figure 11-5. Yellow Freight System's performance chain.

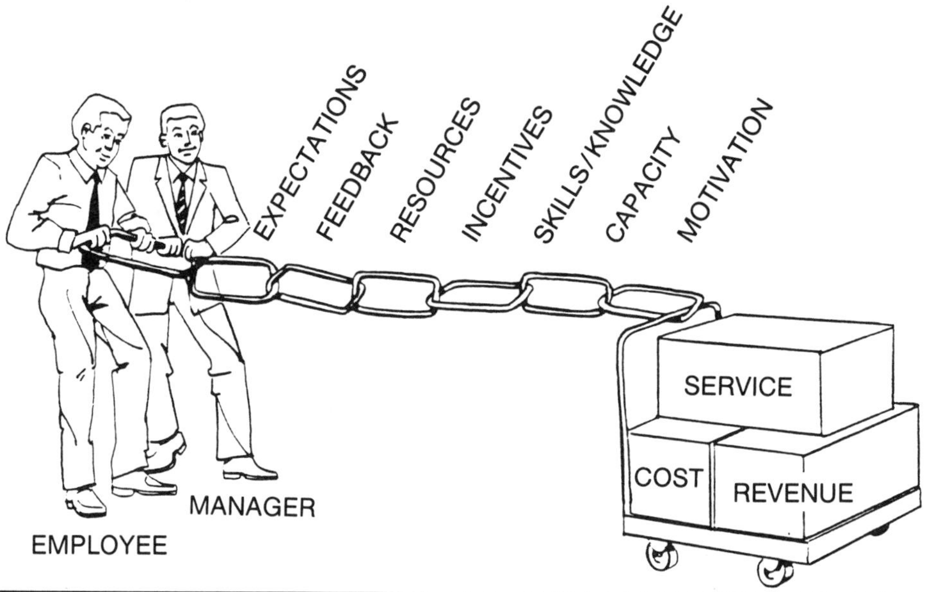

ment. Specifically, after participants attend the training, they need to begin measuring performance of their work groups and individuals in their work groups. These measures are reported to higher levels of management, as well as to the training department. By building in participants' measuring their own productivity and reporting it, CIGNA's corporate management development and training staff do not need to run after trainees to get data on how successful their program is.

Deadline for Implementing Solution

Despite the appeal of this profit improving human resources management technique, companies should not quickly jump into starting performance management training. After all, successful programs require extensive management time and effort, not just the training component of the program. Any human resources department that wants to start such a program needs to garner much-needed support *before* beginning the program. The people providing the training must be skilled at training. They should be trainers with performance mangement expertise or, as Yellow Freight has done, line managers who have an excellent management track record in addition to fine training skills. It takes time to arrange all these components. For that reason, it may take a human resources department six months or more preparation before a company-wide performance management program can be launched.

Deadline for Measuring Profit Improvement

Profit improvements made by each person who receives performance management training should be measured within three months after the person completes the program. Later measures also need to be taken to assure that progress in productivity continues.

Figure 11-6. Job aid from Yellow Freight's Performance Management Program.

SOLVING EMPLOYEE PERFORMANCE PROBLEMS: THEIR CAUSES, TROUBLE-SHOOTING QUESTIONS FOR MANAGERS, AND THEIR SOLUTIONS

Causes	Trouble-shooting Questions	Solutions
Expectations/ feedback	• Do all employees know what their major duties are and the standards by which performance will be judged? • Are employees frequently told how closely their performance matches the standards? • Is each employee told exactly what is acceptable or unacceptable about his or her performance?	• Provide clear expectations • Give feedback about how closely performance matches your expectations
Resources	• Is each employee given the resources necessary to meet the standards: (procedures, tools, materials, time, forms, people, facilities)	• Provide necessary resources
Incentives	• Is each employee rewarded for performance that meets the standards? • Is any employee punished for meeting the standards? • Is any employee rewarded when performance is less than the standard? • Are the rewards for good performance meaningful to each employee?	• Give rewards for good work • Remove punishment for good work • Remove rewards for poor work • Give rewards that fit
Knowledge	• Does each employee know how to do his or her assignments?	• Train employee • Give memory aid
Capacity	• Can each employee tolerate long hours, heat and cold, and acquire the skills	• Transfer person • Change hiring process • Fire employee
Motivation	• Is each employee willing to do his or her assignments to the standards you set, under the work conditions at your terminal, for the benefits which are available?	• Transfer person • Change hiring process • Fire employee

Figure 11-7. Job model from Yellow Freight's Performance Management Program.

BRANCH MANAGER

Major Duties	General Measures	Specific Measures	Performance Standards
Terminal operations controlled	Cost	Overall cost per bill	$14.99–15.25
		Percentage of overtime	3.5–4%
		Raw wage cost per bill	$5.75–6.00
		Claims ratio	1.3–1.5%
		Office cost/bill	(Insert standard)
	Quantity	LTL bills/hour (P & D)	2.90–3.10
		Dock lbs./hr.	3300–3500
		Dock bills/hr.	3.9–4.1
		Office bills/hr.	4.8–5.0
		TL bills/hr.	.50–.60
		Number of bills per power unit	21/avg.
	Quality	Percentage of returns	0–5%
		Number of OD-79's/week	None
		Number of valid customer complaints	0–2/week
		Number of missed pick-ups	0–2/week
		Load average	36,000–38,000 lbs.
	Timeliness	Percentage of delivered on time	Mon 85–100% Tuesday 90–100% Wed-Fri 100%
		Percentage of service spread	10%/week
Revenue Generated	Quantity	Percentage of LTL bill growth	+8–12%
	Quality	Percentage of attainment of sales emphasis quota	80–100%
		Delinquent index	100–125
		LTL revenue/bill	$125–$150/bill
	Cost	Sales expense/bill	$.50–.75/bill
Equipment and facility maintained	Cost	Maintenance cost per bill	$1.50–2.00/bill

Major Duties	General Measures	Specific Measures	Performance Standards
		Wages lost due to equipment breakdowns	Less than $100/month
		Percentage of overtime in shop	(Insert standard)
		Facility cost/bill	$2.00–$2.50/ bill
		City equipment cost/bill	$1.50–$2.00/ bill
Equipment and facility maintained (Cont'd)	Quality	Number of equipment breakdowns	0–1/month
		Appearance of building and yard	Area Manager judges
	Timeliness	Percentage of PMs done by schedule	100% by deadline
Safety procedures followed	Quality	Number of violations on Safety Dept. terminal inspection report	0–2 per inspection
	Quantity	Number of vehicular accidents	0–1/month
		Number of workman's comp. claims	0–1/month
	Timeliness	Number of safety meetings held by deadline	One during month
	Cost	Number of OSHA fines	None
Reports submitted	Timeliness	Percentage of submitted by deadline	100%
	Quality	Accuracy of reports	Area Manager judges
Employee performance managed			
Job models provided	Quality	Percentage of employees with job models on file	100%
		Percentage of employees who know/agree with their job models	100%

(continued)

(Figure 11-7 continued)

Major Duties	General Measures	Specific Measures	Performance Standards
Feedback provided	Quality	Percentage of employees who know how they're doing as often as needed	100%
Resources obtained	Quality	Adequacy of resources	Area Manager judges
Employees rewarded	Quality	Evidence of reward system	Area Manager judges
Employees developed	Quality	Number of terminal functions each employee can perform	Area Manager judges
Employees hired	Quality	Employee job performance	Employee meets job standards
Labor contract managed	Cost	Money paid to settle grievances	Less than $100/month
	Quality	Decisions made are consistent with company objectives	Area Manager judges

These measures should not only be reported to the human resources department, but also must be reported to managers in each participants' department or division, as well as to top management.

PERFORMANCE MANAGEMENT TRAINING TO IMPROVE PROFITS

Based on the experiences of companies that instituted performance management programs, the following scenario summarizes how such training can lead to improved corporate profitability. In general, the *business problem* addresses the concern of how to get all managers in a company involved in *measurably* improving productivity and reducing costs, as mentioned in Figure 11-8. Since the goal is to improve current profit levels, there is no *cost of the business problem* in the usual sense of the term.

The *solution to the business problem* is to operate a performance management program. This program would include five days of training for all the company's managerial personnel. During the training, the participants would learn how to apply the essentials of performance management to their own jobs. These essentials include developing:

☐ measurable performance standards
☐ methods to measure work performed by work groups and individuals

Figure 11-8. Planning Model for a Performance Management Program.

<u>BUSINESS PROBLEM</u>

A company desires to improve its profitability while creating an environment that greatly values outstanding productivity by all employees.

<u>COST OF BUSINESS PROBLEM</u>

N/A

<u>SOLUTION TO BUSINESS PROBLEM</u>

Training in performance management. Training focuses on
- developing work measurement techniques
- conveying work goals in measurable terms
- giving objective feedback and motivation to employees on their productivity
- reporting measurable productivity results

<u>COST OF SOLUTION</u>

$424,000 for first year

Costs included:

A. Trainees' salaries and benefits during training
B. Trainers' salaries and benefits
C. Equipment and training materials

A. Trainees' salaries and benefits
   = Number of trainees × Trainees' average daily salary and benefits × Number of training days
   = 500 trainees × $120/day × $5 days
   = $300,000
B. Trainers' salaries and benefits
   = Number of performance management trainers × Average annual trainer's salary and benefits
   = 2 trainers × $52,000/year
   = $104,000/year
C. Equipment and training materials = $20,000

Cost of solution
   = $300,000 + $104,000 + $20,000
   = $424,000

<u>$ IMPROVEMENT BENEFIT</u>

$1,000,000 for first year

(continued)

(Figure 11-8 continued)

This assumes that each of the 500 trainees uses the performance management knowledge to increase profits by only $2,000 during the first year of the program.

<u>COST-BENEFIT RATIO</u>

2.4:1 for first year

$1,000,000:$424,000

□ techniques to give employees objective feedback on productivity
□ tactics to motivate and reinforce employees
□ methods to improve below par performance of employees
□ reporting procedures to keep tabs on performance improvements

At first glance, the *cost of the solution* looks awesome. If two performance management trainers put 500 managers through the training, the tab would run to $424,000 for the first year of the program. If all managers went through the training during the first year of the performance management program, then the training costs certainly would be drastically reduced for subsequent years of the program, because after the first year of the program, only new managers would need to attend the week-long performance management seminar. Also, a crucial part of the trainers' jobs would be to develop and maintain a record-keeping system that tracks the profit improvement resulting from the program.

If each of the 500 managers who went through the training used his or her newfound knowledge to produce merely $2,000 in additional profits—through cost savings and productivity improvements—then the first year of the program would reap a one million dollar *improvement benefit* for the company. Given the research cited earlier, a $2,000 improvement per participant might prove rather conservative. Still, it illustrates the point that the performance management program can easily more than pay for itself even during its first, and most expensive, year. In fact, such a profit improvement track record would result in the program producing a 2.4:1 *cost-benefit ratio.* In future years, with much lower training costs, the program should produce even greater cost-benefit ratios, even if each participant continues to increase profits by only $2,000 annually.

PART III
POINTERS TO MAKE
THE PROFIT CENTER SUCCESSFUL

Chapter 12
What to Do Now

Successfully turning the human resources cost center into a corporate profit center can't happen overnight. It is an ongoing process. This concluding chapter presents recommendations for how to replace the traditional human resources cost center with a thriving, crucially important profit center. Toward this goal, the following points are most important:

- [ ] When to start the human resources profit center
- [ ] How to start the profit center
- [ ] Publicity to fuel the excitement
- [ ] Incentive pay for human resources managers
- [ ] Snapshot of a successful human resources profit center

WHEN TO START THE HUMAN RESOURCES PROFIT CENTER

Start right now.

Franklin Roosevelt said, "There is nothing to fear except fear itself." Yet, fear is precisely what keeps many human resources professionals from jumping into the profit center method of becoming truly *value-able* to their organizations. They often say that they are not viewed as "real businesspeople," so it seems difficult to change that image.

In practice, improving that image proves incredibly easy. It just takes concentration on business problems, implementing human resources-oriented solutions to those business problems, and measuring the cost-benefits of those solutions. Then, it takes publicity of various kinds to make sure that *everyone* in the organization—especially top management—realizes how very valuable the human resources staff really can be. Nothing stands in the way of human resources managers starting their department's new, profit-focused activities.

HOW TO START THE PROFIT CENTER

The origin of any enterprise's human resources profit center is a *needs analysis*. This needs analysis uncovers exactly what *business problems* the organization faces, along with a sense of the dollar magnitude of the problem. From there, human resources managers can select solutions that will help decrease costs or otherwise increase profitability. The planning schedule for turning human resources into a corporate profit generator (Figure 3-1) proves incredibly useful in this endeavor. It delineates specific business problems, possible human resources-type solutions to each problem, along with other information to solve the business problem of improving profitability. The *Planning Schedule* is an invaluable tool that the human resources profit center uses over and over again.

After uncovering specific business problems and deciding on human resources-type solutions to the business problems, the next step is to present these ideas and plans to top management. Such presentations work best when top management sees the first four steps of the Planning Model, as displayed in Figure 2-1, laid out in detail. Those four steps are:

☐ Business problem
☐ Cost of business problem
☐ Solution to business problem
☐ Cost of solution

Given these four steps, top management can see that human resources managers are thinking of improving profitability in concrete terms. This time may well be the first that they witness human resources staff addressing profit improvement in anything other than *un*measurable platitudes. After all, the usual phrases that human resources managers use to express any connection to profits are rather vague clichés, such as "Good human resources management plays a key role in our company's success" or "By doing a good job, the human resources department helps the company do better in the marketplace." It sometimes shocks top executives to hear human resources managers endeavor to play *business* roles rather than their typical *service* roles.

Once top management sees what human resources staff members might accomplish in turning business problems into business opportunities, they are apt to be quite supportive and encouraging. Later, when the human resources-oriented solutions *do* help overcome business problems, the human resources managers must go back to their company's executives with the last two steps of the *Planning Model* completed in detail. These steps are:

☐ $ Improvement benefit
☐ Cost-benefit ratio

Presentations showing all six steps of the *Planning Model* make even the most jaded, cynical executives stand up and take notice. They become enthusiastic about the profit center approach to managing human resources when they see the dollars-and-cents advantage of doing so.

PUBLICITY TO FUEL THE EXCITEMENT

Whereas top management support and commitment is the first and most important to obtain, there are other constituencies to please. These groups include everyone else in the company, as well as professional, trade, and business groups that might be interested in the successes of the profit center. Many opportunities exist for getting in-company publicity. For example, the human resources staff can:

☐ Write articles for the company newsletter
☐ Deliver presentations to employees and managers
☐ Place descriptions of profit center successes on company bulletin boards
☐ Meet one-on-one with key managers to describe how profit center solutions measurably strengthened company profitability

Even public notice of profit center achievements is possible and also quite often desirable. Most company public relations departments want to publicize how the company is well managed. What better way exists to do so than to contact local or national media with profit center successes. Such stories make good public relations in business, trade, and professional periodicals. They even may appeal to the editors of widely read national publications, such as *The Wall Street Journal, Business Week, Nation's Business,* and *Industry Week,* along with many others.

Such publicity also becomes useful for the human resources managers involved. After all, that sort of media attention is bound to increase the status and worth of the human resources managers who contribute to the success. This sort of attention makes the human resources staff more worthwhile to the company. It also makes them more alluring to other companies that are intrigued by improving their profitability through a profit center approach to managing human resources.

INCENTIVE PAY FOR HUMAN RESOURCES MANAGERS

The incentive compensation techniques presented in this book clearly point out that, whenever possible, employees should be paid for the results they produce for their company. This already occurs frequently for employees in some functions, especially sales.

Likewise, why not pay human resources managers for the profit-oriented results that they produce? If a human resources manager uses the techniques described in this book, he or she could increase profits dramatically. For example, the human resources director in one company used certain techniques described in this book to increase his company's profits by over $4 million in one year. It unquestionably would look ridiculous to pay him only a regular salary, wouldn't it? Would a company pay a sales representative only a salary if the rep increased company profits by over $4 million?

Incentive pay plans can apply to human resources professionals, allowing human resources professionals who use the *Planning Schedule* to dramatically increase company profits to share in the wealth.

PROFILE OF A SUCCESSFUL HUMAN RESOURCES PROFIT CENTER

This book presents a pragmatic approach to managing human resources to improve corporate profitability. The *Planning Model* and *Planning Schedule* provide tools for conceptualizing, planning, and presenting the profit center in action. Toward this end, the question arises: What does a successful human resources profit center look like? Here is a profile of such a dynamic venture. Specifically, the impressive profit center:

1. *Focuses overwhelmingly on corporate profit improvements.* The successful profit center may implement an array of human resources solutions. However, it possesses only *one goal;* improving corporate profitability. All human resources management techniques simply aid in achieving that single goal.

2. *Acts as business improvement specialists in human resources and all other functions.* In other words, the human resources staff becomes in-house business consultants. They bring their expertise and human resources orientation to bear on practically all business problems faced by their employer. Since human resources management concerns span beyond the walls of the human resources department, the staff needs to get heavily involved in improving all departments. They cannot stay cloistered in the human resources department. Indeed, fine profit center professionals are general business advisors in a very special sense.

3. *Creates enthusiasm and involvement throughout the corporation.* A successful profit center is not staffed by shy or falsely modest characters. Instead, it is composed of professionals who know when and how to get publicity for their successes. This publicity emerges in their presentations at top management meetings and other in-company meetings, as well as in company newsletters and bulletin boards. It also comes out in local and even national media that spotlight the successes of the profit center.

4. *Uses business and financial language more than "service" language.* The old way of managing human resources—the cost center method—expresses itself with service language. For example, human resources departments focused on improving morale, communications, and other such unmeasurable matters. Or, compensation programs highlighted equity or comparisons with similar positions, regardless of the actual productivity of each employee. No wonder non-human-resources executives often wondered if the human resources department even was part of the real business.

All that can be history. Successful human resources profit center managers constantly use financial language—the language of business at its very roots. These managers are familiar with calculating costs of business problems, costs of solutions, improvement benefits, and cost-benefit ratios. That is, they are businesspeople whose products just happen to be profit-oriented human resources services.

5. *Implements the 6-step Planning Model to turn human resources into a corporate profit generator.* This easy-to-use *Planning Model* (Figure 2-1) forms the essential framework for almost all activities tackled by the successful human resources profit center. The six steps provide a common, shared perspective for everyone involved in profit center projects. The Planning Model forces human resources staff to *measure* their effectiveness in dollars and cents.

6. *Uses the Planning Schedule to turn human resources into a corporate profit generator all the time.* The *Planning Schedule* (Figure 3-1) accomplishes a few significant feats. First, it provides a useful list of business problems on which the human resources staff might profitably focus, making it an excellent guide for needs analyses undertaken by the human resources staff to discover business problems worth solving. Second, the *Planning Schedule* offers an extensive list of human resources-oriented solutions to each key business problem. Third, the model allows space to indicate the date by which a

particular solution will be implemented to solve a pressing business problem. It affords a fine tool for managing, monitoring, and appraising the activities of human resources staff.

7. *Compensates the human resources staff with handsome incentive pay.* Employees who produce the most money for their employers typically get paid the most. In the past, the cost center approach to human resources management did not produce results worthy of high salaries. But all that is changing. As human resources managers undertake profit center methods, these managers produce results that directly enhance the bottom line. All organizations consider such contributions worthy of high pay. Given this reality, managers and professionals in the human resources profit center get paid using incentive compensation techniques. This affords handsome monetary recognition for the profit improvement created by human resources staff.

CONCLUDING REMARKS AND A SHOT IN THE ARM

As stated in this book's first chapter, business revolves around money. For this reason, the "game" of business measures a player's worth in terms of how well the player creates and enhances profits. This book's *Planning Model, Planning Schedule,* and dozens of examples all show how human resources professionals can—and do—make a very big difference in any organization's ultimate financial success.

Only one more ingredient is needed—action. Human resources professionals and managers need to take the pointers and ideas presented in this book and put them to use. Business necessities mandate that the old ways of the human resources cost center eventually will disappear and occupy only a footnote in management history. The new profit center approach is the wave of the future. It is the only way that human resources staffs can play crucial *business* roles and show their real value to their employers. This value emerges in the organization as increased profits.

At the same time, this value can dramatically enrich the careers of all achievement-oriented human resources managers. The profit center approach provides them a ready-to-use, practical method to advance their careers in terms of promotions, distinguished reputations, and increased earnings.

Source Notes

CHAPTER 4

1. R. M. Kanter, "The Attack on Pay," *Harvard Business Review* (March-April, 1987), p.62.
2. C. O'Dell, *People, Performance, and Pay* (Houston: American Productivity and Quality Center, 1987), p. 77.
3. O'Dell, *People, Performance, and Pay*, p. 77.
4. Jim Coblin, personal communication with author, July 27, 1987.
5. Personal communication to author from Gene L. Johannes of the National Association of Suggestion Systems, July 17, 1987.
6. *Annual Statistical Report–1986*. Chicago: National Association of Suggestion Systems, 1987.
7. A. E. Schwartz, "Are You Making The Most of That Intern?" *Management Solutions*, (July 1987), p. 17.
8. *Productivity Gainsharing Programs: Can They Contribute To Productivity Improvement?* Gaithersburg, MD: U.S. General Accounting Office, 1981, p. 15.
9. R. E. Kopelman, *Managing Productivity in Organizations*. New York: McGraw-Hill, 1986, p. 60.
10. L. Hatcher, T. L. Ross, and R. A. Ross, "Gainsharing: Living Up To Its Name," *Personnel Administrator* (June 1987) p. 162.
11. *Gainsharing at Vulcan*, Birmingham, AL: Vulcan Materials Company, April 1987, p. 1, 2.
12. B. Donovan, *McDonnell Douglas Electronics: Gain Sharing Just One Road To The Future of St. Charles, Missouri, Firm* (Case Study 57). Houston: American Productivity and Quality Center, (April 1987).

CHAPTER 5

1. "Cost of Employee Health Benefits Rose 7.7% in 1986 Despite Cost Containment," *Spencer Research Reports on Employee Benefits* (March 1987), pp. 11–12.
2. B. Handel, "Dealing with The Medical Revolution—Health Care Cost Containment in A Changing Environment" in *Employee Benefits Annual 1986.* (Brookfield, WI: International Foundation of Employee Benefit Plans, 1987), p. 41.
3. T. Lewin, "Shifting Costs To Employees," *The New York Times* (June 9, 1987), p. 30.
4. Handel, *Employee Benefits Annual 1986*, 39–45.
5. Handel, *Employee Benefits Annual 1986*, 40.
6. R. E. Kopelman, G. O. Schweller IV, and J. J. Silver, Jr., "Parkinson's Law and Absenteeism: A Program To Rein in Sick Leave Costs," *Personnel Administrator* (May 1981) pp. 57–63.
7. D. Willings, "The Absentee Worker," *Personnel and Training Management*, (December 1968), pp. 10–12.
8. B. H. Harvey, "Two Alternatives To Traditional Sick Leave Programs," *Personnel Journal* (May 1983), pp. 374–378.
9. W. De Martini, *Twenty-Seven Ways To Avoid Losing Your Unemployment Appeal* (Sacramento, CA: California Unemployment Appeals Board, 1981).
10. B. De Clark, "Cutting Unemployment Insurance Costs," *Personnel Journal* (November 1983), p. 870.
11. C. Trost, "Child-Care Center at Virginia Firm Boosts Worker Morale and Loyalty," *The Wall Street Journal* (February 12, 1987), p. 23.
12. U.S. Bureau of the Census, *Who's Minding The Kids?* (Current Population Reports, Series P-70, Number 9) (Washington, D.C.: Superintendent of Documents, U.S. Government Printing Office, 1986).
13. "Working Mothers' Child Care Arrangements," *Union Labor Report—Weekly Newsletter*, (May 28, 1987), pp. 4–6.
14. K. Christianson, "Child Care as An Employee Benefit," *Compensation and Benefits Management* (Spring 1987), p. 144.
15. L. Silverman, "Corporate Child Care: Playpens in The Boardroom or Productivity Investment?" *USA Today* (May 14, 1987), p. 69.
16. D. R. Tate, Prepared statement for Select Committee on Children, Youth, and Families, U.S. House of Representatives, hearings entitled, *Improving Child Care Services: What Can Be Done?*, September 6, 1984. (Washington, D.C.: U.S. Government Printing Office, 1985), p. 71.

CHAPTER 6

1. *The Corporate Heart.* (Needham, MA: American Heart Association, Greater Boston Division, 1986).
2. "Smokers Beware!" *The Wall Street Journal* (March 17, 1987), p. 1.
3. F. James, "Study Lays Groundwork for Tying Health Costs To Workers' Behaviors," *The Wall Street Journal* (April 14, 1987).
4. Description of LIVE FOR LIFE® Program. (New Brunswick, NJ: Johnson & Johnson, May 1987).

5. J. P. Opatz, ed. *Health Promotion Evaluation: Measuring The Organizational Impact.* (Stevens Point, WI: National Wellness Institute/National Wellness Association, 1987).

6. *Multifaceted Corporate Medical Services Keep Tenneco 'Building on Quality' through Good Health* (Case Study 44). (Houston: American Productivity and Quality Center, April 1985).

7. S. Dillingham, "The Sobering Costs of Alcoholism," *Insight* (December 14, 1987), p. 31.

8. Dillingham, *Insight*, p. 31.

9. C. A. Berry, *Good Health for Employers and Reduced Health Care Costs for Industry.* (Washington, D.C.: Health Insurance Association of America, 1981), p. 28.

10. W. K. Balzer, and K. I. Pargament, "The Key To Designing A Successful Employee Assistance Program," *Personnel* (July 1987), p. 52.

11. *Accident Facts* (1987 Edition)., (Chicago: National Safety Council, 1987), p. 3.

12. *Accident Facts*, p. 29.

13. *Accident Facts*, p. 31.

CHAPTER 7

1. W. F. Cascio, *Costing Human Resources.* (Boston: Kent, 1982), pp. 20–32.

2. "When Employees Talk, IBM Pays Attention," *Communication World* (April 1983), p. 3.

3. R. E. Kopelman, *Managing Productivity in Organizations.* (New York: McGraw-Hill, 1986), pp. 93–94.

4. W. F. Cascio, *Managing Human Resources.* (New York: McGraw-Hill, 1986), p. 187.

5. D. R. Dalton, and W. D. Tudor, "Win, Lose, Draw: The Grievance Process in Practice," *Personnel Administrator* (March 1981), pp. 25–29.

CHAPTER 8

1. W. L. French, and C. H. Bell, Jr., *Organizational Development.* (Englewood Cliffs, NJ: Prentice-Hall, 1978).

2. R. B. McAfee, and W. Poffenberger, *Productivity Strategies: Enhancing Employee Job Performance.* (Englewood Cliffs, NJ: Prentice-Hall, 1982).

3. E. Rendall, "Quality Circles—A 'Third Wave' Intervention," *Training and Development Journal* (March 1981), pp. 28–31.

CHAPTER 9

1. J. W. Walker, *Human Resource Planning.* (New York: McGraw-Hill, 1980).

2. W. F. Cascio, *Managing Human Resources.* (New York: McGraw-Hill, 1986), p. 347.

3. M. W. Mercer, "Making Mergers Work: Successfully Managing The People and Organizational Problems," *Directors and Boards*, Spring 1988.

CHAPTER 10

1. J. E. Hunter, and F. L. Schmidt, "Quantifying The Effects of Psychological Interventions on Employee Job Performance and Work-Force Productivity," *American Psychologist* (April 1983), pp. 473–478.

2. W. F. Cascio, *Managing Human Resources*. (New York: McGraw-Hill, 1986).

3. R. S. Schuler, *Personnel and Human Resource Management*. (St. Paul, MN: West, 1987).

4. R. E. Kopelman, *Managing Productivity in Organizations*. (New York: McGraw-Hill, 1986), p. 88.

5. *Principles for The Validation and Use of Personnel Selection Procedures*. (College Park, MD: Society for Industrial and Organizational Psychology, 1987).

6. "More Companies Are Testing More Workers," *Management Review* (July 1987), p. 10.

7. C. L. Jaffee, *Effective Management Selection*. (Reading, MA: Addison-Wesley, 1971).

8. W. C. Byham, "Starting An Assessment Center The Correct Way," *Personnel Administrator* (February 1980).

9. C. Kleiman, "Fudging Credentials Now Much Riskier," *Chicago Tribune*, (September 27, 1987), sec. 8, p. 1.

10. Kleiman, *Chicago Tribune*, p. 1.

11. Personal communication with author, August 3, 1987.

CHAPTER 11

1. C. L. Finkel, "The *True* Cost of A Training Program," *Training and Development Journal* (September 1987), p. 74.

2. D. L. Kirkpatrick, "Four Steps To Measuring Training Effectiveness," *Personnel Administrator* (November 1983), pp. 19–25.

3. B. J. Licata, and P. M. Popovich, "Preventing Sexual Harassment: A Proactive Approach," *Training and Development Journal* (May 1987), p. 34.

4. B. Paquet, E. Kasl, L. Weinstein, and W. Waite, "The Bottom Line," *Training and Development Journal* (May 1987), pp. 27–33.

5. M. A. Verespej, "Profits through Training," *Industry Week* (June 11, 1984), p. 64.

6. J. Zigon, "Performance Chain Reaction," *Performance Management Magazine* (Fall/Winter 1983), pp. 22–25.

7. R. E. Kopelman, *Managing Productivity in Organizations*. (New York: McGraw-Hill, 1986), p. 164.

Index